Working for Utopia

1937-1953

Working for Utopia

1937-1953

Mark Walker

Quixotic Press--2000
Concord, California

Published by:
Quixotic Press
P.O. Box 60
Concord, CA 94522-0060

Publisher's Cataloging-in-Publication
(Provided by Quality Books, Inc.)

Mark Walker, 1919-
Working for Utopia, 1937-1953 / by Mark Walker
-- 1st ed.
p. c m.
LCCN: 00-132721
ISBN: 0-9700630-3-2

1. Walker, Mark, 1919- 2. Labor Leaders--United States--Biography. 3. Labor unions--United States--History--20th century. 4. United States--Economic conditions--1918-1945. 5. Working class--United States--History--20th century. 6. Cold War. 7. Merchant marine--United States--History--20th century. 8. World War, 1939-1945--Transportation. 9. Socialist Workers Party--History. I. Title.

HD6509.W35W35 2000 331.886'092 B
QBI00-474

Cover by Susan Walker Honey

Printed in the United States of America

This book is dedicated to the memory of the courageous, idealistic young men and women who worked with me, in the face of daunting odds and often at great personal sacrifice, trying to achieve a better world.

Acknowledgments

It is a pleasure to acknowledge my indebtedness to all those who have helped make this book possible. So many have offered advice, encouragement, suggestions, editorial assistance, and constructive criticism that some are sure to be unintentionally omitted. I owe a debt to all of you who have helped, and any omissions are regretted.

First I am grateful to Captain Arthur Moore of Hallowell, Maine, for permission to quote from *A Careless Word...A Needless Sinking*, his definitive work on the disastrous sinkings of merchant vessels and the great loss of lives of mariners during World War II.

I am grateful to Bill Fisk, Susan Walker Honey, Celeste MacLeod, Ethel Ruymaker, Tim Walker, Anita Weiss and Dorothy Witt for their editorial advice and comments. I am indebted to historians Robert Cherny, Richard Condon, Dan Georgakas, Archie Green, Paul Le Blanc, Sally Miller, Harvey Schwartz, and Alan Wald for their constructive comments and criticism.

Others, whose shared memories have made my account more complete and more accurate, include Robert and Margaret Burkart, Dave and Eleanor Cooper, Ada Farrell, Joe Gladstone and Demila Jenner.

I especially want to thank my wife, Maggie, for her support, for her astute criticism, thoughtful suggestions and sound editorial advice.

Responsibility for any errors is mine and mine alone.

Contents

Introduction

The quest for a more humane, a more just world, without the societal evils that have always plagued humankind, extends back twenty-four hundred years to the Greek philosopher, Plato. Against the background of the social disintegration brought on by the Peloponnesian wars, Plato wrote his monumental *Republic* in which he sought justice in the blueprint for an ideal state. Two thousand years later, Sir Thomas More, English statesman and author, wrote *Utopia,* describing an imaginary island with a perfect political and social system. The word Utopia, coined by More, was appropriately derived from two Greek words meaning "no place."

Despite some significant gaps, the dream did not die and enjoyed an explosive rebirth following the popular revolutions in France and the American colonies. Socialist parties, affiliated with the Marxist Second International, attracted mass followings, especially in western Europe and the United States. The late 19th century also saw a proliferation of utopian schemes, some set forth in novels such as Edward Bellamy's *Looking Backward,* published in 1888. This book was immensely popular and was rated in 1935 by philosopher John Dewey and historian Charles Beard as the second most influential book published in the past 50 years — second only to Karl Marx's *Das Kapital.* Bellamy's book inspired a mass movement, organized with the aim of implementing his vision of an ideal society.

The 19th century also saw the founding of scores of model communities, in England by socialist philanthropist Robert Owens, and in France by followers of François Fourier. In America a wide variety of utopian communities were founded, some with a strong religious component and others strictly secular. The names of some of these experiments still resonate —Brook Farm, Amana, New Harmony, Ephrata. All these colonies were peopled by sincere seekers of the perfect society, and all foundered on the rocks of outside influence and internal dissension or, like the Shakers, atrophied in isolation.

The organized labor movement also experienced an unprecedented upsurge during this same period. The Knights of Labor (1869), the American Federation of Labor (1881) and the Industrial Workers of the World (IWW-1905) came into being to champion the cause of the workingman in the industrial arena. Though the focus of their activities was centered on immediate wage/hour demands and defense of workers against employer aggression, most of their founders and leaders were socialists by conviction, seeking a more just society than the one they knew as working men and women. Many of these labor leaders, among them Eugene Debs of the American Railway Union and Bill Hayward of the Western Federation of Miners, participated in the founding of the Socialist Party (1898) affiliated with the Second International. Running for President of the United States on the Socialist Party ticket in five national election years, Gene Debs piled up big vote totals. In his final campaign from the federal penitentiary, where he was imprisoned for his principled socialist opposition to the 1st World War, Debs polled 920,000 votes.

Following that war, which saw the overthrow of capitalism in Russia by disciples of Karl Marx, socialist thought everywhere was heavily influenced by the example of the Russian revolution. In America a new Communist movement, affiliated with the Russian-led Third International, inherited the most militant wing of the Socialist Party and won over many from the IWW.

Believers in the utopian vision of a just society thought victory was attainable, following the example of the victorious Russian Bolsheviks. Despite vicious repression by the U.S. government and a wave of capitalist prosperity in the 1920's, the socialist cause continued to gain adherents. Then came the great depression of the 1930's, sending shock waves through all strata of American society.

And this is where my generation came on the scene. Most of us had no opportunity for higher education, we were without prospects for a job, career or family, many of us homeless and hungry. It is not surprising that many young men and women turned an attentive ear to those who offered hope of basic change. We were offered a vision of a society where we would not only achieve immediate aims of food, jobs and education, we would also be on the road to a glorious future.

We believed we must work untiringly toward that goal: organizing, teaching, preparing for future crises and conflicts that would bring opportunities to achieve a majority following among the workers. Then we, the organized working class, would establish a socialist government that would usher in a new millennium.

Of course, for a time it would be necessary for the new workers' state to suppress any counter-revolutionary attempts to overthrow the new order. However, once a planned economy had ushered in an era of plenty for all, the state as an instrument of coercion would be no longer needed. Over time, people would adapt to the new reality, crimes against property would disappear and police would have little to do, and eventually even the administrative functions of the state would "wither away," being no longer required for the orderly functioning of an ideal society. Inspired by the example of the Russian revolution, a majority of the socialist-inclined youth had joined the organizations of the

Third International, in this country the Communist Party and the Young Communist League. However, events and trends in the Soviet Union convinced many of us that the Stalin regime was an obstacle standing in the way of socialist development both in Russia and in the rest of the world. Many of us would join the left opposition led by Leon Trotsky, parties affiliated with the Fourth International. Undeterred by the Stalinist betrayals, we maintained our revolutionary enthusiasm and continued to work for the socialist future.

We truly believed that, at last, through the scientific-socialist teachings of Karl Marx, as interpreted and expanded by Lenin and Trotsky, and through the instrumentality of the working class, the age-old dream of Plato, Thomas More, Bellamy and those who came after them would be realized. And our generation seemed chosen to lead the way.

The faults of capitalist America were glaringly evident and only the labor movement, and especially its socialist tendency, seemed to offer any hope. I was a country boy just out of high school with no chance for an education or a decent job. I was drawn to a vision of a socialist future and for many years spent all my energies toward that goal.

In our latter-day wisdom, we may ask, "How could anyone have believed all this?"

Well, people have been drawn to such beliefs for 2,500 years and a dream that old is not likely to die, despite all the disillusioning events of recent years. I no longer have all the answers, but I can tell you what it was like to work and hope and believe that a socialist transformation of our society is possible.

1

September 1937

As we crossed Boston Common we heard muffled shouts from the far corner near the bandstand where hundreds of people were milling about. There were men and women of all ages, some well dressed and others as seedy-looking as we were. A riot!? An accident? As we quickened our step and drew nearer, the stentorian tones of a man with a foghorn voice reached us, "World revolution is the only answer!" Other words and phrases reached our ears, floating clear of the general cacophony — "proletariat"; "full employment"; "Kingdom of God"; "social justice".

I looked at Mac, he at me, and we grinned. Hey! This is what we had come to Boston for! Approaching closer we saw not a multitude but a number of separate, unconnected groups — swarms of 30 to 40 people, clusters of a dozen or so, and many clumps of less than 10. One person in each group was loudly declaiming, gesticulating and exhorting his crowd, while members of the audience cheered, jeered, or waited for a chance to deliver a spirited rebuttal. Each grouping seemed to have its own tight nucleus, while many people browsed and straggled, wandering from group to group.

We joined the closest gathering and listened for a few minutes to a well-dressed, middle-aged follower of Henry George expounding the Single-Tax panacea for all the country's social ills. Moving on, we heard a scholarly disciple of Daniel DeLeon, with long white hair and flowing cravat, preach the simon-pure doctrine of the Socialist Labor Party. We stopped briefly to hear another earnest but threadbare gentleman explain the benefits of Lawsonomy, an "environmental science" invented by a man named Lawson. According to its tenets, exhausting all smoke-stack effluents underground would not only eliminate air pollution but enrich the soil, with incalculable benefits to society. We moved on, visiting first one group then another.

We didn't talk, only listened, delighted to be spectators in this lively exchange of ideas on philosophy, social issues, political theory and public policy. There were anarchists present, trade-unionists, syndicalists and single-taxers, several varieties of socialists and communists, Pentecostals, Townsendites, Coughlinites, Jehovah's Witnesses, a Buffalo Bill impersonator and even a de-frocked Jesuit priest. All this was very exciting to two teenagers fresh from the backwoods of Maine. Though we had dabbled at dissidence in high school, this scene on Boston Common plunged us into a whole new dimension of intellectual inquiry.

As Mac and I hastened toward this ideological free-for-all I had no idea I was setting my feet upon a path that would lead to a career as a labor union activist, eventually becoming a full-time professional socialist organizer. Despite the youthful iconoclasm of our rural past, I shared the aims and ambitions of most young people. I was looking for a secure future with a family and a good job that would allow me to pursue my ambitions as a writer. I came to the big city seeking opportunities not available in rural Maine. What I found there led me inexorably into left-wing politics and enlistment in a crusade to change the world and make it a better place, free of war, poverty, unemployment and entrenched greed.

2

On Reaching the Age of Dissent

In high school more than 60 years ago, I aspired to become a scholar and a writer. My heroes were Voltaire and Swift, leading a pantheon of writers whose eloquence had stirred people to think, to ponder the human condition and perhaps try to change it. I arrived on Boston Common on that September afternoon filled with ambition to be of that number, though there was little in my background to indicate I might qualify for such a role.

Born in the hamlet of New Portland, I spent most of my first 18 years in small farming and lumbering communities, the central Maine backwaters of the Carrabassett and Kennebec Rivers. This is a land of rolling wooded hills, rocky terrain and thin soil. Natural habitat of moose, lynx, hedgehog and the black bear, it is a forbidding territory for human habitation. Harsh winters and a brief growing season test the mettle of all who would try to raise crops here.

It is also a beautiful country, beloved of those who know it best. Though they may curse its rigors, most don't consider seeking a more forgiving climate. And those of us who leave Maine remember with nostalgia the land of our birth and regularly return, as the salmon to their native stream.

English settlers from Massachusetts Bay Colony moved into this territory in the late 17th century, my family among them, and for more than three centuries they scratched a subsistence living from the thin soil, supplementing their income by working in the woods. One of my grandfathers had gone into the forest to cut logs and hard wood before he became an orchardist; the other was a farmer who sometimes hired out as a teamster hauling lumber. My father, a lumberjack, teamster and river driver, also did some farming.

When my father, Cephas Walker, married Josephine Williamson in 1917, he was 25 years old and she was 20. Like most of their peers they had only an eighth-grade education, or even less. High school and beyond were regarded as being for the leisure class or those who intended to enter one of the learned professions.

Born in 1919, I was their second child. When they optimistically bought a farm in 1927, I had four brothers, Harland, Laurence, Norman and Richard, and one sister, Haidee May — six of us, aged two to nine years. Proud of their new estate and determined to establish a prosperous home place for their growing family, our parents worked as never before. Both were skilled in all aspects of farm work, having been raised on farms and done chores since childhood. They plowed, harrowed, planted, cultivated and harvested. They raised cows, poultry and hogs. My father worked in the woods for cash income, both as a teamster, and later a jobbing contractor. The farm provided food, but their income was never quite enough for their growing family.

The 1929 stock market crash and bank failures that heralded the "Great Depression" only deepened their problems and in 1930 a seventh child, my sister Anne, was born. Still, they struggled on, probably only vaguely aware of the economic forces that undermined all their efforts. They worked from before daybreak to after sundown seven days a week, just trying to stay even and pay their bills. We lived frugally, but however hard they tried — and I've never known anyone who tried harder — expenses always exceeded income.

In the spring of 1930, when Anne was less than six months old, my father contracted to deliver several hundred cords of pulpwood to the paper mill in Madison. He hired a crew and, since the work site was not too far from the farm, he arranged to furnish board and room to several of the men. At one time there were six of them for whom my mother cooked, made beds and did the washing, in addition to caring for her husband and seven children, and the never-ending farm chores.

My father was a very poor business man and it became evident he would come out of this venture with less money than when he went in, despite all their hard labor. My mother was overworked, under-appreciated and profoundly discouraged by her inability to cope with our chronic financial instability. Then, finally, she fell in love with Earl Moulton, one of the boarders, a man Dad had hired to work in the woods.

There followed a very hard time during which our family was torn asunder, both emotionally and physically. My mother finally left never to return, and to the almost universal condemnation of the adults in the family and in the village. Only my father had no harsh words for his faithless wife. He accepted his share of the blame and never tried to turn us against our mother.

Our grandfather Williamson was very severe in his judgment on his daughter. This made it doubly hard on me and my siblings because for us Gramp had always been the adult who stood out from all others. We loved him for his rare ability to understand and empathize with the feelings of young people and for his way of treating us as rational beings, whether we were or not.

We children were torn by our love for each of our parents, and we listened to Gramp's vitriolic denunciations. Our mother had been central to our existence; it was she who had nurtured and sustained us. But now she had gone and left a gaping hole in our lives. She divorced our father and married Earl Moulton. And we came to believe she did not love us.

After his wife left, Dad tried to keep his family together but what had been difficult before now became impossible. Baby Anne was taken by Aunt May and her husband, Harold Pledger, to be brought up by them. Haidee May, now six years old, was adopted by some people named Douglass who renamed her Marianne. Richard went to live with our Uncle Carl and his wife, Beulah, and Norman was taken in by a childless New Portland farm couple. The three oldest of us, Harland, Larry and I went to Good Will Home and School, a Boystown-type institution on the banks of the Kennebec River in Hinckley, Maine. I was to stay at Good Will for five years and graduate from high school there.

Good Will was founded in 1889 by George W. Hinckley who made it his life work to care for children who needed a helping hand. Hinckley, a young preacher from Connecticut, purchased a small farm between Skowhegan and Waterville and he and his wife took in their first homeless boys. A few years later facilities were added for girls. By 1931 the original farm site had grown to more than 2,000 acres, with five cottages for girls and ten for boys, all funded by gifts and endowments raised by G.W. who never stopped preaching the gospel of helping needy children.

Largely self-sufficient, the school raised most of its own food, having a herd of 60 to 70 cows, many hogs, hundreds of hens and several spans of work horses. Most of the work on the farm and in the cottages was done by students. Under adult supervision we planted acres of gardens, tended the livestock, slaughtered as necessary to feed the community, cut hundreds of cords of wood for heat and cooking, maintained and cleaned the many buildings, mowed the vast lawns, operated a well-equipped central laundry, cooked and served all the meals eaten by the 225 students and 15 matrons.

Tuition fees were based on ability to pay, with many students paying nothing. Dad paid some nominal fee for the three of us. All students had work assignments and the day we arrived at Good Will we were introduced to the system. Harland joined the milking crew and Larry became a dishwasher in the cottage. At the age of 12, I was drafted as cottage cook, preparing three meals each day for our 15 resident boys and the matron, seven days a week, for my first three years at Good Will. Later I became janitor of the administration building and in my fifth year, school barber.

Good Will, founded by a Christian minister, seemed to me a hotbed of religiosity. There was Sunday School in the forenoon, followed by an afternoon service in the chapel and a vesper service each Sunday evening. There was a mid-week Christian Endeavor meeting and Bible reading to start study hour each school night. This was new to me as my family were not churchgoers. My grandfather was irreligious and my father regarded all the Christians he knew as rank hypocrites. I started off resenting the constant compulsory attendance at religious services and ended as a deliberate dissenter from all religion, an attitude that put me into some conflict with the authorities at school.

Academically the Good Will schools were excellent, with a staff of dedicated teachers of very high standards, a rigorous curriculum, and strict requirements. My courses included four years of Latin, two of French, four of Math covering algebra through elementary calculus, world history, American history, English and American literature and English composition. There was a schedule conflict between physics and chemistry and Latin III and IV, and I chose Latin.

I also became known as a vocal dissenter, not only from the religious beliefs of the school, but from the political views of my elders as well. I was 14 years old, late in my sophomore year, when I discovered the "Little Blue Books" published by Haldeman-Julius and sold by mail for five cents each. I sent away for scores of these books on subjects ranging through atheism, Darwinism, socialism, companionate marriage, the bloody events of church history, and many other subjects considered indecorous, perhaps dangerous, by most adults in rural Maine, certainly by the school authorities.

My friends and I read these books, discussed and debated them among ourselves, sometimes passing them on to other students who we thought might be interested. During my last two years at Good Will I tried to enliven class discussions by quoting from Eugene Debs, Niccolò Machiavelli or Clarence Darrow, and received good marks by incorporating the ideas of such thinkers in my written class work.

These years, 1931 through 1936, were among the darkest days of the depression. As students at Good Will we heard about the hard times and the consequent political repercussions, but we were insulated from the worst effects of the depression and the harsh realities confronted by adults.

I owe a great debt to the school. Good Will provided a home, gave me encouragement when I needed it most, gave me an excellent high school education, inspired me with a love for literature and learning, encouraged free inquiry and pursuit of truth wherever it led, and instilled an ethical code that remains with me today. Now more than 110 years old, the school still carries on, helping children in need.

During my senior year, encouraged by my teachers, I applied for admission to Bowdoin College and was accepted. I entered a competition for one of four scholarships to be awarded in 1936, but was not one of the winners. There were no other scholarships available anywhere that I was aware of, and there were then no student loans or any other kind of public assistance to needy students. None of my school counselors was any more knowledgeable than I about opportunities that might have existed outside the State of Maine. No one in my family could help in any way so, though I graduated second in my class, my aspirations toward a scholarly career were rudely extinguished. Others with a much lower grade average went on to college because they were lucky enough to have a family able to assist. I went into the world to make my living, a world of which I knew very little.

Though I would have preferred entering college, I had no objection to going to work, confident I would succeed in whatever I undertook. But I soon learned there were no real jobs to be had. I also found that my Good Will education and work experience qualified me for nothing except unskilled labor, and that for every job opening, however undemanding or poorly paid, there were many eager applicants better qualified.

After a brief stint at farm work for 20 cents a day, dawn to dusk, I worked in the woods cutting pulp, and then tried selling magazine subscriptions door to door in southern Maine, New Hampshire and Massachusetts, a venture at which I was a total failure. Success required misrepresentation and hard sell, and I found myself unable to pressure or trick people into signing a subscription contract when I knew they could barely afford to buy food for their children.

Back in New Portland, I went again into the woods peeling pulp and cutting logs for my father. This was very hard labor at barely subsistence wages, and work for which I was not well equipped by either physique or temperament. Thus, I reached my 18th birthday in August of 1937, determined to get out, to go where there were more opportunities.

Saving my earnings from the summer in the woods, I combined forces with my best friend from Good Will, Preston McMann. Mac had been saving his pay from a summer job in an Ogunquit restaurant. He was my age, a handsome chap, six feet tall and of muscular build. By contrast, I was shorter, lean and wiry, overconfident and wearing wire-rim spectacles to compensate for nearsightedness. Mac and I had been close friends in high school and what I most appreciated about him was his enquiring mind. He was never satisfied with stock answers, always searching, daring to be unconventional.

Together we went to Boston to seek our fortune.

3

Country Boys Come to Town

When we arrived in Boston I was driving a 1926 Model T Ford pickup truck I purchased for $15 from a fellow who'd worked with me in the woods that summer. We were as green as the grass on the hills of New Portland. We carried all our possessions, such as they were — some old clothes and books — in the back of the truck. I also had a recent acquisition, a new L.C. Smith typewriter.

The 200-mile trip had taken all day. The old truck was not capable of speeds over 40 miles per hour and even that was probably unsafe. Fortunately it was a warm sunny day as we had no shelter from the weather, the cab's canopy-like roof having long since parted company with the truck. There were no freeways or turnpikes, so from Portland to Boston we traveled on Route 1, passing through all the resort towns along the way. Mac and I exchanged information about schoolmates and friends. It was late afternoon when we arrived in Boston.

It would be more accurate to say we arrived in Charlestown, Sullivan Square to be precise. We knew little about Boston but we knew we had gone as far as we cared to in that traffic. It was rush hour and the four-lane highway coming into Charlestown was packed with cars and trucks, bumper-to-bumper, cutting in and out from one lane to another, and all going faster than my old Ford was capable of moving. Prior to this trip all my driving experience had been on the back roads around New Portland where you might occasionally meet another Model T or a horse and buggy. I found my first immersion in city traffic unnerving.

So at journey's end we were still more than three miles from downtown Boston, and there we found a furnished room right on Sullivan Square. The square itself was a large, tree-shaded area with paved walkways and benches. Towering above it was the rapid transit elevated track with trains running into Boston. Our room cost $3.50 a week which seemed high to us. But we had money. Mac had his savings from the summer job, and I had what was left of my earnings from peeling pulp and cutting logs on the wooded hills around New Portland. We each had about $50.

Our landlady informed us that we were in Charlestown, but we decided to stay there anyway, temporarily. Our room on the second floor was clean, with a big double bed, dresser, two comfortable chairs and a small table that would do as a desk. The room was bright and sunny with two windows overlooking Sullivan Square. The bathroom was down the hall, but I didn't consider that an inconvenience. I wasn't used to any bathroom at all since leaving Good Will. Indoor plumbing had not yet reached New Portland.

For supper, Mac and I ate bread, peanut butter and apples left over from supplies we'd bought for our trip. We found a map of Greater Boston and spent the evening studying the map, exploring the neighborhood around Sullivan Square and poring over the help-wanted ads in the Boston Globe. There weren't many jobs being offered, and most of those required some special skill or experience. Since Mac and I had little of either, there weren't too many prospects. We had both mowed lawns and cut wood, but the paper listed no jobs for unskilled labor. We had both done some kitchen work. Though I had been a cook in my cottage at Good Will, I was to find that this qualified me at best as a dishwasher or a helper peeling vegetables. Still, we found a few job openings that seemed worth trying. We circled these and studied the map for the job locations.

This was not my first attempt to break out of the Maine woods. The door-to-door magazine crew got me as far as Lawrence, Mass., before I had to give up. My second venture, hitchhiking to Washington, D.C., where I looked unsuccessfully for a job, also ended in ignominy. I was returned to Maine by rail, courtesy of the Travelers Aid Society. However this time, unlike my other attempts, I wasn't starting out broke. I had savings that, with prudent management, would keep me going for a few weeks while I looked for a job. I was determined not to turn back, sure I would succeed.

Rising early the next morning, eager to get started, we went outside to find a policeman thoughtfully eyeing my truck which was parked in front of the rooming house. He was holding a pad in one hand and pen in the other. I think he was about to write me a ticket when we came along. He watched as we approached, looked us over, sizing us up.

"You know who owns this thing?" he asked.

Hearing the contempt in his voice made me look more critically at my 12-year-old pickup, its paint faded almost to disappearance, battered and dented, missing one door, with no roof on the cab and springs popping up through the torn leather seat, crumpled fenders, crank handle dangling sadly below the radiator. It did look very unprepossessing there on the city street.

"I do," I told him. "It's mine."

"And you drove it here from Maine?"

"That's right."

Big, bluff, jowly and red-faced, he was impressive in his blue uniform, and he looked at us two hayseeds with tolerant amusement. Then he asked, "Can you read?"

"Yes," I nodded.

"What does that sign say?" He pointed at a rectangular metal sign mounted above the curb about 20 feet away.

"No overnight parking on the square," I read aloud.

"That's right," he said. "You know what that means?"

I nodded.

"All right," he told me," I won't give you a ticket because you're from Maine and I guess you don't know any better. But you start that thing up right now and get it out of the square and keep it out."

"Where do you think I should put it?" I asked, hoping he'd tell me where it was safe to park without violating any ordinances.

"You might try the city dump."

Perhaps because I looked so crestfallen, he relented.

"If you want to keep it in this neighborhood, you'd better find a garage for it. Go up those streets." He pointed across the square. "You should find some vacancies over there."

Tired of the game, he pocketed his pen and pad and sauntered off down the street.

I'd never had any experience with parking restrictions before. In Maine I had parked my truck wherever I pleased and no one paid any attention. But I knew I couldn't afford any parking tickets, so I decided to take the policeman's advice. We found a place a couple of blocks away in a row of single garages behind a small apartment house. The space would cost me $3 a month and I paid for the first month. The first month's payment turned out to be the last. The unpaid rent soon exceeded the value of the truck so I simply abandoned it. A truck would have been of no use to me in Boston anyway.

Having disposed of the truck problem, we headed for downtown Boston. The rapid transit station was handy, right there in Sullivan Square. We could see it from our rooming house and hear the rumble of the trains through our open window. We were only three or four stations from downtown Boston, a matter of minutes on the fast trains. But it cost a nickel to ride and it was only three or four miles, so we decided to walk. We were young, fit and enthusiastic. We might even find some place that was hiring along our way to town. We did stop at a couple of places and ask for work. One was a job advertised in the Globe for a laundry worker, but the job was already taken. We also stopped on impulse at a big lumber yard just off Main Street in Charlestown. The people there seemed a little surprised, but regretfully told us they didn't need any help.

Our route to town took us past the foot of Bunker Hill, across the Charlestown bridge, past the North Station where we scouted the terminal passenger lounge and found some abandoned newspapers for use in our job search. We crossed Haymarket Square and detoured to take a look at Faneuil Hall, the Cradle of Liberty, as we knew from our history studies.

All this was interesting and exciting for a couple of boys from the country. We were glad to be away from Maine, pleased to be here in this center of history and culture. And I was enjoying the ambience of the city streets, pavement everywhere, on the roadways, the sidewalks and the driveways; people everywhere, singly or in groups, hurrying about their anonymous errands; the bustling busyness of it all. After spending most of my life in the backwoods, living in a village where only the main road through town was macadamized and about 20 yards of sidewalk paved, the urban scene charmed me with its difference and its promise. And it was good to be with Mac, doing things together again as we had for several years at Good Will School.

But the job prospects were not good. We tried a couple more of the advertised openings that seemed to require little or no skills, but found there were other applicants with years of experience and good references. After that we spent the rest of the forenoon enrolling at several employment agencies, filling out long application forms that revealed how ill-prepared we were for most kinds of employment. Some of the agency people were courteous and friendly but said our only chance would be the occasional restaurant dish-washing job that came along. Because neither skill nor experience was required, there was a lot of competition for these jobs. But there were occasional openings.

Around one o'clock of that first full day in Boston, having exhausted the job-hunting possibilities, we decided to splurge on lunch. We each had a great hot dog and a 12-ounce Coke at Joe and Nemo's, a landmark eatery on Scollay Square. This cost us ten cents each and we ate standing up at a counter with sawdust on the floor. We couldn't afford to do this often, but enjoyed the treat, both the food and the ambience.

Our next destination was the main library in Copley Square. We had heard it held two million volumes and had a lecture hall with a schedule of free lectures. We wanted to get our library cards as soon as possible so we could start sharing in the wealth of culture and knowledge to be found there. And indeed that's what we did. All the time I was in Boston, a major part of my spare time was spent in the library reading rooms.

We started for the library but we didn't go there directly that day. Our route from Scollay Square took us out Tremont Street past King's Chapel, Granary Burial Ground and the Park Street Church. We stopped to observe these famous landmarks, reading some headstones in the burial grounds. Then we cut across Boston Common toward Boylston Street. We had read that the 42-acre common, a park right in the middle of the city, had been used by Bostonians in colonial times as a cow pasture, later as a drill field for militia and for occasional executions, duels and religious revivals.

The huge park's green lawn sloped down from Beacon and Park Streets toward Tremont and Boylston, crossed by asphalt walkways with long benches spotted under sheltering oak trees. At the lower end was an ornate raised bandstand with a cleared area. There were people all over the park, crossing, strolling, lying on the grass, sitting on the benches, attending their children, watching the squirrels and birds. It was refreshing to find this oasis in the middle of the city. But apart from what we had read, Boston Common had been to us only a green area on our newly acquired city map.

We were wholly unprepared for what we found down near the bandstand. Nothing in our experience had ever resembled this unfettered forum of ideas where no subjects were taboo and no holds were barred, though the arguments, however heated, rarely exceeded the bounds of civil discourse. This was very exciting to us and we would come back often to the Common, first to listen and later to join in the spirited debates.

I have often asked myself why we took such an interest, even delight, in studying and debating these issues. Most of our schoolmates took no intense interest in such matters. Both my father and my grandfather were skeptical, irreverent men and I must have taken some of my attitudes from them. For as long as I can remember I had been both inquisitive and argumentative. Perhaps at school there had been an element of youthful rebellion in our dissent from the beliefs and strictures of those in authority, and in our early infatuation with texts that scorned the religious and political convictions of our elders at school.

But I believe our involvement with social and political issues was also motivated by an idealism and a genuine concern about the social injustice we had read about if not experienced personally. In any case, we differed with our teachers and the administration of the school on almost every subject.

Certainly most of the issues themselves were real and they compelled the interest and concern of millions. And in the 15 months since leaving school I had learned at first hand about unemployment, about hitchhiking and riding in railway boxcars, about sleeping in flophouses or railroad stations, about missing meals and subsisting on mission handouts of thin soup and stale bread, about walking the winter streets of the nation's capital looking for work without a dime in my pocket and with holes in the bottoms of both shoes.

At Good Will I had seen my teachers voluntarily forego payday because the school had no money, and in New Portland I had seen heads of families out of work, their children going without food, depending on the town for a handout. I had seen how hard my father worked and to so little avail. We were in the midst of a great economic depression and I tried to make some sense of it.

The stock market crash of 1929 had signaled the onset of a deep malaise infecting every organ and inflaming every tissue of the American economic and social system. No person living in this country was immune, but its most virulent ravages were reserved for the poor.

Thousands of banks closed their doors and people lost their savings; mills and factories were shut down and one worker in every four lost his job, while many still working were reduced to subsistence wages; small businesses failed; one farmer out of every four lost his farm through foreclosure, and those who hung on were in desperate straits. Teachers went unpaid, thousands of schools closed their doors leaving millions of children with their education terminated or disrupted. Strong men and brave women fought despair and sent their children to bed hungry.

Economic experts told us the problem was overproduction. We had produced so many commodities no one could buy them any more. So the producers were walking the streets unable to provide their families with simple necessities for life. We had overproduced food to the point where people had to go hungry because they couldn't buy, and the farmers were going broke because they couldn't sell food for the cost of producing it. In my grandfather's orchards the fruit rotted on the trees because there was no market for apples that would pay the cost of picking them. Surely something was terribly wrong with such a "system." Anger and resentment were widespread. Millions of unemployed workers marched and demanded government relief and work projects. A "bonus army" of 20,000 World War veterans marched to Washington to petition for a long-promised bonus payment. On the streets of the national capital they were attacked with tanks and driven out with tear gas. General Douglas MacArthur led the assault against the impoverished veterans.

Then in 1932, when I was 13, Franklin Delano Roosevelt was elected president, receiving 57.4 percent of the popular vote. Conservative Maine was one of only six states that cast their electoral votes for the reelection of Herbert Hoover. At that time 14 million of the nation's workers, more than 25 percent of the work force, were unemployed.

With overwhelming majorities in both houses of Congress, Roosevelt initiated a barrage of legislative activity unprecedented in this country. Labeled the "New Deal" by Roosevelt, its accomplishments were impressive. We heard a lot about the New Deal in Maine and I must have been affected by its wide array of programs, though my memories of it in those early years are sparse.

Some of those I remember reading about, generally identified by acronyms, were the NRA, RFC, HOLC, FERA, CWA, TVA, REA, NYA, NLRA and the AAA. Each of these programs was designed to address specific economic problems ravaging the country when Roosevelt took office.

I don't recall that any of these had an immediate impact on my life, and few had any application to rural Maine. But the Civilian Conservation Corps (CCC) employed young men of relief families in reforestation projects. They were organized in paramilitary units and worked in the national forests for $5 a month, with another $15 going to their families. I knew three or four New Portland boys who went into the CCC, among them one of my father's half-brothers, but I was never tempted to join. I not only scorned the meager pay and rejected the regimentation, I was sure I could do better on my own.

Another New Deal program which was of no immediate concern to me, but would have lasting implications in my life, was the National Labor Relations Act (NLRA) which established labor's right to organize and bargain collectively. These rights, so often denied in the past by employers and local authorities, had for the first time federal sanction and this unleashed an unprecedented wave of unionization all across the land.

These are some of the highlights of New Deal legislation aimed at pulling the country out of the depression. And they had some effect. Surplus food distributions kept many children from going to bed hungry in the New Portlands. Though they didn't bring prosperity, they got some of the hungry off the streets and started things moving again, if creakily. But each of these measures, and all the others, were hotly debated. Republicans and businessmen were sure Roosevelt was going too far and accused him of being a communist. Left wingers of every description knew he hadn't gone far enough; he was only a capitalist quack applying a poultice to the cancer.

Self-anointed saviors appeared and preached their gospels to large audiences, whipping up great enthusiasms and attracting huge followings. Senator Huey Long crusaded on national radio networks under the slogan "Every Man a King" and promoted a program he called "Share our Wealth." Though he had established a virtual dictatorship in his own state of Louisiana, he had a wide following throughout the country and was considered a serious presidential contender until he was assassinated in 1935.

Catholic priest Charles Coughlin of Detroit founded the anti-Semitic, anti-democratic Christian Front and preached hate every Sunday over a nationwide radio network to millions of angry followers. Francis Townsend recruited five million old people into his Townsend Clubs promoting his program of giving $200 each month to every person over 60, funds to be provided by a two percent transaction tax. Called the "lunatic fringe" by Roosevelt, these demagogues nonetheless inflamed their partisans and influenced elections.

And these were only the most prominent of the leaders and groups haranguing the public. In addition, there were scores of parties and organizations that had developed programs intended to quickly solve all the desperate problems the country faced, and they preached their doctrines tirelessly to all who would listen. True believers in the myriad political sects numbered in the millions, eagerly seeking converts to their own particular truth. All of these were represented on Boston Common when I came to town.

The impetus of the National Labor Relations Act and the founding of the Committee for Industrial Organization (CIO) in 1935 brought a mushroom growth of labor unions, with sit-down strikes in automobile plants and union-management confrontations, sometimes violent, all across the country. I was too young to have had any experience with unions, but I had read about police attacks on striking workers in San Francisco and Minneapolis, and I remembered striking shoe workers being tear-gassed in

Lewiston during the past summer in Maine. Labor unionism also became a holy cause for tens of thousands of selfless crusaders.

Young though we were, my friends and I had heard of most of these things and tried to make some sense of them. We were forming our own ideas and opinions on all these issues, and we were ready to debate them with all the arrogant certitude of youth in proud possession of a little knowledge.

However, interested as we were in debating the issues of the day, Mac and I had a more immediate concern. If we didn't find jobs in the city we'd be forced to return to the rural poverty we'd left behind us. Determined not to go back, we stuck to our single-minded pursuit of employment.

4

Ungainfully Employed

Mac and I arrived in Boston during the recession of 1937. That's right. We were in the midst of what was known as the "Roosevelt recession" in the middle of the depression. The president had thought things were going so well at the beginning of his second term in office that he yielded to business-interest pressures and drastically cut federal spending. To add to the economic dislocation, the end of a four-year drought brought huge farm surpluses with slashed prices and widespread dumping and destruction of crops. Unemployment jumped from 7.5 million to 11.5 million. It was a tough time to be looking for a job.

Despite the constant rebuffs and boring hours sitting in employment agency offices, each morning Mac and I would trudge into Boston. Buoyed by our youthful optimism, we answered any help-wanted ad that held the slightest promise and we daily made rounds of the employment agencies. Sometimes we'd make side excursions to Bunker Hill Monument, Faneuil Hall, scene of the Boston Massacre, Old South Meeting House or some other historic site. Then, after the job hunt, we'd generally end up at the Copley Square library or on the Common.

We spent evenings in our room on Sullivan Square where we lived frugally, eating all our meals there — day-old bread, peanut butter, and fruit. Our $3.50 weekly room rent was our major item of expense. My only indulgence was smoking. I used a pipe because it was cheaper and could make a 15-cent can of

Prince Albert pipe tobacco last a week. Only rarely would we indulge in a hot dog at Joe and Nemo's. Sometimes I'd walk slowly past restaurant windows and watch well-dressed people eating big meals at the tables inside, and I'd promise myself that someday I too would be among them. I just had to get a start somewhere.

Reading books from the library and discussing what we'd read provided our only recreation. Some evenings I would peck away at the L.C. Smith, working at a short story I was trying to finish. The story involved the rivalry of two young men, brothers, for the hand of a fair lady, an avalanche, and a denouement in which the loser sacrifices himself so the winner can survive to enjoy the prize. I did eventually finish it, but no one would buy it. We weren't leading a very exciting life and were making no visible progress in the job search. However, we remained confident that if we persevered, we would find employment.

Then, in the middle of our third week of job-hunting, we answered an ad for "willing, conscientious young men for clean, interesting employment. No experience necessary." After my experience in magazine subscription sales, I was suspicious of this one, but it turned out to be a real job and we were both hired. The company was called Rogers Distribution Service and the owner was a prissy little man who had a good thing going.

Mr. Rogers operated out of a garage-type building in Somerville. It was just a large open space with a small office in one corner. The open space held great stacks of baled newspapers. Mr. Rogers had a contract with the publisher of a chain of neighborhood weekly publications. These shopping-news papers were about 80 percent advertising, five percent local news, and the rest pseudo-news filler material purchased by the yard from a feature service. Big trucks brought the papers to Rogers' place of business whence they were distributed door-to-door in the locality served by each publication. Mr. Rogers got paid for the distribution and we did it, about 20 of us "willing, conscientious young men." The work was not very clean and not at all interesting. But it was a job.

For starters, we had to buy cloth bags for carrying the papers. These bags cost us five dollars each, but we didn't have to pay for them up front. It would be taken from our wages. The shoulder-strap bags were made of sail cloth, were boldly lettered "Rogers Distribution," and probably cost Mr. Rogers about 75 cents. The bag held a goodly supply of papers — about 40 pounds worth. Signed-on and bag-equipped, we were assigned to a crew, a group of five who would work together under a crew manager. Mac and I were assigned to the same crew, working under a hearty, tousled, blondish young fellow named Edgar. I don't remember any other name and we just called him Ed.

Before the day's work started, the whole work force was mustered by the crew managers to stand outside Mr. Rogers' office. Mr. Rogers, who earlier had been busily engaged in hiring new workers, selling carrying bags and handling other business details, now came forth to give his assembled crew an appropriate send-off. Short, rather stout, but neatly dressed in a dark blue suit, white collar and tie, Mr. Rogers looked rather like a deacon ready to take up the collection. His ruddy cheeks shone, his sparse hair was parted in the middle, slicked down with something greasy, and he gave off a faint aroma of bay-rum after shave.

Drawing himself up to his full height of about five-foot-four, he'd look us all over, maybe to be sure we all looked clean and conscientious. We would find later that this assemblage was a daily rite and Mr. Rogers could be relied upon to perform it every morning. I used to watch the pecksniffian little man and wonder if he might be moved to lead us in prayer. It would have seemed in character, but he always stopped short of that.

"Good morning, men," he'd start. He always called us men, though most of us were still in our teens. Some of the crew would mumble a return greeting.

"It's good to see you all here, ready to go out and deliver the news to the good people of Shadyside (or whatever district we were working in that day). There are a few rules you should always keep in mind. Don't just throw the paper on the porch. Papers are to be rolled and placed behind doorknobs or behind screen doors. If the screen door is locked, put the paper under the screen door handle. Never put the paper in the mail box. That is against the law and I'm sure none of us wants trouble with the federal government. The penalties could be severe."

He'd pause to let that sink in, leaving the impression that placing a paper in a mail box might result in a lengthy sojourn at Alcatraz.

"Don't skip any houses. I'll find out if you do. The people out there look forward to receiving their papers, and when they don't get one they call the publisher. Then the publisher calls me. I speak to the crew manager and he knows which man was responsible for each street in his district. There have been instances, only one or two, where men I trusted were not worthy of that trust. One of them put a whole bundle of papers into a trash bin. Another shoved a bunch down a storm drain. Those men are no longer with the service.

"So, do your work conscientiously, be worthy of our trust. Do not skimp, dawdle or loiter. We are engaged in important work. Let us do it well." With this he would send us forth.

Each crew, with a manager driving his own car loaded with papers, would go to an assigned section of the city. Edgar had a rather small car for the purpose, I think it was a Studebaker, but he managed to squeeze us all in, along with about 20 bales of papers. Then we moved out to location, Ed driving very gingerly, careful not to break his over-stressed springs. Reaching our district, usually a section of single-family detached homes with an occasional street of up-and-down duplex houses, we would be dropped off, one by one, with a supply of papers and a file-card map of an area to cover. After putting a paper under the door-knob of each home on that map, we would be picked up and brought to another area. Having placed his crew, Edgar then cruised the territory to make sure we didn't violate Mr. Rogers' trust and dispose of some papers illegally, and to minimize time-lapse between maps. I must say he was good at it. He'd usually show up when I was down to my last five papers. Ed seemed a pretty decent sort, but he wanted to keep his job which I'm sure paid a lot better than ours.

At the end of the day Edgar brought us all back to the Rogers garage and we were dismissed and told whether to report the following morning. We didn't work a long day, about seven hours, but that was without respite, time for lunch, or anything else. It was rare we got a chance to pause for a smoke between maps. For this day's work we got a net pay of $1.60, most of the first week's wage going to pay for our bags. There were no other deductions that I recall. Social Security had just been enacted but no deductions were made for that, and income tax payroll levies had not yet been invented.

It was a job, though monotonous and boring, and we could live on the pay after a fashion, though it was rarely more than three or four days a week. We ate all our meals in our room and the major staples of our diet were day-old bread, peanut butter and bargain fruit from the farmers' market. One advantage for us was the easy walking distance from our rooming house to the job, as long as we stayed in Charlestown. It was only about a mile each way. This walk to and from work, in addition to walking the better part of the seven hours on the job, gave us plenty of exercise. Still, many days we walked to the library or the Boston Common after work.

Mac and I both worked for Rogers Distribution for several weeks, but we didn't regard it as a career and continued to look for something else. When I graduated from high school in June of 1936, I had wholly unrealistic expectations. I had thought I might get hired as a reporter at a Portland newspaper because I always received high marks on my written work at school, but I was quickly disabused of this notion. I even turned down a menial job peeling vegetables in the kitchen of Portland's finest hotel. Afterward, I learned better. Now I'd accept any kind of a real job, and I finally found one.

I had learned that restaurant managers sometimes called the employment agencies late in the afternoon because someone had quit or failed to show up for work. By that hour most of the job seekers had given up and gone home. So I started hanging around every day at one of the busier agencies, arriving late in the afternoon and staying until they closed. The agency people got to know me and one day my diligence was rewarded. A last minute call came in for a kitchen helper and I was the only job-seeker left in the office. The employment agency fee of one week's wages would be withheld, in weekly installments, from my pay.

The Century restaurant was on Tremont at the corner of Winter Street, across from Park Street Church. It was an Italian restaurant specializing in seafood dishes. The owner's name was Carbone and he had a rather fancy layout on the street level. The large dining room had white linen cloths on the tables and red leather upholstered chairs; the cocktail lounge was done in natural wood and red leather. It was the sort of place where I used to linger on the sidewalk and stare at the diners through the windows. Some of the menu entrees cost as much as my pay for a week, which was $12 for six ten-hour days.

The kitchen was in the basement, with orders coming down and prepared food going up by means of a dumb-waiter hoist. Supplies were delivered via elevator from the street. I saw no daylight from the time I reported to work until my shift was over, but I didn't mind that. I was just delighted to be working and getting paid twice what I could make distributing newspapers.

The Century's kitchen would not be very impressive by today's standards, but it was big and well-equipped compared to any I had ever seen. Rectangular and about 20 by 40 feet, one half was taken up by big walk-in freezer/refrigerator boxes and by a storage area for canned goods and other food staples not requiring refrigeration. At the other end, the eight-foot-long range with eye-level broilers stood opposite a ten-foot stainless steel table with big drawers, high racks and shelves. Another steel work table ran along the end wall, around the corner and back toward the storage area, interrupted only by the dumb-waiter near the corner and by three huge steel set-tub sinks for pot washing and vegetable preparation. Pots, pans and skillets hung from hooks within easy reach of the cooks working between the range and the worktop. Though not bright, the place was reasonably well lighted and very clean, with every inch of space put to some use.

My duties included peeling vegetables, washing all the pots, pans and implements used in food preparation, keeping the kitchen clean and doing anything else required by the chef and his assistant. I didn't mind the work and liked the guys I was working with, and even learned a lot about professional methods of preparing and serving food.

In addition to learning something, I ate well, getting all my meals on the six days I worked. After a diet of peanut butter and stale bread, I thought I'd died and gone to heaven. My three delicious hot meals every day included not only old favorites like ham and eggs, roast beef, baked fresh cod and spaghetti with meat balls, but I also had Italian dishes I'd never heard of, like lasagna, ravioli and manicotti. My wages weren't high but I was eating better than I ever had before. Unfortunately, I couldn't pass on any of this bounty to Mac. He still lived on stale bread, baloney and peanut butter.

The chef, Steve, was a big man weighing about 250 pounds, but light on his feet and as fast and deft as anyone I ever saw in a kitchen. When I first started I thought he yelled a lot more than necessary.

"More blanched spaghetti out here! On the double!"

"The big skillet! Right now!"

"Do it now! How often do I have to tell you?"

"Don't mix that with a spoon! What the hell you think you got hands for?"

Either I got used to Steve or he cooled off. Maybe he saw that I was fast and willing, often anticipating his needs. And I did admire him as a professional and sought to earn his respect. Maybe he sensed that and calmed down.

I also marveled at Steve's capacity for wine. We kept no cooking wines in the kitchen, perhaps for good reasons. So when we got an order for Lobster Newburg, or other dish calling for wine, the cook had to order it from the bar. Steve had the bartenders trained, so when he ordered sherry for Newburg, they'd send down a full tumbler. Maybe a third of it would go into the dish. The rest went into Steve. But it didn't matter how many Newburgs were ordered during a shift, I could never see any difference in Steve, either in his demeanor or his performance.

I liked Steve, but I think I had even better rapport with the sous-chef whose name was Rocco. A flamboyant, volatile son of Italian immigrants, Rocco was a lean rangy fellow in his mid thirties. He was a jaunty looking guy with olive complexion, black hair and a thin moustache. When Steve was in the kitchen with Rocco, Steve was obviously in charge and Rocco was fairly quiet, working swiftly and efficiently, filling orders as fast as Steve did and talking only about the work to be done.

But after Steve went off duty and Rocco was in charge, he became vocal, constantly talking or singing. He liked me, perhaps because I was a good listener, and I was fascinated by some of the tales he told. Mostly he talked about his love life which, as he told it, was variegated, passionate and not a little scandalous. I never knew how much of his stories to believe but found them entertaining, and they made the time pass quickly. Rocco also seemed to regard me as a sort of apprentice chef and he was always showing me how to prepare some dish or explaining some procedure, between his ventures into autobiography. He advised, "You stick with me for a year, Mark, and you can take over this job. I'm going to be looking for something else, a place where I'll be in charge. Steve likes you and when I leave you can step right in."

Rocco was making $28 a week and Steve was rumored to make $50. Big money compared to my $12 weekly wage. Pleased as I was to have a steady job, becoming sous-chef at the Century and maybe going up from there wasn't exactly my ambition in life. I'd often vowed if I ever got out of that Good Will kitchen I would never cook again, ever. Now I was working back into it, even though I was employed as an assistant and pot washer.

Still I appreciated Rocco's concern and certainly admired his skill. And the most impressive thing to me about Rocco was that he could keep up this chatter no matter how busy we were, and he never slowed down, never hesitated, never got an order wrong. It was as though his mind had two tracks. One carried on the routine of cooking and serving up food, while the other track ranged freely over diverse subject matter. And when he wasn't talking he'd sing arias from grand opera. He had a strong tenor voice and sang mostly popular airs from Verdi or Puccini. I always liked that.

I ate all my meals there in the kitchen and they were always good. Steve would give me a portion of something already prepared, whatever we had a lot of at the time, but with Rocco I could get almost anything I wanted, even specially prepared dishes. I've occasionally wondered what became of Rocco. He was still at the Century the last I had any contact with him.

Now that I had a job in Boston, Mac and I decided to leave Sullivan Square and soon found a big room on Somerset Street, just a few doors from Howard Street off Scollay Square. This room was $5 a week, but now we could afford it. It was a better room, too, bigger and on the ground floor, with two windows looking out on Somerset Street. In addition to the double bed and a dresser, we had a sofa big enough to sleep on, a large table by the windows with comfortable chairs and reading lights. Best of all, we were where we wanted to be. In the center of things.

Scollay Square was indeed a major Boston crossroads and the center of most of the things we were interested in. Tremont Street ended there, as did Cambridge and Hanover Streets. On the west side of the square lay the historic West End, Beacon Hill, and the center of state and city government. To the north was the teeming Italianate North End with Haymarket Square and the busy open-air produce market surrounding Faneuil Hall. To the south was Boston's financial and commercial center. We were within five minutes walk of Boston Common, or any of a dozen historic sites now part of the "Freedom Trail." The main library was a fifteen-minute walk but there was a good branch library on Cambridge Street only five blocks away.

Scollay Square itself was then a rowdy honky-tonk place, bustling with bars, restaurants, movie theaters, snack shops, bowling alleys, a hotel with a strip show, and many less obtrusive smaller shops doing a lively business with the crowds that swirled about the square at all hours. Just off the square and half a block from our rooming house was the famous Old Howard burlesque theater. Scollay Square has since disappeared along with Howard Street and all the old time landmarks. In their place have risen a new City Hall and the JFK Federal Office Building.

With a steady job at the Century I could now afford to go to the movies regularly, and there were a half dozen cinema houses within a few blocks, three right on the square and many more a little farther away. Admission prices ranged from 10 to 35 cents depending on location and the hour of the day. This was wonderful to me and I became an uncritical consumer of the silver-screen magic. In New Portland there had been no movies, and those films that came to larger towns like Farmington or Madison offered little choice and were not easily reached. At Good Will I saw no movies. Now I had a wide range of shows to choose from and only a short walk to get to them. So I went often to see my favorite stars — James Cagney, Janet Gaynor, Charles Laughton, Myrna Loy, Spencer Tracy, Ginger Rogers, Fred Astaire and many others.

However, despite the lure of the movies, we spent most of our spare time at Boston Common or the library. Mac continued working for Mr. Rogers, having had no success in finding another job. But he was also developing, in his spare time, another occupation — scouting for rare books. He had learned that some bookstores would pay well for unusual book finds wanted by their collector customers. Mac would spend hours browsing through the many used-book stores of Boston, on the lookout for rare books for resale. He didn't make a lot of money, but he enjoyed the search and the occasional book sale supplemented his pay from Mr. Rogers. Working long hours at the Century and lured by other attractions, I rarely spent any time at my typewriter and the short story was still unfinished. Neither did I get involved in Mac's book search activity, but he was diligent and may have made as much money as I did, though my income was more certain.

Now that I had a regular job, even though the hours were long and the pay meager, I was beginning to feel that I belonged in Boston. I knew my way around town and felt at home in my neighborhood of Scollay Square. For me there was no longer any question of another humiliating retreat to Maine. I was confident and proud, and knew I'd make it here in the city, and could turn my attention to other things than mere survival and the free attractions of the library and Boston Common.

5

Going into Politics — and out Again

At about the time we moved to Somerset Street we found a leaflet on a bench in the Union Station inviting the general public to attend a rally of the Young Communist League (YCL). And we figured, why not listen to what they have to say? We had a slight acquaintance with this youth auxiliary of the Communist Party, as we had with several other left-wing organizations that we had heard debating on Boston Common.

We had no real understanding of any of these competing groups, but we knew we were in favor of socialism. We had read about it in the Little Blue Books and had discussed it, both at school and in the endless debates on Boston Common. And it seemed obvious to us that something must be done to change an economic system where people starved in the midst of plenty.

A planned economy would produce enough for everyone and distribute goods to whomever was in need of them. It would avoid cycles of boom and bust. There would be no unemployment. Everyone would contribute according to his abilities and talents; he would receive from the general stock whatever he needed. There would be an end to exploitation of one man by another. The end of poverty would eliminate a major cause of crime and the need for expensive and oppressive forces of police and military. The end of capitalism would remove the economic causes of war, thus ending this scourge of mankind. Gradually the need for government itself would cease to exist. All this made sense to us. It appealed to our common sense and to our youthful idealism.

The YCL rally drew nearly 300 people. The speakers were interesting and audience reaction enthusiastic, often interrupting the speakers with applause. We were asked to join and after serious consideration we did. We were for socialism, we reasoned, so why not join the biggest, most successful organization backed by the prestige of the world's first socialist state.

The Communist Party (CP), in an earlier, more militant stage, had led unemployment demonstrations, confronting authority and demanding work and relief. But now the principal thrust of the party's program was building a "popular front" against fascism. At home this meant giving uncritical support to President Roosevelt whom only a few months ago they had denounced as a fascist.

This about-face was explained as a tactic required by Hitler's rise to power in Germany, Mussolini's recent seizure of Ethiopia, the Japanese invasion of Manchuria, and the Spanish Civil War, then going on. All these were causes of alarm to every thinking person and the idea of organizing a broad movement to counter the widespread totalitarian threat seemed not only reasonable but necessary. Mac and I completed application forms and joined without reservation.

As members we were expected to attend a branch meeting every week and try to get our friends to read some of the YCL papers or pamphlets. I tried without much success to interest a dishwasher at the Century in an anti-fascist pamphlet. He read it but didn't think too much of it. Meetings of the West End branch were held in someone's apartment off Cambridge Street on the back side of Beacon Hill.

I don't recall that I learned much at these meetings where discussions were mostly about atrocities being practiced against the peoples of Spain and China. I was getting the same information from reading the daily papers, but there were exhortations about supporting the embattled Spanish and Chinese republics. The only practical measures of support that I remember involved occasionally helping out with a distribution of leaflets at public meetings. Though the meetings were dull and the activities seemed marginal, I continued to attend, feeling that I was making some small contribution toward a better future.

The branch had about 15 members, ranging in age from 16 to mid 20's, more men than women. Though everyone was friendly, the membership seemed to be polarized. On the one hand were those regularly employed at reasonably good jobs. And then there were those like Mac and me whose means of livelihood were marginal or worse.

The two women I remember well, Diana and Sophie, had secretarial jobs, dressed well and had some aura of prosperity. They were both about 20 years old, Diana short, brunette and cuddly, Sophie a cool slim blonde. But they didn't fraternize with us. Bernie Silverstein, a tall dark fellow, worked as a clerk in a store owned by his parents and he seemed prosperous compared to the rest of us. Those three, with a couple of others, seemed to keep to themselves, encouraging no social contact beyond YCL branch meetings.

However, we did make some new friends among those whose circumstances were little better than our own. Joe Russo, a big husky chap with the build of a professional football player and a very sharp mind, had only occasional employment and lived in Charlestown with his parents. His father was a longshoreman, only occasionally employed. John Hamilton, our youngest member, eager, flamboyant and volatile, lived with his parents in Dedham and had no job at all. Lloyd Woodward, whom we called Woody, had no job and was living on his savings. With these three we occasionally attended public forums, hung out on Boston Common, and did things that cost little or no money.

After we had known Woody for a couple of weeks he told us he was looking for a cheaper place to stay. Since Mac and I had the sofa in our double room, we invited him to move in with us. We checked with the landlady who had no objections. So Woody moved to Somerset Street and we split the $5 weekly rent three ways.

Woody could have lived with his parents, but he had moved out and refused to go back. He told us why. His father had worked for many years in some minor supervisory capacity for a small manufacturing plant. When Woody finished high school, his father had asked the boss to give his son a job. So Woody went right to work in the shipping department of his father's shop. Lucky boy. He was practically the only one in his 1936 graduating class at Milton High who got a job of any kind. His wage was $15 a week, which wasn't bad for those times, and he lived at home.

Woody worked hard and saved his money, so he had more than $300 in the savings bank when he was approached by a CIO organizer. Woody joined the union and volunteered to help organize the shop. He had signed up a few of his fellow employees when the boss got wind of this criminal threat to free enterprise and called his supervisors together for a meeting in his office. He told them they had to find out who was at the bottom of this outrage and put a stop to it.

Woody's dad spoke up and told the boss his son was responsible. Woody wasn't even permitted to finish the day. He was out on the street without a job in mid-morning. After a nasty row he left home and ever since had not spoken to his father. He went back to the house sometimes when his father was at work, and his mother would give him a meal. Otherwise he had severed relations with his family.

Woody was a tall gangly fellow, thin and nervous, with a hawkish sort of look about him. Mac and I liked Woody and he had the same interests we had — mostly hanging around the Common and reading at the central library. But Woody wasn't looking for another job. He intended to live off his savings as long as he could and he watched every penny. We were amused, and sometimes exasperated, by his penny-pinching. On rent day we each put up our share of the five dollars. Woody kept careful records and insisted that we take turns putting in the odd penny — $1.67 for two weeks and $1.66 on the third.

Mac and I had worked out a system for eating for little money when we were working for Mr. Rogers. We found a place in the North End where we could get peanut butter in bulk for 15¢ a pound, a big loaf of day-old bread for 5¢, baloney for 15¢ a pound and cheap mayonnaise. We'd hang around the North End farmers' market at closing time when the farmers would practically give away produce rather than haul it back. So bargain fruits from the farmers' market, supplementing our peanut butter and baloney sandwiches, were the staples of our diet. On my day off from the restaurant I shared with Mac and paid my share. Woody joined in, too, but he meticulously counted the number of slices of bread and baloney each of us ate. We found that irritating.

Then one evening soon after I got home from work, Woody came in carrying a huge sack and dumped the contents on his bed.

"What the hell you got there?" Mac asked.

"Pound cakes," replied Woody proudly.

We got up and looked at the pile of cakes on his bed.

"What in the name of God are you going to do with all that cake?" I asked him.

"I'm going to eat it. You won't believe this, but Feliciani's has a clearance sale going on. Pound cakes for 13¢ each, two for a quarter. I bought six dollars worth."

"Forty eight cakes," said Mac, shaking his head in disbelief. "They're going to get pretty stale by the time you get down to the last one."

"Oh, no. They're all sealed up and they told me at the store they'll last indefinitely as long as they stay wrapped. I figure if I eat two a day I won't need anything else. That's just twenty-five cents a day for food and this bunch will last me 24 days."

"You'll get mighty sick of cake," I ventured.

"Oh, no. I like pound cake, and they're very nourishing. You guys want some? They still got a lot left."

"I wouldn't mind having a couple," said Mac.

Woody looked at me and I shook my head. "Tell you what. I'm going back and get another dozen. I'll pick up a couple for you," he told Mac.

Mac gave him a quarter and he went back to Feliciani's, a big north end grocery where we often found bargain foods.

We had a big chiffonier and none of us had any clothes to speak of, so it was no problem cleaning out a dresser drawer for Woody to fill with pound cakes — a 30-day supply. For weeks he ate nothing else. We would occasionally offer him some bread and baloney, but he always refused. They cost more than his cakes and he was determined to save money. And he was very principled. He wouldn't accept the gift of a baloney sandwich, but he didn't offer us any of his cakes, either. The cakes didn't spoil. They did dry out some and got a little stale, but Woody kept eating them and seemed none the worse for it, but he was an awful cheapskate.

Besides spending many days in the library, Woody had one other favorite diversion in which we sometimes joined him when we weren't working. The Old Howard burlesque theater was right around the corner from our rooming house. It opened its doors at ten in the morning and went on until midnight, showing two movies followed by the live show, between four and a half and five hours of entertainment, continuous all day and evening. If you bought your ticket before 11 a.m. it cost only 15¢ in the second balcony. And nobody ever bothered you there. You could stay as long as you wanted, until midnight if you felt like it.

Sometimes the movies were pretty good, sometimes they were lousy, but they changed the bill every week. The burlesque comedy acts were raunchy but we thought they were funny, and the bump-and-grind strippers looked good to us from the second balcony. At fifteen cents it was the best value in town and Woody took full advantage of it. He would put a pound cake and a bottle of water in his bag and head for the Old Howard at 10:30 in the morning. He went two or three times a week, and he never left without seeing the strip show at least twice.

Apart from attending the YCL branch meetings, going to the movies or burlesque and spending time at the library and on the Common, we regularly attended the public forums where prominent speakers addressed a wide spectrum of subjects of general concern. These were usually free or charged only a nominal admission, and there we heard speakers such as Reinhold Niebuhr, Scott Nearing, Norman Thomas and Earl Browder.

One of my favorite forums was the Community Church which, though nominally Unitarian, could hardly be called religious in any ordinary sense. The pastor, Donald Lothrop, was reputed to be a Communist Party member, or at least a sympathizer. He was a handsome, charismatic sort and I got on well with him. Each Sunday morning Community Church would fill Symphony Hall at Huntington and Massachusetts Avenues by scheduling well-known, and often controversial, speakers.

Community Church also had a youth group that met on Sunday evenings in a small hall off Charles Street near the Public Gardens. The youth forum also invited speakers, generally people of local reputation. I recall hearing a popular candidate for Boston School Board. On other occasions we had ex-mayor Jim Curley, a local leader of the Sons of Italy of reputed fascist sympathies, a Communist Party candidate for mayor of Boston and an exchange student from Germany who defended the Nazi party. These youth forums would attract between 30 and 50 people and the audience participation was general and sometimes intense. After a few weeks I was asked to join the program committee, and I always joined fully in the question and discussion sessions that followed a speaker's presentation.

I never developed close relationships with many members of the YCL West End branch. There was the close-knit group that generally kept to themselves, and whom we saw only at meetings. We'd occasionally see Joe Russo at the library, but he was by nature a solitary sort of guy. So John Hamilton was the only member of the branch, besides Woody, who became a good friend and whom we saw often other than at meetings.

Johnny was a little younger than the rest of us, and he had dropped out of high school in the middle of his junior year. He said it bored him. He was a brilliant kid, but he was also erratic and volatile. I always liked Johnny but never knew just what to expect from him. Though he lived with his parents in Dedham, he came into town often and we'd see him at the Common or the library, and sometimes he'd come to our rooming house and spend the evening visiting. I remember the discussions we had in our room as being more interesting than any that ever occurred at YCL branch meetings.

At the YCL meetings most of the discussions continued to be about the fascist assault on the elected government in Spain, the Japanese atrocities in Manchuria, and the new Soviet constitution, touted by Stalin as the world's most democratic constitution. We read it and it seemed to us a good one. There was little said about the Moscow trials, the first of which had taken place in August of 1936, and the second in January of 1937. The third was yet to come and would finish the job of wiping out almost all the original revolutionary leaders of Lenin's party. No one in the West knew, or even suspected, at that time the extent of the slaughter of innocents being carried out by the Stalinist regime. Only recently have we learned that as many as 14 million people were murdered in 1937-1938 alone.

We read about the Moscow trials in the newspapers, and I remember wondering how there could be so many traitors in a country where socialism had triumphed and life was presumably so much better. But generally I accepted the explanation that the capitalist world surrounding the Soviet Union would go to any lengths to entice, bribe and corrupt Soviet citizens, even leaders. And Stalin, we were assured was not only a great leader, but incorruptible, a "man of steel," on whose broad shoulders the future of mankind rested securely. Once committed to the organization, I was not inclined to be critical of our leaders, assuming they knew a lot more about these things than I did.

I don't know how long I might have gone on accepting the rationalizations and disbelieving all negative reports coming out of the Soviet Union. Over the years I have known many intelligent, sincere and idealistic people who could not shed the blinders and went on defending Stalin, whatever atrocities he committed. Many persisted in this state of denial right up to Khrushchev's 1956 speech exposing Stalin's long record of crimes against the Soviet people. Some still apologize for the monster up to the present day. I like to believe that my quest for the truth wherever it led would have kept me from remaining long in thrall to the criminals in the Kremlin, but maybe I was just lucky. In any case, I was soon confronted with a principled issue that I could not ignore. Sometime in early December a special meeting of the Greater Boston YCL was called. We were not told the purpose of the session, but everyone was urged to be present. The meeting was well-attended. I'd estimate between 125 and 150 people filled the hall.

Surprisingly, sitting up front was Phil Frankfeld, the head of the Communist Party in Boston. Frankfeld was a stocky, bullet-headed little man, probably in his mid-forties at that time. I was told he had been a veteran of the YCL from the 1920's before becoming a party leader. Frankfeld was always belligerent when I saw him, but that was probably because of the type of occasions on which he came to my attention. Only recently, I had greatly admired his aggressive testimony at public hearings conducted by the Massachusetts legislature's Committee to Curb Communism. My friends and I had attended all the open hearings held at times when we weren't working. Now, Frankfeld was chairing this YCL special meeting and that alone told us something important was happening.

After Frankfeld called the meeting to order, Dave Grant, Greater Boston organizer for the YCL took the floor. Dave was a tall, clean-cut man in his early thirties, suave and personable in any contacts I ever had with him. He made a little talk about the splendors of socialism as evidenced in the Soviet Union, about the need to defend the achievements of the working class against all enemies, and especially against traitors. For turncoats who would betray the cause of socialism from within, death was too benign a punishment. Our leaders in the Soviet Union knew how to deal with this sort, he proclaimed, referring to the recent treason trials in Moscow.

Then he announced that this special meeting had been called for the purpose of trying a member of the West End branch for treasonous activities. Echoes of the Moscow trials, I thought.

Then Dave told us that the alleged culprit, the snake who had wormed his way into our ranks only to sell out to the class enemy, was John Hamilton. The crime of our precocious 16-year-old friend was that he had been seen talking with some Trotskyites in front of Ford Forum where they were distributing leaflets. ("Trotskyite" was a term of derogation used by Communist Party people in referring to followers of Leon Trotsky. I was to learn that they called themselves Trotskyists).

Dave Grant acted as prosecutor and produced some witnesses who had observed this treasonable conversation from a distance. Bernie Silverstein was the only witness I recall, but there were two or three others. Given a chance to speak up for himself, John didn't deny the conversation, but stated in his defense that he had been trying to convince them of the error of their ways and win them over to the YCL.

Grant seemed to think that Johnny's confession settled the matter. He said it proved the accused was guilty as charged, and he asked for a motion to expel John Hamilton from the organization as a traitor to the working class. Phil Frankfeld joined the offensive, making a vicious attack on Johnny, whom I doubt he even knew, and wound up his denunciation with a call for the vote on the motion of expulsion.

I looked around, waiting for someone of the many people who knew Johnny to speak up in his defense. But no one offered anything. I found it hard to believe this sort of thing could be railroaded through without anyone questioning it. I found it intimidating, but I had never been one to keep my head down and shrink from saying what I thought needed to be said. So I stood up and asked for the floor.

"Is that the only charge against John?" I asked. "That he simply talked with these people on the sidewalk outside Ford Forum?"

My friends sat near me with bowed heads, but I saw other members of the audience turning in their seats to stare at me and I sensed hostility in their gaze. So far I had only asked a question, but I sensed that it wasn't considered good form to rock the boat.

"Yes," Dave Grant assured me. "The charge was that he talked with them and it has been proven. And that's all that's necessary. Such talk is treason. It is forbidden for any member of the Communist Party or the YCL to have any contact whatever with Trotskyites."

"I know John Hamilton," I said, "and if he says he was just trying to convert these people, that's what he was doing."

"It doesn't matter what he was doing. All contact with Trotskyites is forbidden." That settled it as far as he was concerned. As for me, I had never heard of this prohibition, and if I had I might have questioned it sooner.

I was in no mood to passively accept it now. I don't suppose I expected to alter the outcome of the trial but I could not be still. "I have never had any contact with a Trotskyite and wouldn't know one if I met one. But I believe I have the right to speak with anyone I choose to and I won't accept any restrictions on that right. If that is a treasonous view, you might as well expel me along with John. Don't wait until you catch me speaking to somebody I'm not supposed to talk with."

Now the hostility directed toward me by others in the hall was palpable. My friends were silent. Dave Grant moved that I be included in the motion of expulsion and it was seconded by a chorus of toadies.

My friends remained silent as a voice vote roared approval of the motion. Johnny and I left the hall, followed by the hostile stares and occasional jeers of the self-righteous membership. John was shaken but unrepentant and thanked me for defending him. John took the street car home to Dedham and I would not see him again for several months. I walked back to the rooming house to wait for my roommates.

This situation had the potential for causing some bad feeling or embarrassment between us. Mac and Woody didn't actually vote for my expulsion, but neither did they speak up. I may have been a little disappointed in them, but their attitude toward me didn't change. As far as the YCL was concerned, they were guilty of living with an undesirable, but apparently no one made an issue of it. So things continued as they had before, except that we never saw Johnny Hamilton any more and Joe Russo stopped coming around to see us. I never knew exactly why, but I heard he also stopped going to branch meetings. Walking in the streets of our west-end neighborhood, I'd occasionally see someone from the YCL branch. Bernie Silverstein would now cross the street to avoid meeting me on the sidewalk, and the women, Diana and Sophie, snubbed me.

How did I feel about this after it was all over? I was saddened, because I had sincerely believed the Communist Party and Young Communist League were working for the socialist cause and I had no good reason to think otherwise, despite what had happened. I continued to believe in socialism and I knew my friends still in the YCL were idealistic young people capable of self-sacrifice in advancing the ideals we held in common. Still, for me there was something fundamentally irreconcilable between the ideals of socialism and the arbitrary denial of the basic right to free inquiry.

I did not enjoy being considered a pariah, but I was adamant in the position I had taken at the meeting. I thought John Hamilton had been given a kangaroo court trial, based on a precept I found entirely unacceptable. No one could tell me with whom I might legitimately hold a conversation. But I don't remember that I derived from this experience a conviction there was something phony about the CP/YCL dedication to socialism. Nor did I yet doubt the legitimacy of the regime in the Soviet Union, though I found the Moscow trial revelations increasingly disturbing.

I was still working 60 hours a week at the Century, attending the regular forums, going to the movies and the library, and joining the debates at Boston Common, so I had little time to think about it, much less brood over it. Perhaps I started paying more attention to those speakers on the Common who debunked the Soviet paradise and its official representatives in this country, the CP and the YCL. But I did not at this time come to any conclusions.

6

Beantown Winter

Mac was still working for Mr. Rogers with no prospects of finding anything else. Though he continued the rare-book search, there was not enough money in that to live on. Walking about the streets delivering advertising papers in the summer and fall was one thing. Snow or slush on the street and the temperature down below freezing were something else. Mac wasn't dressed for that and hadn't money to outfit himself with winter gear. So he decided to go to California. One cold December day he said goodbye, shouldered a pack with a few belongings and took the street car to the end of the line. From there he would hitchhike.

Mac wrote from San Francisco and we corresponded for a while before losing touch. I was not to see him again until 50 years later when I saw his name in a Good Will alumni publication. I visited him in Portland, Oregon, where he and his wife, Phyllis, had lived for most of the intervening years, raising a fine family. Since 1949 Mac was proprietor of a prosperous bookstore, The Old Oregon, so his early interest in rare books had given him the foundation for a lifetime occupation. He died in 1999.

I considered going to California. But I had an inside job that I didn't mind. Anyway, I decided to stay in Boston and bought enough winter clothes to get by. To cut expenses, Woody and I moved around the corner to a smaller room on Howard Street a few doors away from the Old Howard theater. The room was on the third floor and wasn't nearly as nice as the other, neither as large nor as well furnished. But we spent little time in it anyway, and it cost only $3.50 a week.

I guess another reason for staying in Boston was Elsa Kent. I had met Elsa, a very pretty, petite young lady of about my age, at the Community Church Youth Forum. She was also an active member of the program committee and, as we became better acquainted, we were arriving at meetings together, sitting together and leaving together. This led to our going out for other occasions or to the movies. Elsa had, for those times, a very good job. She was in the steno pool at one of the big insurance companies and was highly regarded there. She made a lot more money than I did and would try to pay her own way. This embarrassed me, but I didn't always insist on paying. If I had, we wouldn't have gone out very often.

Elsa was not only very attractive, she was guileless, fun-loving, intelligent and very affectionate. So, despite the fact that she was not political, I soon began to include her in any plans I made. In my affections she was taking the place of Dorothy, my girl friend at Good Will whom I had missed so sorely after leaving school.

I remember that Elsa was one of the very few people who ever mentioned my eye. Everyone noticed but no one ever said anything or asked any questions. My left eye was noticeably smaller than the right and had developed a film that made it look dull compared to the right. It had become that way gradually and I had no sight in the eye for most of my life. No doubt it affected my attitudes in ways I was unaware of, but everyone seemed to accept me the way I was, so I rarely gave it a thought.

That evening we had been to the movies and were sitting close together on a bench outside the Back Bay apartment building where Elsa lived with her mother. I had my right arm around her shoulders and my left hand held both of hers. The evening was chilly and Elsa remarked on it.

"I'll keep you warm," I told her, pulling her closer and kissing her.

She responded eagerly, snuggling even closer. Then she lifted her face and looked at me very seriously. "What happened to your eye, Mark?"

For an instant I was taken aback. I guess I was more sensitive on this subject than I had known. Then I realized the source of the question and the loving concern that prompted it.

"It was an accident when I was three years old...maybe close to four. I was playing with my older brother and got hit in the eye with a claw hammer."

"How awful!"

"It was pretty bad at the time. They couldn't do anything to save the sight in the eye and it gradually became the way it is now."

"You should have an operation. I'll bet they could do something."

"I'll never see with that eye again," I told her.

"Maybe not, but they could give you a glass eye and that would look better."

"Someday I will, when I can afford it."

That ended that conversation. But though I never forgot it, Elsa seemed unchanged toward me...still lively, charming and affectionate. Remembering Elsa now, I have occasion to consider how lucky I have been over the years in the women I have been intimate with. She was among the first of the bright, talented, beautiful women whom I have loved and who have accepted me despite my evident faults and shortcomings. And incidentally, I did have the operation and acquired a glass eye, but I went about it the hard way. Of which more later.

As it had in our other furnished rooms, my typewriter occupied a prominent place on the table we used as a desk. I used it for my small correspondence, mostly with family, and sometimes I spent an evening writing. There seemed to be a big market for short stories. *Liberty, Saturday Evening Post, Cosmopolitan* and a dozen others ran two, three or more stories in each issue, and I thought I should be able to sell to some of these big magazines. I finished the avalanche story and a couple others and sent them out, but received only rejection forms for my trouble. I still tried, but often my typewriter was just there, a mute reproach to me for not trying harder.

I thought my stories were pretty good but realize now they were very poor. The quality of my prose was barely adequate, grammatically correct perhaps but generally pedestrian, relieved here and there with overblown imagery. But worse was the fact that my stories revealed more about me than they did about the scenes I described. I was a callow youth with little experience in life, and I chose to write about things I knew nothing of. Had I written about life in a boarding school or cutting pulp wood by the cord, my work might have had some ring of authenticity. At least these were things I knew something about. But I chose characters and scenes derived from my reading of other authors, or vaguely imagined, to further romantically conceived and usually tendentious plots. Little wonder I received no encouragement, only postcards or form letters rejecting my work.

Things went smoothly at the Century Restaurant. As I became more adept and accustomed to the kitchen routines, both Steve and Rocco relied on me for details of food preparation that were far outside my duties as a kitchen helper. I didn't mind the extra responsibility. It made the work more interesting and the time passed more quickly. Rocco thought I should get a raise, but

Steve didn't suggest it to Mr. Carbone, so I continued through the winter making $12 for a 60 hour week.

It was during this period that I became reacquainted with my mother. I hadn't seen her since the summer of 1931, before I went to Good Will. Over the years we had exchanged brief letters and I was usually aware of where she was living. But she wasn't much of a letter writer and neither was I. Now I was living in Boston and she and Earl were working on a farm in Amesbury, Massachusetts, about 65 miles away. Mother was cooking and Earl worked in the dairy barn. After an exchange of letters, I arranged to take Saturday off, planning to hitchhike to Amesbury and spend a weekend at the farm where they worked.

What kind of reunion would this be, I asked myself as the weekend approached. For the past eight years I had had no mother and I could still vividly remember those terrible times when our family was being torn apart. Over the subsequent years these wounds had healed but the scars remained. I was the first of her children who had been in touch with her since she went away.

How would I meet this mother whom I no longer knew? I was no longer a ten-year-old child, but had become a young man making my own way in the world. Maine people have justly deserved their reputation for taciturnity, reserve and inability to express emotions. Within the family one rarely hears an adult acknowledge love for a child, let alone another adult. To do so would be considered a weakness, among both men and women. I had developed these qualities to an uncommon degree, probably to shield myself from the hurts I knew could come from commitment. So there was an element of trepidation about the coming weekend, perhaps deriving from an unconscious fear of being hurt once again.

I had good luck with hitchhiking, the second ride letting me off at the driveway of the farm. I walked up to the farmhouse carrying my small satchel. They saw me coming and mother met me on the porch that opened off the kitchen. There was a little strangeness, but we embraced and looked each other over. She thought I looked great and told me so. I thought she looked much older and smaller than I remembered, but I didn't say so. Of course I was nearly twice the size I'd been when she last saw me and she probably hadn't changed that much.

The Binghams who owned the farm were very hospitable to me. They both expressed a high opinion of Mother and Earl.

Mrs. Bingham told me, "Jo is the best cook I've ever seen in this kitchen and I don't except myself." She told me they were pleased to have Josephine's son come to visit.

Mother had always been a great cook and she probably outdid herself that weekend. Though I ate well at the Century, the home-cooked meals were welcome and it turned out to be a very enjoyable visit with Mother, once the awkwardness wore off. She asked about all the others — my brothers and sisters. She wanted to know how her father was getting along, and I told her what I could about all of them.

Following that visit, they came to Boston to see me on two or three occasions. Usually they came just for the day, but once they stayed overnight in a hotel near Scollay Square. They didn't have much money either, but more than I had. We went to restaurants, drank some beer together and saw some shows. Mother was the only family I had close enough to visit and I was glad to reestablish contact with her. We did not discuss the bad times we'd all gone through ten years before. And of course it wasn't the same as before she went away, but it was good in its own way. She was not "Mama" any more. I now called her "Mother," but I still loved her and realized she loved me too. In addition, she and Earl were good company and we became friends.

7

Peddling Oranges and Eggplant

Early in March Woody got the idea of going into business. He had been watching his dwindling reserves and realized that his savings weren't going to last forever. He had no skills or experience except for the shipping room job from which he'd been fired for union activity. If he applied for a job, he wouldn't dare use that employer as a reference. So, casting about for possible ventures, he hit upon the idea of buying a truck and starting a mobile produce market.

Woody couldn't drive but he could hire me for that if I would quit my restaurant job. He had just enough money to put a truck on the street and buy fruit and vegetables for getting the business started. So after a few days of talking about it, I agreed to go along with the venture and Woody sold his bicycle to augment his capital. It was a very good bike for those times, bought while he was still employed. Though it was in mint condition, he realized only a fraction of what he'd paid for it.

I gave notice at the Century and we went shopping for a truck. We found a big used panel truck for $50, tried it out and decided to buy. At the state motor vehicle department I got my chauffeur's license. The truck was registered and we were ready for business.

My experience trying to sell magazine subscriptions had convinced me I was no salesman, but I figured this would be different. I had always been game to try something new. The deal was that I would drive while we both shouted our wares. He would hustle the customers and we'd both serve them. It was Woody's business so he would foot the bills and collect the profits, if any. He would pay me $12 a week and all the fruit and vegetables I could eat. My hours would be a little better at this job and I would have a change of diet, not for the better. Otherwise, it was about the same as the Century. But I liked the idea of being a truck driver and a kitchen career didn't appeal to me. I bought myself a chauffeur's cap to make myself look authentic.

So we'd fare forth at about five o'clock every morning and go down to the farmers/wholesale market by Faneuil Hall, only a few blocks from our room on Howard Street, and buy produce to stock the truck. At that time, the market area in the North End was huge, covering several square blocks where the wholesalers set out the wares and hundreds of farmers came in to park and sell out of the back of their trucks. Most of this has now moved out Quincy way, but in those days that's where all the market action was, and here came restaurateurs and retail store owners to select and carry away their fresh produce each business day. Through the whole area pandemonium reigned in those early hours, everyone jockeying for position, shouting, bargaining and haggling, buying and hustling their purchases to their vehicles.

Woody was a good buyer. He examined the merchandise carefully, bargained skillfully and bought only the freshest and the best, and then only when the price was right. My part was to get what he bought into our truck and arrange it in some kind of order for the day's business. While I drove to the selected sales location, Woody priced all the items, high enough to make some profit on each, but low enough to be reasonably competitive with store prices. He checked out the First National and A&P markets regularly to be sure his prices were right. These were hard times and even households of the regularly employed had to watch every penny. Most just could not afford to pay premium prices for the convenience of home delivery.

I think Woody's planning was good. I thought so then and I still think so. Our problem was that our volume was too low, and we weren't at it long enough to build up a consistent following in any of the neighborhoods where we peddled. We worked hard, going up one street and down another, driving slowly and stopping at any sign of interest. When we weren't serving customers, we were shouting. "Fresh fruit!" "Oranges four cents each!" "Asparagus only twelve cents a pound!"

We had customers. A lot of them, but not enough. We never sold out our stock and some of the stuff didn't keep well. We ate a lot of tomato sandwiches and overripe fruit — anything that wouldn't be saleable the next day. Woody never dumped anything that wasn't already garbage. At the end of the day he'd have me drive to a poor black neighborhood in the South End while he put all the past-prime produce by the rear doors of the truck. There he'd distribute it free to the housewives who came to know our truck. They were very appreciative and Woody rose in my estimation, too. And, of course, I remembered that Mac and I had laughed at him for being a cheapskate.

I got my pay every week, but it was soon evident to me that Woody wasn't making any money. Perhaps less than I was. Every night he'd sit and figure, chew his pencil, scratch his head and pull his hair, entering figures in a notebook with the stub of a pencil. He was getting discouraged. We worked harder, longer hours, but it didn't seem to make much difference.

Once a week we worked a South Dorchester neighborhood out near Woody's parents' home in Milton. Sometimes we'd stop and his mother would give us both lunch. She was a soft, gentle lady, who obviously doted on her only child, but who was also a doormat for her husband. Mrs. Woodward seemed to like me and after the first visit she would talk to her son as though I weren't there.

"Please, Lloyd," she'd say, "won't you tell Daddy you're sorry? Then you could come back home."

Woody would just look grim, trying to ignore her. But she'd persist.

"Won't you do it for me? Please, Lloyd."

Patience was not Woody's long suit so it was just a question of time before he would explode. I knew him well enough by this time to predict it, so I paid close attention to my ham sandwich and tried to look unconcerned. I guess Mrs. Woodward knew her son too, but she couldn't quit.

"Please. It would mean so much to me."

Woody had heard enough. He slammed his sandwich onto the plate and leaned toward his mother, fists clinched on the table.

"You know what he did to me!" he shouted. "He should come to me on his hands and knees to apologize for what he did. Why don't you get on HIM to tell me HE'S sorry?"

The answer to that question was obvious, at least to me. She wouldn't dare. This conversation sort of spoiled the lunch occasion. They would return to this subject at other times when I was present, not always as heatedly.

I saw Woody's father only once, when he came home early from the shop and found us still there. He didn't seem pleased to see Woody and was barely civil to me. A lean, spare man, and graying about the temples, he wore glasses and a permanent frown. Woody seemed to get his looks mostly from his father. His mother was more soft and round. Mr. Woodward, after perfunctory greetings, hung up his hat and coat and went into the bathroom. Woody and I prepared to leave. Then we heard a roar from the bathroom.

"Hey you! Come here!"

There was no doubt in anyone's mind about who "hey you" was. Woody answered the summons. His mother and I listened from the kitchen.

"You get a bucket of soapy water and clean up that mess! Right now!"

Woody made no reply but hurried through the kitchen to find a pail and fill it with suds. Back in the bathroom his father stood over him while he mopped the floor on his hands and knees. Mr. Woodward made a few more comments as Woody mopped, but I didn't catch them all. Then Woody put the bucket away, mumbled some kind of goodbye to his mother and we got out of there.

"What the hell was that all about?" I asked after we got under way.

"He found a few drops of water on the linoleum between the sink and the toilet. So he thought one of us must have pissed on the floor. At least that's what he said."

"I don't think I did," I told him. "Did you?"

"Hell, no! More likely he did it himself when he washed his hands and went to get a towel. But he wanted to blame me for something. I've found it never pays to argue with him when he gets like that."

There didn't seem to be anything more to say on that subject, so we dropped it. We were always careful after that to get out of the house before Mr. Woodward came home. I had the impression he treated his wife the same way he did his son, though I never heard him.

Then one day Woody told me that we just weren't making it and he had to go out of business. "My savings are all gone," he told me. "I haven't been able to pay myself anything out of the business, and it's reached the point where I wonder from day to day if I'll be able to stock the truck in the morning."

"Then I guess it's time to quit," I said. I would be without a job again but it didn't make any sense for Woody to work for nothing and without any hope of improvement. I'd go back to the employment agencies and perhaps I'd get something before I ran out of money.

"Sorry I got you into this," he told me. "You'd still have your restaurant job if I hadn't."

"That's all right. I wanted to do it, and it's been fun while it lasted."

So the next day instead of buying produce we went out and sold off what was left. Then we sold the scale and supply of paper bags back to the people Woody bought them from, at about half what he'd paid originally. The used-truck lot offered $30 for the truck they had sold Woody for $50. Not having much choice, he accepted it. Woody gave me my last week's pay and we were out of business.

I didn't know exactly how much money Woody had left out of all this, but it couldn't have been much. Even at his most frugal, he couldn't last long without some source of income.

"What are you going to do now?" I asked him.

"I think I'll go back home. Mom wants me to, you know."

"Yeah, I know."

He didn't say whether he was prepared to apologize to his father and I didn't have the heart to ask. It was a tough enough decision for him to make without my rubbing his nose in it. I felt sure that if his father had done the apologies, he'd have told me.

It was a few days later that Woody moved out and went back to Milton. I was left without a job and no one to share the $3.50 room rent each week. I had saved a few dollars but they wouldn't last long, maybe a couple of weeks. I would now go back to living on peanut butter, baloney and day-old bread. I could no longer afford the few simple amusements I had indulged in while earning $12 a week. Mostly this was the movies two or three times a week, sometimes with Elsa. Now I couldn't really afford to go myself, let alone pay for her, so now I'd see her even less than before.

Then, with my money almost gone, I thought of my typewriter. I wasn't using it much so I decided to pawn it and get enough money to last until I found a job. The first place offered me five dollars and I was insulted. I'd expected at least $30. It cost $49.50 and had hardly been used. So I tried other pawn shops, but the best offer was $7.50. I accepted, thinking I would redeem it as soon as I had a job. That never happened and it was many years before I owned another typewriter.

Reflecting on my typewriter, I have often thought I'd been foolish to buy it in the first place. I got it by mail order through a magazine ad during my first summer out of high school. I had never before sat at a keyboard so knew nothing about using it. But I had the idea I wanted to be a writer so I sent away a postal money order, paying more than six weeks income from working in the woods. I didn't have that first machine long enough to acquire any proficiency, but over the subsequent years I have become a reasonably competent self-taught typist.

In those days I was a sucker for merchandise advertised in magazines, perhaps because I'd never lived anywhere with retail outlets other than the village general store. In high school I had been an avid consumer of the five-cent books distributed by mail from Girard, Kansas. A stereotypical 97-pound weakling, I was the natural target for Charles Atlas' body-building ads. Bigger, tougher kids were always figuratively kicking sand in my face and I dreamed of retribution. I read the Atlas ads, was tempted, but was kept from answering by the cost, far too high for me.

I recall being similarly attracted to the magazine ads for condoms, recommended for both disease and birth control.

Having heard other, more experienced boys, discussing problems of accidental fatherhood, I thought it well to be prepared. I also had a strong urge to couple, though I'd had no opportunities and was too shy to try and create some. The rubbers advertised were a great bargain, less that five dollars for a gross, so I optimistically sent in an order. Soon I was in hopeful possession of 144 rolled latex sheaths. Never was a 16-year old boy better equipped for a sudden access of sexual opportunity.

I wish I could report that all these devices were suitably employed and that a replacement order was soon indicated. Alas, that was not the case. I recall that I sold or gave away a few to friends but don't remember what happened to the others. The only thing I know for sure is that I never used even one of them for its intended purpose.

My typewriter was a marginally better mail-order investment and proceeds from the pawnshop loan paid another week's rent and kept me eating my austerity diet for another few days while I spent many long hours in the employment agency offices. I tried not to think about what I'd do if my money ran out before I found a job. I knew there were missions where a homeless man could get a bowl of soup and a place to flop. But I'd do that only if I had no other option. I'd been that route in Washington, D.C., my first winter out of school, and knew how demoralizing it was. Being homeless meant never to be really clean, never to have a decent meal unless you were willing to beg at restaurants. It meant losing what few possessions you have and wearing out your clothes with no hope of replacing them. There were no public agencies that would help unless you were a resident, and then they wouldn't do much. I knew I wouldn't qualify and would be told to go back to New Portland. The Traveler's Aid Society might send me back as they had from Washington, but they wouldn't do anything else.

The New Deal agencies, the WPA and the NYA, were helping some people — those who qualified, which I didn't. The WPA had a program for writers and artists, and I thought I might get accepted on the writers' project. They were not unkind, but made it clear they did not consider me a writer, whatever I may have thought of myself. The only things I'd ever had published were a couple of pieces of doggerel written when I was in high school and I didn't even have evidence for that. Furthermore, I had no family to support.

I wasn't a student, so the NYA was out. About the only program where I could have qualified was the Civilian Conservation Corps (CCC), and I'd already rejected that. If I was to work as a lumberjack for $5 a month, I might as well go back to New Portland. I could do better than that there. But I was determined not to go back. I'd find some way. So far I hadn't tried panhandling. It was so damned demeaning, but maybe I could bring myself to do it. The closest I'd come so far was offering to work for food at restaurants, knowing they were unlikely to need any help but might give me a meal.

8

Moving up to Butter and Eggs

On Wednesday afternoon, after the employment offices had closed, I walked down to the central library on Copley Square. It was one recreation I could still afford. There I saw John Hamilton in the main reading room. I hadn't seen him since the night we were both expelled from the YCL. He looked just the same and I was delighted to see him.

Johnny was feisty, exuberant as always. He told me he'd gone back to talk to those Trotskyists to see what it was that made them so dangerous that he got expelled just for arguing with them. He found out, Johnny told me, that the principal reason for existence of the Communist Party and Young Communist League was to cover up Stalin's crimes against the Russian workers. Trotsky had Stalin's number. He had exposed Stalin's crimes and that's why the Frankfelds and Grants hated him so much. Johnny gave me a pamphlet that expanded on this theme.

"And hey! How're you doing? Still working in the restaurant?" he asked.

"No. I'm looking for a job right now."

I told him what had happened since I last saw him. About Mac leaving for California and Woody returning to Milton after the failure of the produce business.

"Just hanging on, now," I told him. "I'll be all right if I can find something before my rent runs out. I don't think the landlady will let me go much beyond the due date. That's Saturday."

"Oh boy, that doesn't sound very good. I guess I'm lucky, living with the folks and I've got a job too."

"What're you doing?"

"Well, it's a business my father started. A butter and egg route. Dad let me take it over as soon as I was old enough to get my driver's license...a couple months ago. It's going pretty good. Got regular customers in some nice neighborhoods."

"Making any money?"

"I can clear $15 a week. Could do better if I took time to hustle more customers."

"Sounds good, John."

"Might be some way we could fit you in. I'll talk to my folks about it and let you know. I'll be in to see you anyway. Bring you some more literature."

I didn't really expect anything to come of that but gave Johnny my new address on Howard Street. I believed he would bring me more pamphlets. John was earnest and enthusiastic about his new political creed and I could depend on his proselytizing zeal.

Then on Friday, the day before another week's rent fell due, Johnny came to the rooming house. He had talked with his folks and I was invited to go with him to Dedham and live at their house. I would help out with the egg business doing some of the work his dad had been doing. For this I would get my room and board, plus two dollars for each new customer I added to the route by canvassing, while riding the route with Johnny. And sometimes I could work with his dad who sold and installed canvas awnings. For this I would get 50¢ per hour. That was a more than I had ever earned before. I eagerly accepted the offer and we loaded my belongings into Johnny's car.

The Hamiltons lived at the end of a quiet street not far off Washington Street in Dedham in an area that seemed almost rural at that time. They had about a half acre of land, and 20 yards from the house their lot was crossed by a small brook from which Mrs. Hamilton harvested watercress for salads. It was a modest two-story house with a basement and three small bedrooms on the second floor. I arrived in time for supper, put my suitcase in one of the bedrooms, and found that Mrs. Hamilton was a good cook.

Mr. and Mrs. Hamilton seemed old to me, as parents go. They must have been in their early sixties, which would have made them about 45 when their only son was born. By contrast, my parents were still in their forties. Mr. Hamilton was a stout jovial man with close-cropped gray hair. His wife was also heavy, neat and clean, but a little bedraggled looking, with long gray hair usually pinned up in a bun behind her head. They were both very welcoming to me and I was glad to be there.

The butter and egg business was conducted out of a shed-like structure Mr. Hamilton had attached to the side of the house. The shed was well equipped for efficient handling of the eggs and the work was easy. We would go to a big chicken ranch not far away and pick up cases of fresh eggs. This place was owned by a colonel in the Salvation Army and his wife ran it, and that's about all I remember about it.

Back home, we'd run the eggs over a scale to verify their weight. On this scale, an ingenious device built by Mr. Hamilton, the eggs rolled down a gentle carpeted incline and were separated by weight into small, medium and large. After grading, we'd candle all the eggs and pack them a dozen to a box. For candling we'd pass each egg before a hole in a light-box to view its insides and sort out any that were fertile or had a tiny blood clot. We'd eat these ourselves. Mr. Hamilton used to say these were the best eggs but the customers didn't know it. We guaranteed all our eggs were 100 percent fresh, infertile and bloodless.

The butter came from some friend of the Hamiltons. It was very good creamery butter and it brought a premium price from our customers. Our only other product was home-made sausage. Mr. Hamilton made it about once a week and we took orders in advance. He used one half lean pork, one half veal, and spices known only to himself. He wasn't equipped to stuff it into casings to make link sausages, so it was simply bulk-wrapped in one-pound packages. It was the best sausage I ever ate and it was prized by our customers. As I recall, we ran the route three or four days a week. Once a week we'd make a morning restocking run to the chicken ranch, then spend a few hours packaging our eggs. On the route, while Johnny served the regular customers I would canvass their neighbors and managed to add enough new clients to keep me in spending money.

Occasionally Mr. Hamilton would have an awning to install and I would go with him for a day and earn big money. The jobs I went on were all residential, and the houses were in some of the nicest neighborhoods of suburban Boston. They were houses of people who could obviously afford to shade their windows from the sun to protect their furniture and drapes, even during a depression. Mr. Hamilton was skilled, thorough and conscientious. He was also patient about showing me the rudiments of the trade and I enjoyed working with him. I don't recall that Johnny ever went out on any of these jobs. He seemed to take no interest in working with his dad.

Johnny was a good friend to me and his parents couldn't have treated me better if I had been their own son. Mr. Hamilton was a droll sort who read widely, and we often discussed the books he had read and passed on to us. A free-thinker, he was scornful of all religions. His wife, on the other hand, was a Pentecostal devotee who never missed a gospel meeting and prayed all the time for her scoffing husband and atheist son.

She would pray at the slightest provocation, or for no evident reason at all. Sometimes the urge would take her and she'd drop to her knees, whatever she might be doing. I have a vivid recollection of Mrs. Hamilton in the midst of the evening meal, down on her knees in the middle of the kitchen floor, bun loosened and long gray hair streaming down the sides of her face, eyes uplifted to the ceiling, earnestly praying for all of us. At the table we continued eating, Mr. Hamilton sometimes telling a wry tale or joke about the misadventures of Pentecostal preachers he had known, and Johnny and I laughing, though I was never entirely comfortable with the scene.

One story I recall was about Mrs. Hamilton's spiritual father, the local tub-thumper, who was never very generously supported by his constituents and often ran short of food for his family. When the larder was getting low, the preacher would go into the back yard. He would, Mr. Hamilton related, raise his eyes to heaven and pray for food. He had a powerful set of lungs and his voice when raised to peak volume could be heard all over the neighborhood. He knew, of course, that his loud eloquent prayers would be heard by the kind-hearted Irish Catholic woman who lived on the other side of the fence and that she would answer them as best she could with donations from her family's meager supplies.

Mr. Hamilton was a good raconteur and I thought his stories and jokes were funny. Nonetheless, I felt sorry for Mrs. Hamilton. She never challenged the truth of his stories, just prayed the harder for his salvation. I'd glance at her, down there on the floor praying for all of us. She was such a good old soul, I hadn't much heart for making fun of her.

She must have thought I was a prospect for conversion and kept urging me to accompany her to prayer meeting.

"Go ahead," Johnny told me. "They put on great show. You never saw anything like it."

"Then why don't you go? Come on. I'll go with you"

"Oh no! I've already been. But you should try it. Just for the experience."

Finally, I did go with Mrs. Hamilton and it was like no church meeting I had ever attended. My church experience had been limited to Good Will where I resented the compulsory attendance. But the nondenominational church services at Good Will were always solemn and dignified, and the sermons were occasionally thoughtful appeals to reason as well as faith. I questioned their premises and rejected their faith but learned to love the church music even as I tuned out the rest.

This Pentecostal affair was something else altogether. I recognized one or two of the hymns, though they were somewhat jazzed-up versions from what I remembered. But the "sermon," if you could call it that, was a few simple ejaculatory statements, endlessly repeated with slight variations and increasing emphasis, while the congregation responded with banging of cymbals and shouts of "Hallelujah" and "Amen."

The preacher's objective seemed to be to work the audience into a frenzy and he succeeded, at least with some of them. Individuals left their pews (actually folding chairs) and leaped about the aisles, having fits, ululating and jabbering meaningless non-words. I was told they had been seized by the Holy Ghost and were talking in tongues. This seemed to be a good thing in the eyes of the other parishioners.

Mrs. Hamilton didn't perform, at least not at that meeting. The whole affair had its comic aspects, but mostly I found it pathetic. Needless to say, I didn't go back for a second helping, and I understood why Johnny had urged me to attend but wouldn't come along. Johnny asked me if I had seen anything of the "holy spook" that was causing such a ruckus at his mother's church.

The street cars ran out to Dedham on Washington Street and connected with the Boston elevated trains. The car stop was only a few blocks from the Hamilton house, so I could easily go to town whenever I wanted. With a free transfer, it cost only a nickel. I went in often to the library, to attend forums or go to the movies with Elsa. Also, Johnny drove in regularly and I usually went with him. He attended meetings of the Young Peoples Socialist League (YPSL) and invited me to go along. The YPSL was the youth organization of the Socialist Workers Party (SWP-Trotskyist). I had been reading Johnny's SWP pamphlets and papers and realized how very ignorant I had been during my time in the YCL.

The people I met at these Trotskyist meetings were far better informed than their counterparts in the YCL. They knew more about what was going on in the world and their analyses of events were clear and penetrating. As for Stalin, they pointed out that the third Moscow trials, then going on, had the last of the old Bolsheviks in the dock. When these trials were finished, Stalin would have wiped out the entire Central Committee of the party that led the revolution of 1917 — all except Trotsky who was in exile in Mexico, and Lenin who may, or may not, have died a natural death. Stalin had deified the dead Lenin and called all the others traitors, but Stalin was the traitor and they proved this to me conclusively. He had to wipe out all opposition in order to maintain his dictatorship in the Soviet Union.

I learned that Trotsky had publicly offered to turn himself over to Moscow if an independent international commission of inquiry should find him guilty of any of the charges in the Moscow trials. A commission, chaired by philosopher John Dewey and including Suzanne LaFollette, Benjamin Stolberg, Carleton Beals,

Carlo Tresca and several other prestigious and independent intellectuals, held hearings in Mexico City, questioned Trotsky and examined reams of evidence. I had seen nothing about it in the press, but in September 1937 shortly before I was expelled from the YCL, the Dewey Commission released its report finding Trotsky innocent of every charge brought by the accusers in Moscow.

My basic beliefs had been formed under the influence of socialist leaders like Eugene Debs and Norman Thomas. Despite my disillusioning experience with the YCL, I had never abandoned my conviction that socialism was a more rational ordering of society than the system of capitalist boom or bust that had resulted in the catastrophic times the United States, along with the rest of the world, was enduring.

Talking with my fellow job-seekers at the employment agencies, I had heard endless variations of misery suffered by men desperately looking for the means to feed and house their families. Though needing a job myself, I sometimes felt sick about using any advantage to secure placement over someone whose need was greater than my own. Walking the streets of Boston I saw homeless men clad in rags waiting for a bowl of watery soup while I knew food crops were being destroyed and milk dumped. And at the same time farmers like my grandfather were losing their land because they couldn't sell their produce for the cost of raising it.

I was also keenly aware of events abroad — the Japanese military occupation and atrocities committed against the people of Manchuria, General Franco's rape of the Spanish Republic, Mussolini's brutal invasion of Ethiopia, Hitler's occupation of the Rhineland and recent annexation of Austria, with certainly more to come. All these I regarded as rotten fruits of capitalism and the only answer seemed to be a reordering of society along socialist lines. I considered it my duty to participate actively in working toward such a solution. To see the misery and injustice all around me and do nothing except seek my own selfish ends seemed intolerable to me. Realizing that I had joined the YCL on impulse, uncritical and poorly informed, I now read the basic Marxist texts, Leon Trotsky's books and the pamphlets of the SWP. I became convinced that Marx and Engels had spelled out the laws of historic change that led inexorably toward a more rational socialist society, requiring only the intervention of the workers of the world organized as a class and led by class-conscious socialists.

Comparing the SWP positions and programs with those of all the competing socialist organizations, I also became convinced that the Trotskyists had the most penetrating analyses and most cogent answers to the problems of achieving such socialist change. I came to believe that the Russian revolution of 1917 had set an example for all the world to follow and that the tragic bureaucratic degeneration there had been the result of isolation and the failure of more advanced countries to follow suit.

Leon Trotsky had been active in the revolutionary socialist movement in Russia since 1898 and was the outstanding leader of the unsuccessful 1905 revolution for which he was banished to Siberia. Escaping, he carried on from abroad, returning to Russia after the February revolution of 1917. Elected chairman of the Petrograd Soviet of Workers' and Soldiers' Deputies, he was the undisputed organizer and leader of the October seizure of power in the capital. As foreign minister he negotiated the peace treaty with Germany, then became commissar for military and naval affairs, organizing the Red Army and leading it to victory, fighting on 22 different fronts, not only against white resistance armies but also against British, American, French and Japanese armies of intervention. During the revolution and the years immediately following, Trotsky was universally regarded as the outstanding leader and thinker of the Bolshevik party, after Lenin.

Though they worked to consolidate the gains of the October revolution, none of the leaders had believed it was possible for socialism to succeed in a single, isolated country, least of all in a country as backward as Russia with its meager industrial development, its lack of democratic tradition and largely illiterate populace. A unique set of circumstances had made revolution possible there, but if it was to survive it must be supplemented and supported by workers' power in advanced industrial nations. Both Lenin and Trotsky stressed that the Russian experiment, in isolation and without such support, was doomed to degenerate or revert to capitalist power.

Then Lenin died in 1924 leaving a vacuum no one could fill. Stalin, who had always been considered by all the party's leaders a consummate mediocrity, turned out to be a devious schemer and an accomplished machine politician. As party secretary he built a machine that would eventually eliminate all his colleagues and instituted a regime that tolerated no disagreement with the line as laid down by him and those who may have formed a temporary alliance with him. Opponents were silenced and persecuted.

Trotsky and the "left opposition," in keeping with the tradition that any member could criticize freely any leader, or offer and argue for an alternative policy, refused to be silenced. Their perspective considered a revolution in some major industrial countries as the only way to assure the continued existence of the Soviet Union. "The authentic rise of a socialist economy in Russia," wrote Trotsky in 1922, "will become possible only after the victory of the proletariat in the most important countries of Europe."

To justify his oppression, Stalin evolved the concept of "socialism in one country," calling for endless sacrifice and abject submission as the only way to maintain Soviet power. In practice "socialism in one country" meant no socialism anywhere else. The Communist International became an instrument for the preservation of the Stalin bureaucracy and, veering from ultraleft posturing in Germany to betrayal in Spain, the Comintern engineered one disaster after another. As for the American Communist Party, its zig-zag course from ultraleftism to popular front was dictated not by the interests of the American workers but by the needs of Stalin's foreign policy.

In 1927, at the 15th Congress of the Russian Communist Party, Trotsky's left opposition, his colleagues and followers, were expelled from the party. In January of 1928, Trotsky was banished to Alma-Ata, a high desert crossroads in central Asia, 4000 kilometers from Moscow, 250 kilometers from the closest railroad. A year later he was deported to Turkey where he stayed for four years. Then, driven by Stalin's pressure and threats, he moved to France for two years, then to Norway. After one year, during which the first great Moscow show trial was being carried on, Trotsky was placed under virtual house arrest. Norway threatened to cave in to Stalinist pressure and deport Trotsky back to the USSR executioners. Then President Lazaro Cardenas granted him asylum in Mexico where he arrived in January, 1937.

A prolific, brilliant writer, Trotsky never gave up the struggle against the Stalinist bureaucracy in the Soviet Union, turning out book after book. In addition to his political works, he also wrote on military theory and problems of cultural life. Some of the titles published after he went into exile include *My Life* (1930), *Problems of the Chinese Revolution* (1932), *History of the Russian Revolution* (three volumes, 1932-3), *The Suppressed Testament of Lenin* (1935), *The Third International After Lenin (1936), The Revolution Betrayed* (1937), *The Stalin School of Falsification* (1937), and *Stalin* (1946). *Literature and Revolution,* published in 1925 was Trotsky's answer to the vulgar fad of proletarian writing that engulfed the Soviet Union and seduced many leftist writers in America. Trotsky argued that a socialist literature could not be artificially created by decree but would be a natural growth arising from a socialist culture and would take forms we could not foresee.

While Trotsky lived in Mexico, many of his books and articles were published by U. S. commercial publishers, but he never received a visa to visit the States. He stayed in close contact with the Socialist Workers Party. James P. Cannon and his closest associates were among the first to take up the cause of the Russian Left Opposition, and for this they were expelled from the American Communist Party in 1928. Trotsky's role was that of an advisor and mentor to his American followers, and the force of his presence across the southern border was felt by all of us. He contributed to the party magazine and offered his opinion in party political discussions. His heroic record and the brilliance of his writing assured him enormous prestige among his followers, but I never knew of any instance where he presumed any sort of authority other than that of a counselor.

While in the SWP, I never encountered the closed-minded attitudes that had driven me out of the YCL. My new associates were not only convincing, they were dedicated idealists engaged in a pursuit I considered essential. I joined wholly convinced that for me there could be no higher calling than a life devoted to creation of a more rational and decent world.

Several of the Trotskyists I met were merchant seamen who told me I should get my seaman's papers from the Maritime Commission. Equipped with the proper credentials, I could try to get a job aboard a ship as the first step toward becoming a member of one of the seafaring unions. They showed me the ropes, and I secured a set of passport-type photos, filled out all the necessary applications and had a brief interview with an official at the Maritime Commission offices. Then I received my papers certifying that I was a merchant sailor authorized to ship as an ordinary seaman (lowest deck department rating), wiper (lowest rating in the engine department, requiring no skill or experience), messman (waiter/busboy), or second cook and baker. They were impressed enough by my Good Will experience to give me this rating.

My new seaman friends told me that the Sailors Union of the Pacific (SUP) was picketing the Maritime Commission offices in New York City over an issue they referred to as the "fink book."

If I went to New York and signed up for picket duty, they told me I would have a good chance of getting an SUP trip card and a job aboard a ship. They were giving preference to men who had done picket duty. For me this would mean leaving the Hamiltons, Elsa and all my other friends in Boston. I would miss them all sorely, and I'd be giving up the small measure of security I had found there. I would need to find a way of surviving in New York City while I did my picket duty at the U.S. Government offices, waiting for a chance to go to sea. However, encouraged by my new seamen friends, I was game, confident I'd find a way to become a sailor myself.

But before leaving for New York City I wanted to visit Maine. I had been away nearly a year now and missed my family. I had good luck hitchhiking, getting a ride from just outside Revere all the way to Portland. A second ride dropped me in downtown Auburn, and it was still only the middle of the afternoon. I guess it was being in Auburn that made me think of my sister, Marianne.

I hadn't seen Marianne since early in 1931. She had been only five years old then and her name was Haidee May. She had been our first sister and we five boys adored her, but we lost her when the family split up.

I rode the interurban electric streetcar out to East Auburn and I did see my sister. She was at home alone when I arrived, now a slim, pretty girl of 12, with long blonde hair. She was as delighted to see me again as I was to see her, and after the ice was broken we had a pleasant reunion. After Mrs. Douglass, known as "Bibber," came home she told me how well Marianne was doing in school and had her show off her talents as a musician, but made it plain no further visits from me were encouraged. I came to know later that she held Marianne's family in snobbish disdain and wanted to shield her from contact with them. Bibber gave me a snack and I left there at suppertime to hitchhike to New Portland. I didn't see my sister again for another 15 years.

Dad was living at the Wymer place on the Chick Road, hauling mail between New Portland and Farmington and doing a little farming. I stayed with him and visited with my brothers. I also spent a couple of days with Gramp Williamson who was still hanging on at his farm on New Portland Hill. Only three places were still occupied on the hill where once there had been scores of relatively prosperous farms. We had a good visit as always. Gramp was interested in everything I had been doing since leaving New Portland and our talks ranged over all that had happened since.

Gramp had always been the adult with whom I could discuss anything. He might not agree with me, but he would always listen carefully and discuss rationally, whatever the topic. Now, of course, I told him about the things I had learned and my determination to work for a better, a socialist society.

Gramp agreed that the present system left much to be desired and that the socialist ideal of a classless, non-exploitive society seemed to be a big improvement. However, he didn't believe we'd ever convince a majority of the need for such a change. He cited the closed minds of his neighbors and saw little chance for radical change. Nonetheless, he wished me well and I gave him a six-month subscription to the SWP weekly paper, *The Socialist Appeal.*

On the other hand, my father (and my mother too, later) showed little interest in trying to understand my ideas. They did conceive the notion these ideas might be dangerous — to me. Generally, they just warned me to stay out of trouble.

Back in Boston, I said goodbye to the Hamiltons and to all my new friends. Leaving Elsa was the hardest. Though she hadn't joined the party and I hadn't pressed her, she agreed with me on all major issues and often backed me up in debates at the Community Forum. I would miss her very much, but she knew why I was going and encouraged me to go. She accepted my belief that a career as a seaman was a step up from any opportunities available to me in Boston. With my few belongings in a battered suitcase, I hitchhiked to New York City.

9

The Sailors Union and the Fink Book

It was early in the late-July afternoon when the truck driver let me off below an elevated train station in the Bronx. He told me that from there I could get to any place I wanted in New York City for five cents. I carried my battered old suitcase up the long stairway to the train platform and put my nickel in the turnstile. The truck driver was right about being able to go anywhere on this system, but I had to ask several people for help before I got to Union Square. It wasn't that complicated, but I had trouble understanding the directions. I had thought Bostonians had a peculiar accent, but some of these New Yorkers might as well have spoken a different language. I'd get used to this, but my first immersion was a shock.

Getting to Union Square was really very simple. The Bronx elevated station was on the IRT Seventh Avenue line which became a subway at about 121st Street in Manhattan. Changing at 14th Street for a Crosstown subway train, I got off at Union Square Station and was only about three or four blocks from my destination.

I found New York an awesome place. The sheer immensity of it, the impersonal architecture, the unaccustomed odors, the crushes of people crowding the subway trains and platforms, the frenetic pace, the constant noise. Boston, too, was a metropolis. But there, even in the heart of the city, things were on a more human scale. It would be some time before I began to feel comfortable in this city and know my way around using public transportation. Though in later years I was to spend a lot of time in New York, I never felt at home there as I had in Boston.

The headquarters of the SWP/YPSL occupied the three upper floors of a narrow building on the corner of 13th Street and University Place. There was a vegetarian restaurant on the ground floor. The Trotskyist headquarters was a beehive of activity with scores of people coming and going, working at various tasks at desks crowded together in tiny offices, an unceasing babble of voices and clatter of office equipment. Organized pandemonium. It was interesting to me, if confusing. And it was exciting to see so many people engaged in routine tasks or earnestly discussing how best to work for a way out of the impasse into which the capitalist system had plunged the country.

After consultation with several people, I was directed to a house on Washington Square where I could get free lodging. This fine old three-story mansion fronting on the north side of the square had seen better days, but it was still imposing. It belonged to a Doctor Lusinger who had his office and residence on the main floor, up a few steps from the street level. The upper floors were occupied by resident party leaders. The basement level, down a few steps from the street, was turned over to party seamen on the beach (a euphemism for being out of work). These accommodations, I would find out later, were the doctor's contribution to the party. As an aside, I should comment that the phrase "the party" for most radicals of this era meant the Communist Party. For me and my comrades, "the party" referred only to the Socialist Workers Party.

It was a short walk from the party headquarters down University Place to Washington Square. When I knocked on the basement door, it was answered by a tall, slim young woman who told me her name was Kay. She appeared to be the only person there at the time. She was, I learned, the secretary of the party seamen's group and the girl friend of one of the seamen. She showed me the bathroom, gave me a choice of two or three vacant single beds. Several others showed signs of occupancy. Kay outfitted me with some sheets, a blanket and a key to the basement entrance. She told me to be sure to return the key when I shipped out so it would be available for the next man.

I made up my bed, unpacked a few toilet articles and a book. There was not room for much more on the small table beside the bed. The suitcase went under the bed. I asked Kay for directions to the Sailors Union headquarters, and getting there turned out to be easy. Maybe I was getting the hang of it. Getting off the downtown subway train at South Ferry, I had only a few blocks to walk to the union hall.

The SUP in New York occupied the second floor of a narrow commercial building on a side street down near the Battery. The entrance door, with a barroom on one side and a defunct cafe on the other, opened on a stairway leading up. The union hall at the top of the stairs was a big open area with a few tables and lots of folding chairs and benches. One corner of this space was walled off as an office with a closed door, and a window opening onto the hall. The window was open, and framed in the opening with his elbows on the sill was a big ugly fellow with red face and cauliflower ears, wearing a white cloth cap.

I went to this window through which I could see some desks, file cabinets and a couple of men sitting at the desks. They also wore white caps, as did most of the men in the hall. I was to learn that this was the unofficial uniform of the west coast sailor and these SUP men were very proud of their west coast heritage.

I showed my brand-new seaman's papers to the guy in the window who I later learned was known as the dispatcher. He was a union official elected by the membership at a regular port meeting. Dispatcher was an important job and a position of trust, as he was the one who first received word of all openings aboard ships, posted the jobs and selected the men to fill them.

The dispatcher just glanced at my papers, then told me, "We don't have any jobs."

Dismayed, but still determined, I said, "But I heard you were picketing the Maritime Commission. Couldn't I go on the picket line and maybe get a chance of a job later on?"

He looked at me more closely now. I guess he didn't get many greenhorns coming in off the street to volunteer for picket duty at a U.S. government office.

"You'll have to talk to the port agent," he told me. He turned and spoke to the man behind the furthest desk. "Morris, this guy wants to go on the picket line." Then he opened the door to admit me to the office beyond.

The man at the desk was a stocky, powerfully built chap in his early thirties with black curly hair. He watched me approach, his eyes narrowed in what I felt was hard, suspicious scrutiny. "I'm Morris Weissberger," he told me with a curt nod.

"Mark Walker," I said.

"What do you want?"

"I've been told that if I go on the union picket line I could get a chance for a ship when there's a job no member wants."

"Who told you that?"

"Bernie Goodman."

For the first time his features softened and he gave a brief nod of acknowledgment.

"And Frank Lovell," I added.

Now he even smiled a little. The embattled SUP had gone through a long siege of attempted infiltration by Stalinists, and its leaders were also apprehensive about possible government retaliation for their unyielding opposition to federal regimentation. I realized that the names I'd mentioned had identified me as a Trotskyist, and that we were welcomed in the SUP as union militants and the most effective opponents of Stalinist intrigues. Harry Lundeburg and the other leaders of the SUP thought, rightly, that the Stalinists would like to seize control of their union and use it to serve the current Communist Party line. They had seen it happen to other organizations.

Frank Lovell and Bernie Goodman, both able seamen, were known as Trotskyists to the leaders and to the ranks of the sailors' union. Quite different in appearance, Bernie was stocky, rough and tough looking, while Frank was slim, suave and even debonair. Both were articulate rank-and-file leaders and highly regarded by their fellow seamen. Frank, a college graduate with a scholarly bent, would later write a book, using the pen name Frederick Lang. *Maritime—A Historical Sketch, A Workers' Program,* was issued in 1943 by Pioneer Publishers. It was a definitive study of the history of the U.S. maritime industry and its relationship to the government, of the maritime unions and their long struggle to define themselves and to develop an adequate leadership. The book describes the impasse facing the maritime unions in the 1940's and sets forth a socialist program for breaking out of the blind alley in which they found themselves. *Maritime* was well-received by union militants then and it still reads well now, 55 years later.

In later years, Frank would become a national leader and Trade Union director of the party. Though Frank's book was not yet written in 1938, he was certainly not unknown to Morris Weissberger.

Weissberger spoke to the dispatcher. "Give this guy a picket card, Joe, and put him on the list."

Thus I was duly enrolled for picket duty at the Maritime Commission offices on lower Broadway, a short walk from the union hall. On the picket line and in the union hall I was to learn what the "fink book" issue was all about.

The SUP was responding to a renewed effort of the Maritime Commission to implement a clause in the Merchant Marine Act of 1936 which called for issuance of what were officially known as "Continuous Discharge Books." The book, patterned on one issued to all British seamen by the Trade Board, contained a description of the man, his rating, and space for a continuous record of his sea service. Under prior U.S. law a seaman was given a discharge at the end of each voyage. Since he had a separate piece of paper for each voyage, he might produce as many, or as few, as he wished to prove his qualifications. If he was an active union man with many short trips, or if he had quit the ship before completion of the voyage, this would not be immediately evident to a company shipping master. But with the Continuous Discharge Book, the entire sea record of the man would be there. Anyone could tell at a glance whether it belonged to a "loyal employee" or an "agitator." Thus, in one neat, handy little pocket-sized book each seaman would carry his own blacklist.

The Sailors Union had, over the years, endured a series of employer-sponsored "grade books" which seamen had been required to carry in order to find work in hard times. The books not only recorded the dates of a man's service, they had a space for the captain to comment on the quality his work. The man who complained about the food or was not sufficiently servile got a bad rating. The shipowners associations had used the books and shipper-controlled hiring offices to discriminate against union activists, and these were known to seamen as "fink books" and "fink halls."

The federal government's initial drive to force all merchant seamen to carry the fink book coincided with the west coast maritime strike of 1936 and the issue was heatedly debated in the councils of the Maritime Federation of the Pacific and among men on the docks. The Sailors Union denounced the fink book and all militant seamen refused to accept them. The Stalinists were in a position to make a difference. On the west coast they had captured control of the Marine Cooks and Stewards Union and pulled a lot of weight in the Marine Firemens' union. But the Communist Party of the U.S. was more concerned with supporting the reelection of Roosevelt than in the welfare of the seaman. First they equivocated, then three months into the strike and on the eve of settlement, they came out openly for acceptance of the fink book. Even Harry Bridges, Stalinist leader of the longshoremen, came out in favor of accepting the fink book, though it was none of his business.

The long-entrenched leaders of the American Federation of Labor's International Seamen's Union (ISU) had expelled the militant west coast Sailors Union in January of 1936. These misleaders' continued collaboration with the shipowners at the expense of their membership resulted in widespread desertion and dissatisfaction on the Atlantic and Gulf coasts. Stalinists had moved into the vacuum created by the policies of the ISU leadership, first as leaders of a rank-and-file movement, then as organizers of the National Maritime Union (NMU). Joe Curran, President of the NMU came out in favor of accepting the fink book and a lot them were issued on the Great Lakes, but most deep water sailors, following the lead of the Sailors Union of the Pacific (SUP), continued to reject them.

Faced with the recalcitrant rank and file refusal to take the fink book, the Stalinists tried to divert the struggle. Their slogan became, "Take the Fink Book — and burn it on the Capitol steps on May Day." How then would thousands of seamen scattered on ships at sea and in ports around the world get to Washington for the bonfire? The militant seamen did not fall for this impractical and dishonest tactic. They followed the advice of the SUP leaders.

Coastal ports had stopped requiring fink books, waiting for a more propitious time. The Maritime Commission issued Certificates of Identification which carried nothing about an individual's sea service record, but the compulsory fink book had been their fond dream. Until the summer of 1938 it had been a standoff. Now the SUP was reacting to a renewed effort to foist the fink book on the seamen and was picketing Maritime Commission offices on the west coast and in New York, the only east coast port where the SUP had a hiring hall. The purpose of the picket line was to force the Maritime Commission to rescind the "fink book." On the line we were often joined by militants from other unions, but the National Maritime Union, by far the biggest on either coast, officially ignored our picket line. The Communist Party leaders didn't want to embarrass President Roosevelt, their favored candidate, whom they believed would collaborate with their hero, Stalin.

My picket card was date-stamped each day I went on the picket line, and it qualified me for a chance at any job that came along for which I was certified and that no union member wanted. The stamped card was also good for a noontime meal. This was welcome because I had only a few dollars to see me through until I got a ship. Now my number one priority was to wait it out and get a job aboard ship as the first step toward becoming a bona fide seaman and member of the party's maritime section.

The seamen's group was a tight-knit organization within the party, known as the "maritime fraction." I was to learn that the fraction held regular meetings of those seamen who were on the beach. At these meetings we discussed policy questions involving the seafaring unions and planned strategies for increasing our influence and numerical strength in the maritime unions.

The basic issues in dispute between the SUP and the NMU seemed clear-cut to us. The Stalinist leaders of the NMU were following class-collaborationist policies, giving in to the government and the shipowners because they believed that thereby they were helping the cause of the Soviet Union. To the rank and file Communist Party member this meant working for socialism. Only their top leaders knew where these policies originated and that they were designed to benefit their Kremlin masters. Our policies in the union, which I heartily endorsed, were based on the belief that the interests of the seamen and those of the shipowners are diametrically opposed and that in all these fights the government acted as the agent of the shipowners. The militant, though generally non-political, sailors agreed with us and we had some influence on their thinking. And it was our aim to broaden that influence in all the maritime unions.

All of this flowed from the conviction held by Marxists that only socialist revolutionary change could solve the fundamental problems of society and that the working class would be the instrument of that change. From that it logically followed that the place to influence the workers was within and through their own organizations formed to fight for economic justice. Thus, in seeking a ship through the Sailors Union of the Pacific, I was not just looking for a job. I was looking for an entree into one of the powerful transportation unions that would play a major role in coming revolutionary struggles. I was taking a significant step toward realization of the ideal of a socialist society.

With my bed and one meal a day secured, I had little worry. I could get by without any money if I had to. The subway cost five cents, but I could always walk the three or four miles between Washington Square and the union hall if necessary. Meanwhile, I had enough to ride the train for a while and even buy something to eat to round out my diet.

Picket duty meant marching from the union hall with a group of sailors and carrying a picket sign for four hours before the entrance of the building housing the U.S. Maritime Commission. But after I had been picketing for a couple of days, the dispatcher noticed that I had a steward's department endorsement for second cook. He told me they needed a cook more than they did another picket and asked if I would like to work in the union kitchen. That sounded all right to me, so from then on I did my picket duty in the kitchen.

The Sailors Union kitchen was a primitive operation. Through some arrangement with the landlord, we used what was left of the equipment from the onetime restaurant below the hall. We had a big range, a small refrigerator and sinks and tables. We also had some pots and dishes either left over from the defunct cafe or given by well-wishers. Much of what we cooked was donated by supporters of the union or collected by sailors who did their picket duty by canvassing and scavenging. We bought some things with money donated to the cause, and we did cook some good meals, hearty, filling and cheap. I no longer had to make my meager savings stretch for food. A cook who goes hungry has only himself to blame.

I spent my days at the union hall, cooking in the morning and then sitting in the hall reading, doing crossword puzzles, visiting with friends I'd made among the sailors, waiting and watching the dispatch board for job openings. The system worked this way: when a seaman became unemployed either through quitting a ship or layoff, he would register with the dispatcher at the union hall. He would receive a card stamped with the date and hour of his registration. When a ship called the union office for men, the dispatcher would chalk on the blackboard a list of all the ratings requested.

A typical listing of jobs on the blackboard might read:

2 AB's	SS Pilgrim
1 OS	SS Pilgrim
1 Bosun	SS Sequoia
1 Crew mess	SS Marie
1 Galleyman	SS Flintlock
1 QM	SS Boston

Then, on the hour, the dispatcher would call out the jobs to the assembled men. The member with the oldest card (the one who had been on the beach and registered the longest and who was present in the hall) would show his card at the window and get the job if he had papers for that rating. Non-members present in the hall got assigned, also in rotation by the date stamped on their picket card, but only when there were no members present who wanted the job.

Evenings, and weekends when the union hall wasn't open, I mostly spent hanging around the party headquarters on University Place, reading in my space at the Washington Square house, or doing things that didn't cost anything with other members who were also just hanging around. Often in the evening I would go to street meetings where party speakers would set up a "soap box" on a busy street corner and address crowds of shoppers, neighborhood idlers and passersby.

The soap box was actually a folding speaker's stand something like a stepladder, with a platform for the speaker about 30 inches off the ground and a narrow lectern top, handy for notes if needed, good for leaning on or pounding for emphasis. We always tried to have a contingent of supporters present at these street meetings to protect the speaker, deal with troublemakers and sell the party's weekly, *The Socialist Appeal*. The *Appeal* at that time was four, sometimes six, full-size pages with news and commentary from a socialist viewpoint, and sold for five cents. Occasionally I sold the paper at these street-corner meetings.

At the offices on University Place I would sometimes fall in with a group of young native New Yorkers, most of them attending City College, the free university of the City of New York. They were bright, articulate and seemed to me very sophisticated. Though I enjoyed their company and their conversation, with them I felt like an ignorant rustic. I don't think they did anything intentionally to make me feel that way, but I was acutely aware of the limits of my education and reminded that my aspiration to become a scholar had been thwarted by lack of money to attend college.

Of that group I remember particularly Hal Draper and Irving Howe. Hal was a tall handsome young man about 24 years old, national secretary of the YPSL and no longer in school. I admired Hal but he was always cool toward me, not unfriendly, just reserved. Perhaps he was that way with everyone. I never knew him well enough to find out.

Irving Howe was about my age and at that time a sophomore at City College. A tall, slender youth, amiable, and a brilliant talker, Irving was very friendly to me — not all of them were — and I admired him and enjoyed his company. I lost touch with Irving at the time of a split in the party (more about that later) and never saw him again, though I followed his career as one of America's foremost authors and literary critics. I have enjoyed his books and admired his steadfast refusal to compromise his principles or temper his views to the prevailing winds of political fashion.

My big break came after I had been living in the basement on Washington Square for about four weeks. On August 24th in the late afternoon a call came in from the SS HARPOON for a chief cook, a second cook, a galleyman, a messman, two OS's (ordinary seamen) and three AB's (able seamen). The HARPOON was bound for San Francisco via the Panama Canal.

The AB and OS jobs were immediately taken by Sailors Union members. The SUP had always been a west coast deck sailors' union and ordinarily would not have been filling jobs in the steward's department. But since the west coast Marine Cooks and Stewards Union (MCS) had no hall in New York the SUP was handling hiring for the stewards department on west coast ships. This was a temporary situation and lasted only while the SUP was setting up a new organization on the east coast known as the Seafarers International Union (SIU). The SIU would embrace all three departments, deck, engine room and stewards.

There were cooks in the hall with more experience than I had, so I took the galleyman's job and was given what is known as a trip card which entitled me to the job for one month, or until the end of the trip, whichever was longer. Or I would be able to continue on the job if no full member of the MCS wanted to replace me.

The ship was at a West Side pier and I was told to report immediately. Taking the subway uptown, I picked up my seabag. On the advice of a seaman friend, I had paid about three dollars for the trademark cylindrical canvas bag which was standard equipment for merchant seamen. I said goodbye to Kay who happened to be at the house and returned my key to the Washington Square basement. Then I caught a bus across town and another down to the pier, reporting aboard in time to help the new cooks get some supper together for the crew. We were scheduled to sail that evening for Philadelphia.

10

The Seafarer's Life for Me

The Steamship HARPOON, was one of four or five freighters belonging to the Shepard Line. She was not a very big ship, about 6,000 tons, but she seemed immense to me. The biggest ships I had ever seen up close were the little ferries that served the islands in Casco Bay in Maine.

The HARPOON had a high midships deckhouse and five cargo holds, three forward and two aft of the engine room which was amidships. Through open cargo hatches at the well-deck level, longshoremen were lowering sling loads of crates, boxes and bags to be stowed in the holds. The ship was in general-cargo service, hauling a variety of dry cargoes in the intercoastal trade, back and forth between the east and west American coasts via the Panama Canal.

Most of the crew ate and slept in the after deckhouse on the well-deck level, the deck and engine crews in separate fo'c'sles with a messroom between. The crew messmen had to hustle all the food for the crew from the midships galley, down a ladder and the length of the after well deck. They carried all hot foods in special stacking containers kept warm by boiling water poured into the bottom compartment. I was glad I was galleyman and not a crew messman. The poop deck above the crew quarters was used as a fair weather lounging area for all the unlicensed crew. The forward deckhouse was used only for storage, the bosun's locker and the carpenter's shop.

All the ship's officers and the steward's department crew slept amidships. I was assigned to share a small cabin with the room steward, a friendly older man, a long-time member of the MCS, whom I knew only as Warren. The narrow room had two bunks, one above the other, two lockers and just enough space to walk between to reach the porthole. Toilets, showers and washbowls were down the passageway a few doors from our cabin. Warren already occupied the upper bunk — told me he thought he got more breeze through the porthole up there. I was pleased to take the lower bunk.

Warren's principal duty was to clean the officers' cabins. I believe the HARPOON sometimes carried a few passengers, and their cabins would have been his responsibility. But on this trip there were no passengers aboard. On the main deck, in addition to cabins for the steward's department and engine room officers, were the galley, walk-in refrigerator and freezer, the officers' mess (called the saloon), and its adjoining pantry. Above us on the boat deck there were, besides the lifeboats, the radio shack, the radio man's quarters and rooms of some of the higher deck officers. Above that was the bridge deck and the captain's quarters.

Soon after supper on that 24th of August, the SS HARPOON left the dock and moved down the harbor. My work in the galley done for the day, I watched the deck crews swing into place the steel beams that bridged the hatches, place the big hatch-cover planks, roll out the heavy tarpaulins and batten them down, secure against any heavy seas we might encounter on our way to Philadelphia. At dusk we passed through the Verrazano Narrows into the Lower Bay and the green Atlantic. I stayed at the rail as the lights of New Jersey faded from view and only our ship was out there between the sea and the sky.

I can vividly recall how exhilarating it was for me to watch the land fall away on the horizon, feeling the throb of the ship's engines and slight roll of the ship beneath my feet. An avid reader of Joseph Conrad, Jack London and Richard Henry Dana, I was embarked on a whole new adventurous way of life. I not only had the papers, I was now a real seaman, and on the way to making a genuine contribution in the struggle for a more just society. My 19th birthday had passed unnoticed five days earlier.

Unlike the deck and engine departments, the stewards crew were all on daytime work. My duties in the galley were not unlike what I had been doing in Boston restaurants and in school before that, and more recently at the SUP hall helping cook for the pickets. I peeled and chopped vegetables, fetched, measured and prepared meats and fish for the cooks, cleaned pots and pans and in general made myself useful to the cooks. I soon became used to the motion of the ship and the need for roll bars on the range to keep pots from sliding around during rough weather. The cooks on the HARPOON were men I'd been with in the Sailors Union kitchen, so we already knew each other's ways and worked harmoniously together. When I wasn't working, I explored the ship and became acquainted with the other departments, talking with the other crewmen to learn all I could about this new life.

Steaming south from New York there was a moderate sea running, enough for the ship to roll, and occasionally salt spray would reach as high as the deck house. But I enjoyed the motion and often I stood by the rail watching the rolling swells of blue-green sea, the turbulence of the ship's wake, the occasional porpoise stitching the waves across the bow of the ship. It would be a long time before I saw anyone really seasick, and I was fortunate never to be seasick in all the years I followed the sea.

The ship stopped at Philadelphia to take on more cargo for the west coast. We stayed there only one day and overnight. I went ashore only once, had a glass of beer, paid 89 cents for an emblematic white cloth cap, and came back aboard. Then we headed south with good weather and calm seas. The work became routine and I had plenty of time to become acquainted with my fellow crew members. They were all friendly and some had stirring tales to tell about the strikes on the waterfront in 1934 and 1936. I found these sailors generally to be a very militant bunch of unionists and I was proud to be among them.

From crew members I learned that the HARPOON and her sister ships of the Shepard Line had recently been involved in a dispute that has entered maritime labor history as the "Shepard Line Beef." The Shepard ships, which were usually in intercoastal trade running between the east and west coasts, were under contract with the SUP and the other west coast unions.

However, during an interval when some of the Shepard ships were working up and down the Atlantic coast, replacement crewmen had been supplied by the NMU with whom the SUP had a working relationship at that time. It had become strained when the NMU started signing substandard contracts just in order to gain representation rights. The relationship had fallen apart completely the preceding fall when the NMU, in collusion with the company and the National Labor Relations Board (NLRB), set up a union representation election on Shepard ships and neglected to put the SUP on the ballot.

Harry Lundeberg had lodged a serious protest with the NLRB, but he was ignored. The SUP took the only course available if it was not to give up jurisdiction over ships under contract. SUP men left Shepard Line ships arriving in west coast ports and picket lines were set up at the piers. In most cases they were supported by the Marine Firemen's Union, and sometimes by members of the Marine Cooks and Stewards. In some ports the longshoremen supported the sailors and refused to cross their picket line.

But Harry Bridges was not going to stand by while the SUP ousted the NMU, another CIO union led by fellow Stalinists. He denounced the SUP action as an attempt to destroy the International Longshoremen's and Warehousemen's Union (ILWU), though this far-fetched charge failed to rally the majority of old-time longshoremen. In Seattle, while police looked the other way, Bridges personally led a crowd of 300 longshoremen through an SUP picket line at the pier where the TIMBER RUSH was docked. A few days later in San Francisco, unable to convince enough longshoremen to go through a picket line, Bridges mustered a crew of warehousemen, scalers, and cannery workers for an assault on several hundred Sailors' Union pickets at Pier 41 in San Francisco where Shepard's SEA THRUSH was moored.

The fight lasted fifteen minutes and many noses were bloodied before the police entered the fray on the side of the scabs and forced the sailors back from the pier. The SUP lost this skirmish to the combined forces of the cops and goons herded by longshore boss Bridges. The war went on in every west coast port visited by a Shepard Line ship, with scenes similar to that at Pier 41. In the end, however, the SUP won. Against the combined pressures of the company, the waterfront employers' associations, the federal government and the communist bloc seamen and longshoremen, the Sailors' Union had forced the Shepard Line to recognize its contractual agreement.

My shipmates on the HARPOON were proud of their union and its stubborn battle against what they regarded as the forces of reaction. They scorned the leaders of the NMU and the ILWU, not because they were "radicals" but because they regarded them as finks with a political agenda to which they subordinated the interests of the workers.

Shipmates offered these opinions to me unsolicited. I had been advised not to initiate any political discussions with crewmen during my probationary trip-card days. I was not there to instruct but to learn. This whole life was new to me and I had everything to learn from old hands aboard the ship. When one of the crew would offer an opinion or state political beliefs that were not far from my own, I generally refrained from comment. Thus the days went by pleasantly as we worked our way toward the Gulf of Mexico and Panama.

In Panama I had my first glimpse of a tropical land and its inhabitants. We arrived at Colon in the morning and spent most of the day passing through the canal. Whenever my presence was not required in the galley, I was out on deck looking at the jungle scenery and watching the activities of the scantily-clad black men who came aboard to handle our lines as we went through the canal's locks. These Canal Zone workers kept pretty much to themselves during our passage, having no reason to interact with the ship's crew. I could hear them talking among themselves, but their patois was incomprehensible to me.

For most of our crew, passage through the canal was an opportunity to relax when not on watch. But it was an interesting passage for me, everything new and strange, making it more memorable than any subsequent trip I made through the canal.

From Panama we headed up the Pacific coast of Central America with clear skies, calm seas and warm weather. I slept nights on a cot on the poop deck, along with others who wanted to get out of the heat and stale air of their foc's'le or cabins.

The first day out from Panama City my roommate, Warren, told me our captain had cut his finger which had become infected. If it became worse there was a question whether he would make it to San Francisco, our next scheduled port. Since Warren cleaned all the officers' cabins, including the captain's, he was a good source of information. A day or two later, he told me the captain had developed blood poisoning and we were heading for Acapulco, Mexico, where he would be taken to the hospital. Thus I got to see another, unscheduled, foreign country.

But I didn't see very much of it. The HARPOON was met by the pilot boat, a harbor pilot came aboard and the captain went over the side to be whisked ashore to the hospital. With him went the chief mate to attend to any necessary paperwork resulting from our unscheduled stop and to communicate with the company offices in San Francisco. The ship proceeded to an anchorage in the harbor, a beautiful, semicircular bay.

It was a bright sunny morning, the heat tempered by a slight on-shore breeze. We lay in fairly close to shore not far from a towering cliff that arose abruptly from the water. Acapulco occupied a narrow strip of land between the bay and the encircling grayish-green mountains.

The town was too far away to be distinctly seen and appeared more as an impression of red-tiled roofs and pink/yellow pastel walls broken by the pale green of palm trees. It appeared to be a sleepy Mexican coastal village, but I was told Acapulco was a regional shipping center and resort. However, it was not yet the tourist mecca it was to become.

Within minutes, two or three small boats had put out from town docks, and soon clustered at the side of the ship. A Jacob's ladder was dropped over the side and several traders swarmed aboard, along with three or four teenaged girls. The girls disappeared into the crew's quarters, while the traders did a brisk business in coconuts, souvenirs and tequila.

I never knew whether the captain's being incapacitated and the mate ashore had anything to do with the freedom permitted these visitors, or whether it would have been the same with the captain in command. In any case, the crew seemed to be left to its own devices for a while. Some of the men purchased souvenirs, some bought tequila, and some the favors of the Mexican girls.

Others just stood by the rail and watched young boys dive from the cliff after coins thrown by a tourist.

After an hour or so, the chief mate returned to the ship, now the acting captain. He immediately asserted his authority and ordered all the traders off the ship, had the girls rounded up and ejected, and gave orders to prepare for sailing. But by this time a lot of tequila had been consumed and a good time had been had by many. One able seaman, a huge fellow of Mexican extraction, was running around wearing nothing but his skivvy shorts, threatening other crew members. During the attempts to quiet him down, he got hold of a fire axe and swung it at the second mate. Finally subdued, he was locked up for the balance of the voyage and, according to shipboard scuttlebutt, would be charged with mutiny and some other offenses when we got into port at San Francisco.

He wasn't the only one the worse for tequila. I had never heard of this beverage before. It was probably 80-proof, but I figured anything that cost only forty-five cents a fifth couldn't be very strong. I bought a bottle and the first drink made me feel better. So I drank some more, a lot more, and was very sick. I spent the mid part of the day lying on a folding cot on the poop deck wishing I'd never heard of tequila. I wasn't any help in the galley for a while, but since hardly anyone aboard wanted lunch that day, I don't think I was missed much. By supper time I was back on the job, not feeling too well but functioning.

The rest of the trip north was uneventful. In San Francisco we tied up at one of the piers along the Embarcadero, not far from the center of town. From the ship I could look up and down the Embarcadero, and it seemed that every pier had ships alongside, loading or discharging cargo. It was just as I'd imagined the San Francisco waterfront would be — busy, vital. The fabled strike actions of 1934 and 1936 by seamen and longshoremen were of recent memory making San Francisco an exciting place for me.

Our pier was also very close to the bars and other waterfront centers of entertainment for seamen, and these were the only places I visited while in port. In the evening, when I was off duty, I'd go ashore with shipmates. Apart from the pleasure I took from just being in San Francisco, our visit was memorable to me for another reason. Here, at last, I lost my virginity.

With my several girl friends I had indulged in a lot of necking and petting and groping, but we had never "gone all the way." Lack of know-how, and some prudent restraint on the part of the girls, had always kept us technically chaste. However much I may have wished to follow through, none of my bargain condoms was ever suitably employed. Two of my friends aboard the ship offered to take me to a place they always visited. The girls there were young, comely, clean and inexpensive, they told me. And I could have my pick of the lot. It was as they said.

Leaving San Francisco after a couple of days, the ship went south to San Pedro, port of Los Angeles, where we tied up at a pier on Terminal Island. San Pedro in 1938 was very much a seaman's town, with the Sailors Union hall on a corner right in the middle of town and the other maritime unions all nearby. There were palm trees and occasional cacti, the whole place having for me a sub-tropical appearance, with a small-town ambience quite unlike San Francisco.

This was late September and the weather was balmy, in the eighties every day, with blue skies and few clouds. It seemed an ideal climate. But I didn't stay there very long. Times were tough, shipping was very slow, and there were a lot of members from the west coast Marine Cooks and Stewards union on the beach. Since the trip-card men of the HARPOON had completed a voyage, their jobs were open to MCS members who wanted to claim them. So we were paid off.

Up to this time I hadn't had a payday. I had made a $10 draw against pay due and run up a small account with the slop chest. The slop chest is a store of clothing and personal articles carried on all ships for the convenience of the crew, charges for items being made against wages due. The only thing I bought was a carton of cigarettes which, at sea, cost thirty-five cents. And I hadn't spent for much of anything else. Just a few nickel beers and one girl (three dollars, if memory serves).

Seamen's wages were very low at that time, even though there had been a little improvement resulting from the big strikes. The major accomplishment of the strikes had not been wages but union recognition and control of hiring. Prior to unionization, seamen were at the mercy of labor contractors, known as crimps.

Most of the crimps operated flophouses and gin mills, where sailors were encouraged to get drunk and run up bills, sometimes fictitious or at least padded. Once in debt, they were obligated to go where the crimp sent them and the crimp had first claim on their wages. For a seaman to wake up from a drunk and find himself aboard a ship at sea with his first four month's wages already paid to a crimp was not an uncommon occurrence. Sometimes the sailor was walked onboard in a drunken stupor. Often he was drugged or knocked cold in an alley then carried onboard ship, a practice familiarly known as "shanghaiing." The shipping companies, their agents and some ship's masters were in collusion with the crimps and the seaman was at their mercy.

Sometimes the crimps didn't even wait for the seaman to spend his money and run up a debt. In some documented cases, boarding-house runners would board an arriving vessel, give the departing crew a lot of free booze, steal their money and deliver them unconscious to another ship ready to leave port. The seamen woke up at sea, broke, hungover, and never having set foot on shore, their wages on the new ship already advanced to the crimp who delivered them to bondage. These criminal acts were not prosecuted because of connivance between the police and the shipowners.

Much has been written about the conditions under which seamen lived and toiled in times gone by. Many of the authors who wrote stirring tales of the adventure and romance of the sea — Dana, Conrad, London — have also told the story of virtual slavery at sea. Seamen had no legal rights, their wages were abysmally low; they were subject to beatings and other corporal punishment by their officers with little or no recourse; they were fed hardtack and salt horse; they worked 12 hours a day and more when called upon; and they could be imprisoned for desertion if they left a ship without the captain's approval.

In 1887 Andrew Fureseth became secretary (the union's highest office) of the Coast Seamen's Union (CSU) , founded by socialists in 1885. In 1891, Fureseth led the CSU into a merger with the Steamshipmen's Union and the new organization became the Sailors Union of the Pacific, which later affiliated with the International Seamen's Union ISU).

From the time Andy Fureseth accepted office in the CSU he was in the forefront of the fight to win civil rights and decent treatment for seamen. Living frugally, sometimes going without salary, he worked tirelessly for his seafaring brethren, organizing, negotiating and lobbying Congress for legislation freeing seamen from serfdom.

Mainly through his efforts, some of the worst of these conditions were alleviated, on paper at least, by the seamen's acts of the 1890's and by the LaFollette Act of 1915. All these laws were partially written and tirelessly lobbied for by Andy Fureseth, and after their passage he worked for many years to thwart employer/government schemes to circumvent the law and try to keep seamen in a condition of servitude.

For more than 50 years Fureseth labored in this vineyard with scant concern for his own comfort or safety. Once, when brought into court and threatened with a jail sentence for his activities on behalf of seamen, Fureseth summed it up for all time in his statement to the court.

"You can put me in jail. But you can't give me narrower quarters than as a seaman I have always had. You cannot give me coarser food than I have always eaten. You cannot make me lonelier than I have always been."

Little wonder that Andy Fureseth was revered by seafaring men, especially the west coast sailors. Freeing seamen from the grip of the crimps was a major accomplishment in the long struggle led by the Sailors Union of the Pacific against the notorious shipowner-crimp cabal. The issue was not finally settled until the establishment of the union hiring hall under contract in 1937 at the conclusion of a 99-day strike. I was an early beneficiary of that settlement.

By the summer of 1938, an able seaman made $72.50 a month, in addition to his bunk and food aboard ship. An ordinary seaman, wiper, or messman got $55 which was my wage as galleyman on the HARPOON. Not very big pay, but as good or better than I had been getting ashore, and enough so I had a small nest egg when I was paid off the SS HARPOON in San Pedro at the end of September.

11

Cross Country Disaster

My stint on the SS HARPOON ended, and with little chance of getting another ship out of San Pedro I went into Los Angeles which was about 25 miles on an antique interurban trolley car. I had the address of the party headquarters so I went there first to get advice about the best place to stay and to consult about my next move. Someone at the office told me there were several seamen members on the beach, either from choice or necessity. Tom Kerry, editor of the west coast *Marine Fireman*, was also in town. Talking with him, I decided my best bet was to go back to New York. The bulk of the Seafarers International Union (SIU) was on the east coast and most of the shipping companies under SIU contract were there, so I would have a much better chance of getting a job in Boston or New York than on the west coast.

I fell in with a fellow seaman, Tony Marino, also a member of the party, who was in about the same position I was. He had had trip cards out of the SUP hall but his home was in New York and he wanted to go back and ship from there. He'd been hanging around in Los Angeles for several weeks and his money had almost run out. Tony had been sleeping on a cot in one of the party branch headquarters halls in L.A., along with a fireman named Murphy. Rather than spend money on room rent, I went there too. There was some spare bedding but no cot so I slept on the floor.

In Los Angeles I enjoyed getting acquainted with the local people, attending meetings and at least one Sunday social affair with about 50 present at a big, beautifully landscaped home that seemed palatial to me. Among the local comrades, I especially remember Abe Harkavy, a young fellow of about my age and good company. He showed me some of the local sights and took me to his parents' house in Boyle Heights where his mother set out a meal for us whenever we showed up.

Though all this was pleasant, my job prospects here were non-existent. So after a few days, Tony and I decided to go back to New York together. Murphy was a permit man in the west coast Marine Firemen, Oilers, Watertenders and Wipers Union (MFOW) so he decided to stay where he was. Besides, he had a girl friend in Los Angeles. A permit man was a sort of probationary member of the union, a step up from the trip card.

Instead of hitchhiking, or even taking a Greyhound bus, I not very sensibly purchased an automobile for the trip. It was a 1931 Chandler touring car in pretty good shape, for which I paid $25. It was a big open type car with a wooden superstructure, canvas roof and comfortable leather seats. It was capable of high speeds but was not very safe by today's standards.

Tony and I left Los Angeles about the middle of October, taking turns driving, and stopping occasionally for a short sleep in the car. We didn't plan on making many stops because Tony had no money, and I had little left by this time. We couldn't afford to pay for lodging. But the weather was good and we didn't mind sleeping in the car. Then, somewhere in the desert near Yuma, we picked up a hitchhiker named Russ who needed a ride to New York, could share the driving and would put in a few dollars for gas. So we decided we wouldn't stop at all any more, except for food and gasoline. We would drive in turn, on four-hour watches around the clock. Those not on watch could sleep on the go, taking turns in the back seat where it was possible to stretch out.

I chose the 4 to 8 watch, Tony took the 12 to 4, leaving Russ the 8 to 12.

We made good time through Arizona, New Mexico, the Texas Panhandle, Oklahoma and halfway across Missouri. I didn't get to see very much of this country we were passing through. Much of the time I was sleeping, or it was dark and there was nothing much to be seen. I regretted that, but we had to keep moving if we were going to reach New York before we ran out of money for food.

Then one morning I finished my stint at the wheel. It was just before daybreak as I pulled over to the side of the road and awakened Russ who was sleeping beside me in the front seat. Tony was snoring in the back. I got out of the car, stretched and walked around to the passenger side. Russ slid across under the wheel.

"We're about a hundred miles from Saint Louis," I told him. "Just stick on this road, then look for Route 40 out of St. Louis heading for Terre Haute."

Russ grunted something unintelligible and we started to roll again. Closing my eyes I lay back in the passenger seat.

After a few moments I realized we were going very fast and I opened my eyes to look at the speedometer. We were going over 75 miles per hour heading into a curve and I could see a steel-cable fence with a rocky gully coming at us.

"Slow down!" I yelled. "For Christ's sake, slow down!"

I looked across at Russ as his head jerked up, but it was too late to change our course or brake the car.

The car tore through the cable fence and plunged toward the gulch. I heard the tearing of metal and the snapping of breaking wooden fence posts, then a thud as we hit our first boulder. Then I crashed through the car's roof. Cars had no seat belts then. Airborne, I continued toward the opposite bank of the gulch as the car bounced and careened down the hillside strewn with boulders, finally stopping at the bottom where a small stream bubbled among the rocks.

I remember the hard landing and don't think I lost consciousness even for a moment. Looking around I could see Tony. We were both lying on a huge rock pile on the far bank of the little stream. In the early morning light I could see the car, its roof and wooden framework completely gone, with its front wheels in the brook. But couldn't see Russ. I learned later that he ended up under the car's front bumper.

Some people on their way to work were emerging from a side road above the opposite bank just in time to see our car fly off the road. They stopped traffic and organized help for us. First they lifted the car to free Russ, then they helped get us into an ambulance which arrived from the nearest town. This was Rolla, a sleepy town of about 8,000 people, best known as the site of Missouri's State University. Rolla's only hospital was a seedy-looking two-story brick structure right in the center of the downtown, with about 15 or 20 patient beds. We soon occupied three of them.

Russ had a cut on his head, sustained when the car landed on him. Otherwise he didn't seem to be much the worse for the experience. He was up walking around the hospital that same afternoon. Tony had some broken ribs and a broken arm. He was soon wrapped in adhesive tape to hold his ribs together, and his splinted arm was in a sling. He had a lot of pain in his ribs when he tried to move around but felt pretty good if he kept still. I had many surface cuts and abrasions and required a lot of stitching and bandaging. My principal complaint was severe pain that extended throughout my midsection, from the ribs on down, both front and back. But apart from the surface bruises and lacerations I had no visible signs of injury. They brought us meals and Tony and Russ ate them. I didn't feel like eating and when I tried whatever I swallowed came back up.

I never knew whether the hospital had no X-ray or whether they didn't want to waste it on someone who couldn't pay. Whatever the reason, they took no X-rays. The doctor, the only one we ever saw at that hospital, was middle-aged, with a sad face and a rather gray personality. He came in to see us each day.

Tony and Russ seemed to be mending and had no complaints, but I had a lot of abdominal pain. The doc would thump my abdomen and listen. I don't know what he was listening for, but his conclusion was always the same. He'd turn to the nurse and say, "Give this boy another two ounces of mineral oil." And she would. The only other thing they did for me was to stick an enema tube up my rectum on the theory that it would vent some of the gas which might be giving me abdominal pain.

The nurses were very kind and did all they could for us, but they could do only what the doctor ordered. And he didn't order much. After four days of this Tony and Russ were ready to go. Both up and around, they didn't see anything more the hospital could do for them. I hadn't yet been out of the bed or taken any nourishment. I didn't feel much worse, but I didn't feel any better. I figured we might as well go.

We told the doctor we were leaving and he said okay, but it was on our own responsibility. We agreed to that, as we couldn't see that it made any difference. We each signed some kind of release paper stating we were leaving on our own initiative and that the hospital wasn't discharging us as cured. I also signed over title to my wrecked car and they accepted that, not as full payment exactly but figuring it was all they'd ever get, which it was.

I was to learn later from friends who had lived in Rolla and gone to the University that the doctor owned the hospital and had a reputation locally as a chronic alcoholic. My friends said that while they were still in Rolla, a few years after I was there, the doctor lost his hospital and his right to practice as a result of his affliction. While I was in Rolla I had no idea what the doctor's problems were, but I had a low opinion of the treatment we were getting and was pleased to be leaving the place.

Though I was very critical of this doctor and the treatment we received in his hospital, it never occurred to me that he was guilty of malpractice. Both the term and the concept were unknown to me at that time. Just like Russ sleeping at the wheel, I accepted the doctor's failures or shortcomings as simply my bad luck. It was my fate and I accepted it. And on reflection, I think it was better that they took no X-rays in Rolla, and I'm fortunate to have got out of that hospital alive. I probably would never have survived continued treatment in that place.

I got up, dressed and counted my money. Then I walked to the bus station which was in a drugstore a half block down the street from the hospital. Rolla was just a small midwest town with one main street. The hospital was on that main street, about in the center of town, sharing the block with the post office and a Woolworth five and dime. From the station agent I found I had enough money left for two bus tickets to New York with two or three dollars left over. I bought Greyhound bus tickets to New York City for Tony and me, saved out two dollars for food on our trip and gave the rest, maybe a dollar, to Russ who would continue hitchhiking to New York.

Returning from the bus station, we stopped at a grocery store next door and got some cardboard cartons and twine. Tony and Russ had had suitcases but they were destroyed in the accident and our few belongings scattered all over the stony hillside. Either the ambulance crew or some of the bystanders had picked it all up and brought it to the hospital where it was dumped in a heap in one of the unused rooms. We bundled those of our belongings we considered worth saving into a couple of small cartons to take on the bus, and I gave Russ what was left of my seabag to carry his things in.

Then, with Russ's help, I got our cartons across to the bus station. Tony wasn't much help with his broken arm in a sling and unable to use the other without hurting his ribs, so Russ and I did most of the packing and toting. We said goodbye to Russ and he headed for New York. The cross-country Greyhound stopped in Rolla in the early afternoon and Tony and I got aboard.

I don't know what route we followed. I wasn't really paying attention to the scenery or anything else. I know we stopped in Saint Louis long enough for us to shop for some peanuts and candy for the trip. I wasn't hungry but thought I should eat something. There was nothing wrong with Tony's appetite, though it was painful for him to move around or try to do anything. Back on the bus, we traveled east.

The bus must have made some rest and meal stops along the way, but I have no recall of them. I know we kept going all night and all the next day, and I was getting sicker as we went. The pain in my gut and my back was worse and I couldn't do anything to be comfortable or relieve the pain. During the afternoon of the second day I lay on the back seat of the bus, the only one where I could stretch out. Fortunately, the bus was not full so I was not disturbed back there. Tony stayed with me and offered me things to eat and talked with me when I felt like talking.

It was early evening of that second day that I got much worse and started having fits or convulsions. I don't know just what I was having but it scared Tony. Probably scared the bus driver, too. I was too sick to be scared. We were somewhere in the mountains of Pennsylvania and our next stop was Harrisburg. By the time we got to the Harrisburg bus station along about 9 p.m., I was almost comatose. I was vaguely aware of what was going on around me but unable to do anything about it.

Tony got me into a taxi and out to the Harrisburg City Hospital. He had no money so I guess he used the dollar and change I had left in my pocket, but I have no memory of it. I don't remember the taxi ride but have some vague recall of the emergency room and being admitted to the hospital.

I don't remember just when Tony left but I do remember his being with me when we arrived at the hospital emergency room. He probably left as soon as it was evident he could no longer do anything to help. He had to get back to the Greyhound station and use what remained of his ticket to get home to New York, and he wasn't in very good shape himself. Tony wrote to me in the hospital but I didn't see him again for many months.

I have a vague recollection of the concerned people at the hospital emergency room asking me innumerable questions which seemed irrelevant to me. Increasingly impatient with their seemingly endless questioning, I remember giving them obscene answers and asking them why the fuck they didn't leave me alone and let me die in peace.

They stabbed my fingers trying to get blood for typing and found no blood. They found a little in my arm. They X-rayed me and found my abdomen was full of blood from a ruptured liver. That's where it had all gone. They hooked me up to an intravenous tube and started feeding some fluid into my arm, and I dozed after they stopped talking to me.

I had given them my parents' addresses. Mother and Earl had left Massachusetts some months before and were at this time working in Freehold, New Jersey. When they got the phone call from the hospital, they left at once for Harrisburg, but first called my brother Tex (Harland) who was working in the dairy barn at the Rockefeller estate in Tarrytown, New York. Tex immediately arranged for someone else to do his chores and was on his way to Harrisburg, hitchhiking. They couldn't reach any of my other brothers and Dad had no phone, so I guess they sent a wire. Somehow Dad found out where I was. He called and talked to Mother but there was nothing else he could do.

I was only 19 years old and they told me the doctors couldn't operate on a minor without a parent's permission, so they had to wait for Mother to arrive. Meanwhile, I lay behind some curtains in what seemed to be a kind of holding area. I must have appeared unconscious because that's the way they treated me. Doctors stood beside my bed and discussed me as though I weren't there. But I could hear them.

"Pritchard lost one like that last week. And another just last month."

"Yeah. I wouldn't give a plugged nickel for this one's chances."

"Well, if anybody can do it, Brightman can."

I heard them but I couldn't move or say anything. Not even to tell them to go to hell, which is what I felt like. Then Mother arrived and gave permission to operate. I knew she was there, sitting beside my bed, holding my hand. That made me feel a little better but not enough to be able to say so or give much thought to it, though I was glad she cared enough to come immediately on getting the phone message.

They would need blood for my operation and Mother was going to be the first to donate. But the doctors found her blood vessels so deeply embedded that it would require surgery to get blood from her. So Earl said he'd give twice and they drew two pints of blood from him. Then later that night, or the next morning, Tex arrived and they took another two pints from him. Altogether they gave me six or seven pints of blood before I was through and I think they got all of it from Tex and Earl.

I don't know when they took me to the operating room but I was told afterward they had removed about two thirds of my liver and it took five hours to do the job. The next thing I remember was waking up in a 16-bed ward, thirstier than I had ever been in my life. I'd been dreaming about Gramp's water barrel and how good that water was, and feeling that I could drink a whole barrel of it. Of course, all they would give me was a sip or two of not very good water. But it was welcome.

Doctor Brightman came in and told me that since I'd survived the operation he thought I'd make it. He was in his forties, a big, bluff, hearty-looking fellow with a red face and an air of confidence. He told me not to worry about losing all that liver. He said it would regenerate and soon I'd grow enough new liver to make up for what I'd lost. I didn't feel much better yet, but for the first time since the accident I believed I was in good hands. I felt that these people at least knew what they were doing.

12

Life in Limbo

All the time I was there the nurses were very good to me, and I wish I could say that I had been as good to them. But I wasn't. I guess I was too low and miserable to be pleasant. Anyway, as I recall it I was cantankerous and argumentative. They seemed to like me anyway and did all sorts of nice things for me. I stayed in that bed for three months — most of November, all of December, all of January and part of February.

Mother, Earl and Tex all stayed until I was out of danger, then had to get back to their jobs. But they came to visit. Tex came down once or twice, but Mother and Earl who were closer came every couple of weeks. For them it was a four-hour drive each way and even longer in bad weather. I really appreciated their visits and looked forward to them, though of course they never stayed very long. Earl would have to make up any time he lost from the job.

As I began to feel better, I became more aware of what was going on in the ward. The 16 beds were always full, so there was something happening all the time, day and night. Though I had neighbors in the beds on both sides, they were older men and we rarely had anything to say to one another. Then, after I'd been there about ten days, Miss Fisher, the head nurse on the ward, asked me if I'd like to move down to the other end of the ward next to Nick, a fellow nearer my age. I said that sounded like a great idea.

I may have known Miss Fisher's given name, but since it was never used, I have long forgotten it. She was a tall, strikingly handsome woman in her early thirties and she seemed old to me, a 19-year-old. Efficient, decisive, but always thoughtful and kind with both patients and staff, she was one of the most admirable people I had ever met. This move was just one of the many thoughtful things she did to make my stay on the ward more comfortable.

My new neighbor, Nicholas, a wan, handsome Greek boy of about 16, was the youngest patient in the ward and the oldest patient in terms of tenure. Nick had already been there several months. I never found out just what ailed him, or even if the doctors knew what he had. Though he was very thin and weak, Nick was a charming lad and unfailingly cheerful. At the end of the ward, farthest from the nurses' station, Nick's bed was by a window where he could look out and see some of the city outside. From my bed, next to his, I might have seen something too if I had been able to sit up. But lying down I could see only the sky, which was better than nothing.

Nick and I didn't have a lot in common, apart from being in our teens, but he was so lively and outgoing that he did much to raise my spirits. I never stopped being grateful to Miss Fisher for placing me next to him. While I had visitors only once every two or three weeks, Nick had someone coming in everyday, usually twice a day. In the afternoon, his mother would come and sometimes his sisters. Though I never really got to know them, after a time they tried to include me in their circle of warmth. And every evening Nick's dad would come, and though he was less at ease with me than his women were, he was totally devoted to his son.

Nick's father made a living selling roasted chestnuts on the streets of Harrisburg. Whether he'd always done this, or it was a depression expedient, I never knew. A heavy, stolid, square-built man, he smelled strongly of the smoke from his chestnut cooker, and he looked sort of smoked himself. He'd always bring Nick something to eat, chestnuts, candy, and occasionally small roasted birds. These were squab Nick's dad had captured on the street and cooked in his chestnut roaster. Nick always shared with me whatever his dad brought him. I was a little dubious about the street pigeons at first, but they turned out to be delicious and a welcome change from the hospital's evening snack offerings.

So for most of my three months on the ward I had a good companion in the next bed. This did much for my disposition, though I still found some things to gripe about. One of the things I complained about was my back. It ached almost constantly. They told me it would probably improve once I got up and had a little exercise.

After about three weeks I got all the stitches out and the drains removed from the 10-inch slit in my abdomen. Then I was ready to sit up in a wheelchair. Sitting up for an hour made my back feel much worse and I complained some more about it. Then they decided to take some more X-rays. I was up already when the time came, so they pushed my wheelchair down to the X-ray rooms.

Back upstairs, I sat in my wheelchair in a little visiting room just off the ward, arguing politics with an old Macedonian Stalinist and waiting for the results of the X-rays. Then here came Miss Fisher, in a hurry and closely followed by two male orderlies.

As she approached, she held up both hands and called to me, "Don't move! "Don't move!"

I thought she'd flipped. But when she got to me and put her hands on my shoulders to make sure I stayed put, she explained they had seen my X-rays and had to put me back to bed—very carefully. They did that, first reversing ends of the bed and jacking up the knee section, then picking me up and putting me down very gently, my back arched over the raised leg rest.

Then a doctor I hadn't seen before, an orthopedist, came and explained they could now see my spine for the first time, since my abdomen was no longer full of blood. He showed me the X-rays and I could see how the first and second lumbar vertebrae were crushed, crumpled together on one side. The doctor called it a compression fracture. Before the X-rays, they had pulled me around and rolled me from side to side to make the bed. Now they handled me as though I were fragile. They asked me a lot of questions about where I'd been and what I'd done since the accident. They couldn't believe that I had walked around, packed my belongings, carried the box to the Greyhound station and ridden more than a thousand miles on the bus.

I was to stay in that position, on my back, bent over the section designed for a patient's legs, for another ten weeks. To change the bed, the nurse would roll me very gently onto one side, keeping my back in its bent position, then she would make the half of the bed behind me. Having completed that half and tucked the folded sheets close against my back, she'd roll me the other way and do the other side of the bed. I was not permitted to move, even to roll onto my side by myself.

Any books I may have had with me at the time of the accident, and I had a few, did not survive the crash. But the nurses provided me with reading material, and as soon as I felt well enough I spent a lot of time reading. Mostly they brought popular magazines, light fiction and detective stories. All good for passing the time. I had one of the student nurses write a postcard for me to Johnny Hamilton telling what had happened to me. In response I got a couple of letters from comrades in Boston, as well as a package with three or four paperbound books. This added some variety to my reading matter.

I had only one problem with reading and that was the lighting. There were no bed lamps and, lying as I was forced to, I looked straight up into the big ceiling fixtures that provided general illumination for the ward. This not only made it hard to see the print, but I found the glare of the lights hurt my eye.

A large part of patient care on the ward was done by student nurses. On any given shift there would be one registered nurse in addition to the supervisor. Then, depending on the time of day and what classes might require their attendance, there would be three to five student nurses on the ward. They brought the meal trays and took them away; they gave baths and back rubs; brought and took away the urinals and bedpans; they read to the patients and wrote letters for them. They were a constant presence and a pleasure to have around. Most seemed to be robust, healthy-looking young women from the surrounding farm country, corn-fed, pink-cheeked and generally good-humored. I remember them with affection and wonder at the grace with which they did all the menial tasks involved in caring for us.

The student nurses were younger than the RN's, and easily identified by their differently-colored shirtwaists and their headgear, or lack of it. They were not yet qualified to wear the distinguishing cap of the RN, so most wore no cap at all. But I noticed that two or three of the student nurses wore little white linen skull caps, plain and not at all like those worn by registered nurses.

One day, as one of the girls, Gretchen, was finishing my bath and making the bed, I asked her, "Gretchen, why do you wear that little cap? Bridget doesn't have one. Neither does Alice."

"It's my religion," she told me.

I pondered that for a few moments, then told her, "That seems a strange religion to me." She said nothing to expand or clarify her statement and I continued, "Down through the ages people have worshipped just about everything, but this is a new one to me. But I don't suppose," I added thoughtfully, "that it's any more absurd than the things most people believe in."

Gretchen was a sweet girl and had always been very good to me. I would not have intentionally hurt her, but I had, in my callous zeal to show that I was above that sort of superstition. Gretchen finished what she was doing, and said no more about it. But later Miss Fisher told me that I had hurt Gretchen and should be ashamed. Well, once I considered it, I was.

Miss Fisher told me that a lot of their best nurses were Dunkards, belonging to a German Baptist denomination that refused to take oaths or bear arms, and their single girls wore those caps because they had some religious significance for them. Gretchen's family were Dunkards and she was required to wear the cap as long as she was unmarried. It was a symbol of her faith. Defensive, I told Miss Fisher that I had no intention of hurting Gretchen but that I considered all religions ridiculous.

"You can believe anything you want to," she told me, "but you might consider the feelings of others. Especially those who are trying to help you."

I respected Miss Fisher and admired her very much. I was ashamed of treating Gretchen as I had and apologized to her at the next opportunity. I asked and she told me a little more about her family's religious beliefs, trying to inform me, not convert me. I got the impression from her that the Dunkards were some sort of Mennonites, but that's not quite accurate. Actually, the Church of the Brethren (otherwise known as Dunkards), though originating in Germany, was a distinct pacifist sect unrelated to the Amish. Anyway, Gretchen never changed toward me, remained always kind, cheerful and willing. And I learned something from the incident — that irreligious intolerance is no more admirable than religious intolerance.

The incident was to have one repercussion. Two or three weeks later, Miss Fisher came to my bed to tell me I had a visitor. It was mid-morning after all the routine morning chores were completed on the ward, a quiet time with some of the patients catching a nap before lunch. It wasn't visiting hours and I wasn't expecting anyone. Miss Fisher seemed to be amused by something but I had no reason to believe it had anything to do with me. She told me it was all right for my visitor to come back and see me even though it was outside usual visiting hours. All this seemed a little strange but I told her to send the visitor in.

Miss Fisher returned to the nurses' station smiling happily. If there was a joke, several others of the nursing staff were in on it and gathered by the nurses' station looking on. By this time everyone in the ward, staff and patients, were watching as a young man whom I had never seen before came sashaying down the aisle, turned in and stopped by my bed. He was well dressed in a suit with tie, and clasped a book to his bosom. He grabbed me by the hand.

"God Bless You Brother Walker!" he shouted. At least it sounded to me like a shout. I'm sure everyone in the ward could hear him.

"I beg your pardon," I answered, trying to release my hand.

But he wasn't letting me go. "Sister Hamilton wrote and told me what happened to you. It's a sign from God. Surely you can't doubt Him now! Let us pray!"

So Mrs. Hamilton was still trying to save my soul. Well, I really wasn’t in a mood for that sort of nonsense.

"Taking revenge on me for not believing? Is that what He was doing?"

"He was protecting you from evil. He was by your side the whole time. Let us give thanks!"

Now I jerked my hand from his grasp, raised my voice and shouted back, "If He caused my accident, I haven't anything to thank Him for. Tell Him to keep His nose out of my business, next time you talk to Him."

"Oh, Brother Walker. I'm praying for you!"

"Do it somewhere else. Now get the hell out of here and don't come back!" I called up to Miss Fisher still standing at the other end of the ward. "If this guy comes here again, don't let him in!"

Reluctantly, he left, praying his way back up the aisle and out of the ward.

Miss Fisher came back to see me.

"Well," she asked smiling, "did you have a pleasant visit?"

"Yeah. Thanks a lot." I told her, then started laughing. She laughed, too.

"I couldn't resist," she told me.

I guess some of the patients and nurses were shocked and some amused. I never knew what Miss Fisher's religious convictions were, if any. I never asked and she never told. But after that incident I felt closer to her than I had before and did not at all mind her having had a little sport at my expense. She never let any more preachers in to see me, though I don't know if any others tried.

For some reason, all during my stay at Harrisburg City Hospital, the nurses, student nurses and orderlies, seemed to like me, always treating me well no matter how cantankerous I became. Miss Fisher called me "the grump," and sometimes joked about my ill nature. They also seemed to be entertained by my Maine accent, which I had been convinced I no longer had. At Good Will school I had learned to speak standard English rather than the rural idiom of New Portland, and I thought I had shed my Down East accent. Apparently I hadn't altogether lost it, and sometimes I'm told even today there is a trace of Maine in my voice. Usually the nurses understood what I was saying, though sometimes they looked a bit puzzled. I guess my most common variation was the presence of r's where they didn't belong and their absence in words where they did. I had no problem spelling these words, but sometimes added an "r" or left one out of my pronunciation.

On one occasion, Alice had brought my dinner tray and I noticed immediately that there was no fork on the tray. So I called her back.

"Alice, would you please give me a fork?" Unwittingly I had omitted the "r" from fork.

Alice looked startled. "What did you say?"

I raised my voice to a volume that could be and was heard throughout the ward. "I said I want a fok!"

Alice looked not only startled but offended...also puzzled because this was not what she would expect from me or any other patient.

Wondering why Alice was being so dense, I made motions of eating with a fork and said, "A fok! A fok to eat with!"

"Oh!" She laughed and so did everyone else on the ward, except me. I was mortified as I realized what she thought she'd heard. After that I carefully enunciated the "r" in fork.

As time went on, the lights in the ward became more and more bothersome. At times they hurt to the point where I had to cover my eye and couldn't read. Miss Fisher reported all this to my doctors and they called in an eye specialist who did some tests, examined my good eye and asked me about my blind left eye and how I'd lost sight in it. He said he thought the blind eye was affecting the other and it would be a good idea to have it removed. I could then get a glass eye that would look much better than my shrunken left eye. That seemed a good idea to me, and he set a time for the operation.

The surgeon gave the option of general or local anesthetic for the operation and I chose local. General meant ether and that I would probably be sick from the anesthetic. So when he did the cutting and snipping, I could watch the hands and tools at work over my face, hear the crunch and snip, and listen to the doctor and his assistants. The whole thing took only about an hour and a half, including the bandage and returning me to the ward.

After the eye healed from the operation, Miss Fisher got me a black eye patch to wear instead of the bandage. The surgeon had given me the address of Mager & Gougleman, the foremost glass-eye people in the country. The company had offices and labs all over the U.S., but the New York outlet was the closest to where I expected to be after leaving the hospital. The glass-eye people didn't make house calls, so I would wear the eye patch for the rest of my stay in Harrisburg.

As I recovered from the shock of the crash and all the operations, I gained strength and became more cheerful. I really did like these people at the hospital very much, but I was also anxious to be out of there. Miss Fisher would bring me newspapers and I read about the sorry state of the world. It was obvious things were going to hell out there, and here I was helpless, flat on my back and not able to do a damn thing about it. Of course I've long since learned that this state of the world is chronic and my inability to do anything about it has nothing to do with the state of my health. But then I was young, idealistic and impatient with the necessity of lying on my back while my bones mended.

But finally I was ready. I was growing a new liver, my empty eye socket was ready for a new eye, and my backbone was fused so there was no risk of damaging the spinal column as long as I wore a heavy brace that kept me in a stiff upright position.

The brace, for which I was carefully measured, was ordered by the orthopedist. It was built around a stainless steel welded frame, with a curved member that circled my hips at the bottom, with two vertical bars running along beside the vertebrae, and at the top two horns like bicycle handlebars that went under my armpits and held my shoulders back. The whole thing was padded and had a heavy canvas body vest with leather straps and buckles to hold it securely in place.

It fitted me perfectly. All strapped in, I could move my head, arms and legs but little else. And it was uncomfortable. Very uncomfortable, at least at the start. I practiced rolling into this appliance and strapping it tightly in place preparatory to getting out of bed. Wearing my brace, I learned how to walk again and tottered up and down the ward for several days, gradually gaining strength, until the doctors decided I was capable of making it on the outside.

13

Shaping Up

It was the second week of February, 1939, that I was discharged from the hospital. Mother and Earl came to get me and the hospital gave them my bill. I don't remember how much it was, but it seemed astronomical to me then. My bill for the three months would probably pay for about 48 hours at today's rates. Anyway, Mother paid part of it. I'm sure she couldn't have handled it all and the remainder was absorbed by the City of Harrisburg. Neither of my surgeons ever gave me a bill or mentioned payment.

I said goodbye to Nick and wished him well. His condition seemed just as it had been when I came in, and he had no prospects for getting out soon. As I left the ward, Miss Fisher and all those wonderful nurses and aides lined up to say goodbye. Ornery though I had been, they seemed sorry to see me go and some had tears in their eyes. I did too, glad as I was to get out of there, and I thanked them all for their kindness to me. Then Mother and Earl brought me to their house in Freehold, New Jersey, a drive of about 170 miles.

They rented a small but comfortable place on the main street of the small town within walking distance from the dairy barns where Earl worked. Here, for the first time that I knew of since she left the family and farm in New Portland, Mother didn't work. But Earl worked long hours. They milked the cows three times a day — at 4 a.m., at noon, and at 6 p.m. — and he had to work about three hours at each milking. And cows have to be milked seven days of the week. He came home between milkings and tried to get some rest.

They gave me a bedroom on the second floor, small, but adequate for my needs and the single bed was comfortable. I had no clothes except a few things Mother had bought me to wear coming out of the hospital. Otherwise I had a couple of books, safety razor, comb, toothbrush and a back brace. Somehow, everything I'd had before the accident had disappeared. I would acquire a few more things while I stayed with Mother.

My instruction from the back doctor was to wear the brace at all times, except in bed, for six months. So I kept it beside the bed on the floor where I could reach it. I'd put it in place, roll into it and strap it on before I got up each morning. When I went to bed I lay down, unstrapped it, rolled out of it, and placed it on the floor until morning. I don't think now that all this was necessary for that long, but I stuck with that routine for most of the six months.

Soon after I came to Freehold, Mother and I took the bus into New York City to get a glass eye. The Mager & Gougleman office and lab was in a high-rise building on Madison Avenue, somewhere in the fifties, where they occupied one of the upper floors. The receptionist put me in the hands of a technician who was an expert in outfitting customers with prostheses that fit their eye sockets and resembled their own eyes as closely as possible. M&G had both ready-made eyes you could purchase from stock on hand, or made-to-order eyes designed especially for the customer. The ready-made eyes cost $20, while the custom jobs were $50.

We opted for the ready-made, and in less than 15 minutes the technician selected an eye that was the right size, shape and color from huge sliding trays holding thousands of models. He gave me instructions on the care of the prosthesis. Mother paid the $20 and we departed. I left Mager & Gougleman's walking on air. For the first time since childhood my two eyes were the same size! And the color match was close enough that the casual observer wouldn't even notice that my eyes were not just like everyone else's. It had been only a little over a year since I told Elsa I would do this sometime. Now I could hardly wait to see her and watch her reaction! I admired myself in the mirrors on the elevator and in shop windows after we reached the street.

Standing on the avenue back against the store fronts, we waited for an empty cab for the ride back to the bus station. Though the new eye was generally comfortable, I was not yet used to it and quite aware of this foreign object in my socket. Feeling a minor itch in my left eyelid, I put my index finger there to scratch it. It happened so suddenly it's hard to remember exactly how I did it, but I dislodged the eye and it fell to the pavement, smashing into a dozen pieces. Dismayed and disgusted with myself, I picked up the pieces. Fortunately, we were still right in front of the Mager & Gougleman building.

"Let's go back up and get another," Mother said.

"God, I'm sorry."

"I know. But it was an accident. Let's go back."

So we returned to the office we had left only five minutes before and told them what happened. They assured us it was not the first time. It was a good lesson in what is possible if the wearer of a glass eye is careless. Incredibly to me, they fitted me with a new eye without charge. I did learn the lesson and never broke another eye.

Over the next few years I had to replace the eye a couple of times due to discoloration. Then Mager & Gougleman developed a plastic eye guaranteed not to discolor. I paid $75 for a custom-made plastic eye, drawn by an artist to match my right and guaranteed for life. I'm still wearing that one after more than 50 years. The eye has some movement and is such a good match that many people who have known me for years are surprised to learn I have an artificial eye.

I stayed with Mother and Earl through April. There wasn't anything to do in Freehold and not much I was able to do anyway. When the weather was nice, I could walk down the main street and back again. There was a small lending library where I got a few books to read after I'd worked my way through all the books and magazines Mother had in the house. I listened to the daytime soap operas on the radio and became interested in the love affairs and sordid misadventures of the characters.

Mother and I talked a lot about many things and we had much to talk about. Apart from her visits to the hospital, I'd seen her only two or three times since she left us almost ten years ago. She told me about the places they had worked, usually hiring out as a couple, Mother cooking and Earl working as a dairyman. From her accounts, they got on well with their employers, but kept moving on, looking for something better. They had been saving and it was her hope that someday they would have their own place, and she would no longer have to work in someone else's kitchen. But though they had always found employment, the continuing depression had thwarted their efforts to pull ahead. Earl's present job paid enough so Mother didn't have to work out as a cook, but it was only barely enough and they were just getting by with little to spare.

She asked about my school, my friends and my ambitions. Of course I told her of my political views and my intention of working toward a better, more rational, more humane society. Like my father she agreed that improvement was desirable, but her principal concern was that I might get into trouble. I assured her that what I was doing was not only entirely legal but in the best American tradition. If Samuel Adams, John Hancock and their colleagues had been more concerned about getting into trouble than about fighting injustice, there would be no American republic. She could accept that argument, but still urged me to stay out of the forefront and try not to get into trouble.

One thing we talked little about was the time of our family's disintegration. Mother had never been one to bare her feelings, to complain, or to try to justify herself. So she never really told me her side of the events that tore our family apart. I was too diffident to question her closely about it, but did learn through indirection much that confirmed what my father had already told me.

She did not want to leave her children and the farm into which she had put such high hopes and so much hard labor. My father did not want her to go and would have agreed to reconciliation at almost any price. She was 34 years old and had an awful choice to make — either give up her children or give up the man she loved and go back to economic circumstances which had been endlessly frustrating, against which she had fought a losing battle for years. This, in addition to the scorn of her father, the sworn enmity of her husband's sister and a covey of local gossips.

Mother made her choice and lived with the inevitable remorse for the rest of her life. She never talked about it, but over the years she and Earl helped all of her children and often lent money and found jobs or rentals for my father and brought gifts to his new family. She and Earl had a good marriage. They were affectionate with one another, they enjoyed the same recreations, they played and laughed together, went on many trips and holidays together, and their major decisions were made jointly after frank and open discussion. Their union lasted until his death in 1976.

I had been conditioned to hate Earl Moulton and blame him for the havoc that was wrought on our family. My grandfather, whose opinions I respected above all others, had drummed this attitude into us boys. Though Gramp eventually became reconciled to his daughter and her husband, some of my brothers never really accepted Earl. They were civil, but it was more like toleration than affection.

It took me a long time to fully accept Earl, though he was unfailingly generous, good-humored, considerate and helpful to me. And he was obviously devoted to my mother. Remembering Earl, I also recall his dry Maine wit, a whimsical humor that made his company a pleasure. By the time of my visit to Freehold I had started to appreciate him for his good qualities. In later years I came to have some genuine affection for him, though of course the past was always there in memory.

I was steadily getting better, gaining strength, walking a little farther each day and getting more impatient to leave. Though I had enjoyed my long visit with Mother, I felt I was just marking time until I could get moving again and had no doubt I could make it on my own now, though no one else thought I was ready. Dad had kept in touch and wanted me to come and stay a while with him in Maine. I thought if I didn't go now, no telling when I could get up there again. I did want to see them all — my brothers, Gramp, Dad and his family. So about the first week of May I got on a bus and went to Farmington.

Since my last visit to Maine, Dad and my stepmother, Hilda, had moved from New Portland and were now living in a small two-story house in Fairbanks, a little hamlet about two miles north of Farmington on the New Vineyard road. Another contractor had underbid him on the star-route mail job, so he had to find something else. He had been working all winter on construction of a new bridge across the Sandy River at West Farmington. It was hard work and the weather had been brutal, but in a way it had been a good job for him. It paid fairly well, as such things went in Maine, and he was highly valued on the job where they kept him working with his axe most of the time. He liked that, being able to do something at which he was skilled.

There was even less for me to do in Fairbanks than there had been in Freehold. The weather was less clement than in New Jersey and the roads were bad, covered with either snow or mud. The house was very small and always a mess. Hilda had three children now. Joanne, a daughter born before she met Dad, was six, and went to a school nearby. The boys were four and two years old, so she had a lot on her hands. She tried to make me feel at home, but I never was very comfortable there. I really had little to discuss with Hilda, and the children made reading difficult.

When Dad got home from work he always had chores to do — splitting and bringing in wood for the two stoves and doing other things Hilda wasn't strong enough for. I would have liked to help, but I still wore my cumbersome back brace and was not supposed to do anything without it and could do very little with it on.

I enjoyed talking with Dad for a while in the evening when he had finished all his chores. But he left the house before daylight in the morning so had to go to bed early. New Portland was only 16 miles away but I had no way of getting there. During most of my visit to Maine I was bored and impatient to get back to Boston.

I had been in correspondence with my comrades in the YPSL ever since I was able to write them notes from my hospital bed. They had sent me books and papers, both to the hospital and to Mother's in New Jersey, making me even more eager to return. So after a couple weeks at Fairbanks, I boarded the bus for Boston.

It would be great to be back in Boston with my friends, to be back on Boston Common, to attend the forums, to read at the public library, to go back to political activity. And I wanted to see Elsa again. I had written from the hospital and received a get-well card from her and her mother. But that was all. I wasn't sure how I'd make a living now but was confident I'd get by somehow. I'd done it before and was sure I could again. Held stiffly erect by my back brace I rode the Greyhound, watched the scenery go by and eagerly awaited my first view of the city I now considered my home.

14

Back to Boston Politics

When I arrived in Boston, I went to stay with friends in a small cold-water flat on East Dedham Street in the south end. I didn't want to go back to the Hamiltons, though I might have been welcome. Johnny hadn't written to me for a long while, and I was surprised to learn from others that he had left the YPSL to become an Oehlerite. The regular Trotskyist organization was not radical enough for him.

Hugo Oehler had split from the party a few years prior more or less on this ground and taken with him his wife and a few other people. He had founded a new organization called, if memory serves, the Revolutionary Workers Party and published a mimeographed, monthly, one-page organ full of incendiary bombast. At the time Johnny Hamilton joined him, Oehler's organization had dwindled to less than half its original scant numbers. Johnny Hamilton was the only member in Boston. He was still enthusiastic and full of rhctoric, but I never found out just what motivated him to join a sect that was visibly disintegrating.

Dedham Street was in a slummy area, not nearly as attractive to me as the Scollay Square neighborhood where I had lived before. But it was reasonably handy, located just off Washington Street and a short walk from the Dover Street rapid transit station. The apartment had only one bedroom where Kim and Mary Dolson slept. They gave me a cot in the corner of the big kitchen.

Kim cooked in restaurants but he was not steadily employed during the time I lived at the apartment. He was a stout, moon-faced man of 30, from New York City, wearing glasses, very bright and a stimulating conversationalist. Mary, an attractive young woman of 18 years with reddish blonde hair, went to art school and was intent on becoming a first class painter. I liked her work, but my knowledge of art was so meager that my opinion would have had little value. Her father was an Episcopal bishop who had served the church in China for many years. That's where Mary and her sister, Jane Huntington, had been brought up.

Jane also lived on East Dedham Street part of the time. I had met Jane on Johnny's egg route, recruited her to the party and was very fond of her, though never romantically involved. She had written me several letters while I was in the hospital. Jane, a couple of years older than Mary, was in college and sometimes stayed at school or at her parents' house in Wellesley. Both had some kind of allowance from their parents and paid their share of the expenses. When Jane was in residence, she slept on a cot in the living room. I was to stay there through most of the summer of 1939, sharing expenses with the others. We all chipped in to pay the rent of $12 a month and to buy groceries, though at first I got a free ride because I had no income.

There were few types of work I would be able to do and still obey the doctor's instructions about care of my back. Restaurant work was out as I had neither the stamina nor the agility, so I didn't go back to the employment agencies. I did get a few hours modeling at Mary's art school. I just had to sit reasonably still, holding a model ship in my hands, while the students sketched and painted. They were considerate of the model and I got plenty of opportunities to move about, stretch and observe what the students were doing. There were about 20 in the class at all levels of competence. I thought Mary was the best of them, but I may have been prejudiced. Modeling was pleasant work and paid well, but there was no future in it. I had to find something else.

With no other prospects in sight, I applied for home relief, what would now be called welfare. After careful interrogation and several long interviews, I was accepted as worthy of aid. They gave me a grant of four dollars a week, and in order to get my check I had to submit to another interview each week to establish whether I was still in need. The four dollars helped our communal budget a little.

After a few weeks on home relief, I had stopped wearing the brace while sitting around, putting it on only if I was going to do some physical activity that might put some strain on my back. I was doing so well I decided I should be able to do some kind of work that required no lifting or bending. Driving a taxi seemed a logical choice. I still had my chauffeur's license from Woody's ill-fated venture into the produce business, and with that it was easy to get a hack license.

The major taxi companies, Checker and Town, were not hiring, but I was taken on by one of the independents operating out of a garage in the Back Bay. My company had only five or six cabs, and there were a half dozen other little companies and maybe 50 cabs working out of that garage. It was strictly commission. No salary or minimum pay. Just 40 percent of the take. The company provided the vehicle and put in gas. The driver kept a log of all fares and turned in all of the daily proceeds when he returned the cab to the garage. He kept whatever tips he might have received. At the end of the week he would receive his 40 percent of the fare proceeds, less any deductions.

The minimum taxi fare was twenty-five cents. That's what the meter showed when you threw the flag. This twenty-five cents was good for a quarter mile or three minutes, depending on whether the meter was running on mileage or time. Driver's option. Many fares were only that first quarter and many passengers didn't tip. The two big companies had tied up the best taxi stands through agreements with the railroads and hotels. Sometimes an independent driver could wait on a stand an hour or even two hours before getting a fare. It was a tough way to make a living but it beat home relief. I wore my brace for the first month or two of driving, then decided I could get along without it.

I had thought when I started driving a taxi I could join the teamsters union, but soon found out otherwise. The union had an agreement with the Checker cab company, the largest in Boston. The contract called for a minimum weekly wage, not dependent on the gross fares turned in by the driver. In practice, I don't think this mattered much, because the guarantee was so low, only $12.50 a week. Checker had sole access to the taxi stands at South and North stations, as well as several of the major hotels. So if a Checker driver put in his time, he could count on booking the minimum in fares. The taxi union contract called for little else as near as I could find out from a couple of friends who drove for Checker Cab.

Thinking I might help the union organize the independent cab companies I called at the teamsters' union office. They were not only uninterested, they seemed hostile to the idea. I never knew why, unless they had some kind of understanding with the owners. Perhaps, to give them some credit, they may have thought the independent drivers too transient to form a stable base for a local. It is true that many of the independent drivers came and went, drifting from one little company to another, leaving for a season or longer, finding something else to do. Speaking to a few of my fellow workers, I found them no more interested in the union than the union was in them.

One offered this friendly advice, "If you want to keep this job you'd be better off keeping your mouth shut about unions."

Since I looked on the taxi job as a means of making a few dollars to live on while I recovered enough to go back to sea, I took the advice and stuck with the taxi company through the summer. I probably averaged about the same income I would have had washing dishes in a restaurant, except that I didn't get my meals. Anyway, I liked it better than restaurant work and was making enough to pay my share of our communal expenses on East Dedham Street.

Early in my taxi career, as soon as I had a few dollars, I wanted to see Elsa. I hadn't yet told her about my eye operation, so I called to ask her to go to the movies. She said she was glad I was recovered and back in town, but she didn't seem nearly as eager to see me as I was to see her. But she did agree to meet me at a cafe near her apartment, and seeing her again I was struck by how pretty she was.

She looked at me, did a double-take and ran into my arms. "Oh, Mark! You did it! Your eyes...you look wonderful!"

It was the reaction I had expected. I held her tightly and sought her lips, but she pulled away.

"There's something I have to tell you, Mark."

"Yes?"

"I'm engaged. I'm going to get married next month."

Surprised and hurt, for a few beats I didn't answer. I would miss Elsa but I knew I couldn't offer her anything except occasional companionship. She deserved better than that. "Congratulations," I told her, and I could see she was crying. I held her again and said, "I'm very happy for you, Elsa. Truly I am."

We had coffee together and she told me about her engagement to an insurance company executive. She had started going out with him soon after I left for New York. Her mother liked him and Elsa was sure they would be very happy. I hoped so too. I knew her mother didn't approve of me, though she had always been civil. Elsa and I parted friends and I used to see her occasionally at Community Church Youth Forum.

One hot summer morning on East Dedham Street when we were all still in bed, there came a loud pounding on the door, with shouts of, "Open up! Police! Open up!"

Sleeping in the kitchen and closest to the door, I opened it. Two burly Irish cops barged in. Standing there just inside the door, they could see Jane on her cot in the corner of the living room, and through the open bedroom door, Kim and Mary in a double bed.

The one with officer's chevrons on his sleeve seemed to be the spokesman. He started with me. "Who are you?"

I told him.

"Where do you sleep?"

I pointed to my cot in the kitchen. I guess they wanted to be sure I didn't sleep with Jane on her cot. It was obvious where Jane slept because she was still in bed. They now turned to the bedroom where Kim had managed to get up and slip on some pants.

"Who're you?" the cop asked him.

"Kim Dolson."

"And who's that?" he pointed to Mary.

"That's Mrs. Dolson."

"Can you prove it? Where's your marriage license?"

"We don't have one. It's a common-law marriage."

"There ain't no such thing! Get your clothes on. You're both coming with us. We charging you with L&L, and we've seen proof of it ourselves."

Kim and Mary got dressed and went with the cops in a squad car. As soon as they were gone, Jane and I hurried over to Washington Street, found a phone and called Jane and Mary's parents.

I must give Bishop and Mrs. Huntington a lot of credit. They got to the court house from Wellesley almost as soon as we did from about a mile away. Whether it was standard procedure for Boston law enforcement I don't know, but they went to court that same morning. In the course of the proceedings I found out that L&L was Boston police shorthand for Lewd and Lascivious Cohabitation. These Irish Catholic lawmakers had a way with words.

The police gave their evidence of this criminal activity. The judge asked Kim and Mary what they had to say. They said what they had before, that it was a common-law marriage and didn't think there was anything wrong with that.

The judge allowed that he saw plenty wrong with it. It was against the law. He then asked Bishop Huntington whether he knew his 18-year-old daughter was cohabiting with this man.

The bishop, a very dignified gentleman with grey beard and clerical collar, said he and his wife knew about it and saw nothing wrong or sinful about it. The judge contemplated that for a few moments, no doubt wondering what kind of a man of God this was who didn't object to his daughter having a loving relationship sanctioned by neither the majesty of the law nor the sacraments of the church. Actually, I don't think Bishop and Mrs. Huntington were overjoyed by their daughter's choice, but as parents they were wise enough not to object. If they had their reservations, they had little to do with religion or the sanctity of the law.

After thinking it over, the judge said, "I'll dismiss the charges if they are married before noon today."

Kim and Mary assured the judge they would be, and they were. By judicial order, the statutory three-day waiting period was waived, and Jane and I were witnesses to the shot-gun wedding held right there in the court house with Mary's parents also present. Then we all went out for lunch before going back to the apartment. An exciting and enlightening morning. I had given no thought to whether Kim and Mary had a license to sleep together and hadn't realized that it was illegal to do so without one. Lewd and Lascivious indeed!

We never did find out how the police happened to raid our apartment in their war against sin. Somebody must have put them up to it. But we had never had any problems with any of our neighbors and little contact with them. Nothing the cops or the judge had to say pointed to any political reason behind the raid. It remained a mystery.

In addition to driving cab and witnessing weddings, I was also busy with the activities of the YPSL. I attended meetings and classes, and participated in leaflet distributions and paper sales. I was learning a lot and becoming more confident about defending the precepts of the Trotskyist organizations in debates on Boston Common and elsewhere. I was able to attract some new adherents to the cause and was well thought of by the branch members. Also at this time, having served my "apprenticeship" in the YPSL, I was admitted to the Socialist Workers Party.

I'd occasionally see John Hamilton or Woody, either at the library, on the Common, or outside one of the public forums. They were friendly and we might have a glass of beer together and josh a bit, but the old relationship was gone and none of us wanted to renew it. By tacit agreement we didn't argue or discuss our various political beliefs.

In the YPSL I was highly enough regarded that I was offered an opportunity to work full time as branch organizer. One of the party members, Dr. Konikow, was willing to provide free board and lodging, and the branch came up with enough pledges to pay me four dollars a week. I accepted and immediately quit my job driving taxi. I worked very hard for the organization through the fall and early winter of 1939-40.

My work as organizer involved planning and expediting all the activities of the branch; meeting with all the committees and sub-groups (e.g. the student section at Harvard-Radcliffe) and helping them plan their activities; speaking before other organizations where members had arranged an appearance; visiting subscribers to our paper and encouraging them to join and become active in the YPSL; and participating in all actions of the branch — picket lines, paper sales and leaflet distributions, classes and regular weekly forums.

On Sundays, weather permitting, the party branch would conduct soapbox meetings in the Boston Public Gardens, adjacent to the Common, and I always participated in these. A group of six or eight members would volunteer each Sunday. Our headquarters on LaGrange Street was not far from the Common, so we'd walk over carrying the folding platform, and a supply of papers and pamphlets to sell.

Setting up on the margin of the park that runs along Arlington Street, one of our speakers would mount the stand and start haranguing the crowd of passersby. On a nice day, there would be hundreds of people, shopping the line of speakers that lined the strip or just out for a walk. We attracted good crowds, varying from 15 to 60 people, depending on the weather and the speaker. Some of our best speakers were very eloquent and persuasive, and all speeches were extemporaneous. No one even used notes. I always liked to listen to Larry Trainor. Incisive, sardonic and sometimes funny, he always got a good response. Kim Dolson would assail the crowd with all the fervor of a revivalist preacher. Poet John Brooks Wheelwright was also popular, with his patrician looks and formal bearing, Boston Brahmin/Harvard accent and careful, erudite delivery. I reached the point where I sometimes took over the soapbox for short spells of 15 or 20 minutes. I'd generally talk about some item in the news and relate it to our socialist solution.

Though some of the work could be considered drudgery and some of the meetings were tiresome, I was inspired by a higher purpose, a vision of a better world and found pleasure and took sustenance from the fellowship of shared work and common cause. There were no days off and no holidays. I wouldn't have wanted them in any case. I was doing what I wanted most to do and only regretted there were so few hours in each day.

I liked living at the Konikows. There were two Dr. Konikows, Antoinette and her son, Willy, whose wife and teen-age daughter completed the household. Willy was in his mid-forties, stout and jovial. Antoinette must have been in her late sixties, grey-haired and looking her age, but still going strong. Both doctors were Genital/Urinary specialists and they had a large three-story row house in the Back Bay, big enough for both family living quarters and the doctors' offices.

Antoinette was the matriarch of the movement. She had first become a socialist in 1888 at the age of 19, while a Russian student studying in Switzerland. On coming to the United States in 1893, she had joined the Socialist Labor Party, then the Debs wing of the Socialist Party, and following the Russian revolution she had gone with the newly formed Communist Party. Though practicing medicine in Boston, she followed closely the events in the Soviet Union, reading the debates between the Stalin-Bucharin faction and the United Opposition (Trotsky and Zinoviev). She and Louis Schlossberg, along with some other associates, were expelled from the CP in Boston, even before Cannon and his group were kicked out in New York. They published one issue of their own little paper called *Bulletin No 1.* She had been a founding member of the first American Trotskyist organization, the Independent Communist League.

Antoinette was also a pioneer birth-control advocate and she and Willy had fought many battles with Boston's Irish politicians who denounced birth control and legislated against it.

Catholic men ruled the roost in Boston politics, but the wives of these same politicians came to Antoinette to be fitted for diaphragms. She derived some ironic pleasure from this knowledge but would never have betrayed the confidence of her patients.

I had my own room on the third floor, the food was always very good and they treated me like one of the family, making me feel entirely at home. I also had free medical attention if any was required. Antoinette seemed to take a motherly interest in my welfare and Willy was a pleasant companion and an amusing raconteur. My four-dollar weekly wage was enough for my incidental needs and I enjoyed the work. We made some progress, added a few new members, and everyone seemed satisfied with the investment.

Terrible things were happening in the world during this time. Hitler, taking his cue from the Chamberlain's appeasement at Munich, seized Austria and part of Czechoslovakia in 1938, then completed occupation of Czechoslovakia in March, 1939. In August Stalin signed a mutual assistance pact with Hitler, turning the U.S. Communist Party 180 degrees, like a flock of sheep. For several years the principal thrust of all their propaganda had been anti-fascist, urging the "peace-loving" democracies to unite and do something about Hitler and Mussolini before they destroyed democracy everywhere.

Then suddenly with the Stalin-Hitler Pact, the warmongers became peace lovers chanting, "The Yanks are not coming!" They denounced the democratic imperialist nations and campaigned to keep America out of the conflict. Some went so far as to make apologies for Hitler, comparing him favorably with the perfidious western democracies. Then in September Hitler invaded Poland, and Stalin joined him in dividing that country. Hitler followed up by invading Norway and Denmark.

I would still occasionally see someone I had known in the YCL. Some had long since dropped out, a few completely demoralized. One young fellow who had been a member of the West End branch had joined a Nazi group that got together to march in uniform and "Sieg heil" one another. At least that's what he told me and he seemed totally unabashed about it. But most were still hanging in, going along and trying to justify every twist and turn of the Stalin line. The YCL and CP members I saw on the streets of Boston would rarely speak to me, though I would sometimes try to engage them. I would have liked to discuss our differences but they were not permitted, and maybe didn't care to hold their political positions up to close scrutiny.

A couple of those I saw had been in Spain, volunteers in the Abraham Lincoln Brigade fighting against Franco's fascist forces. These people were not political tricksters or trade union bureaucrats. I knew them to be sincere, courageous and selfless fighters for workers' rights, against racial discrimination, tireless in their devotion to the ideal of a socialist world without wars, hunger and exploitation.

I held in low regard their continued devotion to the dictatorial regime in the Kremlin and couldn't quite understand their willingness to let someone else do their thinking for them. At the same time I was saddened to see the idealistic ardor of so many of my generation used, manipulated and warped. These men had risked their lives and many lost theirs in Spain, but they had been betrayed and didn't even know it. Their leaders had systematically murdered the leaders of the Spanish left socialist parties (FAI and POUM), as well as those of the Spanish anarcho-syndicalists who had spearheaded the revolution in Catalonia. Yet the volunteers fought on against the combined forces of Franco, Hitler and Mussolini, never realizing that Stalinist treachery was helping to defeat the Spanish Republic they were fighting to preserve. And, of course, they joined in savaging the reputations of those like George Orwell and John Dos Passos who told the truth about what they found in Spain. I was saddened then, as I was saddened then, as I am today, by the terrible waste of these young idealists and the awful consequences of their betrayal.

We, the followers of Leon Trotsky, tried to make sense of all this, regarding Hitler as the mailed fist of the dying capitalist system, calling upon the workers of all countries to rise up and overthrow their exploiters. We denounced Stalin for his pact with the Nazis and called for the overthrow of the Stalin cabal by the Russian workers for its betrayals of the working class of the Soviet Union.

These critical events — the Moscow trials, the betrayal of the Spanish revolution, the pact with Hitler, as well as all the earlier crimes committed against the workers and peasants of Russia — were to have serious repercussions in our movement. Some came to believe that the totalitarian Stalinist bureaucracy represented a new exploiting class in the Soviet Union, and dubbed the new order "bureaucratic collectivism." They argued that there was nothing worth saving of the achievements of the 1917 revolution, and that the workers and peasants of Russia should overthrow their new ruling class. Trotsky, on the other hand, argued that the basic achievement of the revolution, the overthrow of capitalism and nationalization of industry and the land, still survived and were worth fighting for. The Soviet Union was still a "workers state," however degenerated. What was needed, he urged, was a political revolution to oust the usurping bureaucracy and restore socialist democracy. The situation, he said, was comparable to that of a trade union taken over by a corrupt bureaucracy — still a union, worthy of defense against capitalist assault though badly in need of internal housecleaning.

This may seem a semantic dispute, but it was taken very seriously by all of us at that time. It was a regular practice of the party, when there was disagreement on political issues, to establish a pre-convention period of internal discussion, to publish every dissenting opinion— all the arguments pro and con— in special discussion bulletins distributed to all party members. Special meetings were called for debate and every member was encouraged to participate. When the issue was finally resolved by majority vote at the convention, all members were expected to publically support the majority decision and suspend further debate until the opening of another period of internal discussion.

This concept of free discussion followed by united action was known as "democratic centralism," and it worked well when the party's work was prospering and when the issues in dispute were minor. Then, unity of purpose outweighed differences of opinion. However, when the differences were considered of major importance they usually led to a split or the expulsion of the minority by the majority. This became especially true of small isolated groups whose every effort seemed ineffectual.

In the dispute over the essential nature of the Soviet Union, a faction of the party led by Max Shachtman and Martin Abern enlisted a wide following in the party to support the view of the Stalinist bureaucracy as a new exploiting class; the issues were hotly debated in the internal discussion bulletins and meetings called for that purpose. Shachtman's faction won the support of most of the intellectual leaders of the party, including James Burnham, Hal Draper, Dwight Macdonald (whom I had known slightly and whose writing I admired), and Irving Howe, my old friend from New York.

James P. Cannon, the SWP National Secretary and probably the outstanding leader of the party, supported Trotsky's position. Cannon had been a fighter for socialism since 1910 and served an apprenticeship as an IWW organizer among western hard-rock miners under Vincent St John in his younger days; but after the Russian revolution he became a Leninist and was one of the founders of the American Communist Party. Recognized as one of the CP's top leaders, he went to Moscow in 1928 as a delegate to the 6th Congress of the Third International. There he came into possession of a translation of Trotsky's "Criticism of the Draft Program of the Communist International." Impressed, Cannon managed at some risk to smuggle his copy out of the USSR. Back home he showed the thesis to colleagues, several of whom joined him in defending Trotsky's position against the new phenomenon of Stalinism. Summarily expelled from the CP, the group continued to defend the program of revolutionary socialism, publishing a newspaper, *The Militant,* and founding the Communist League of America (CLA) in mid-1929. It was the CLA that eventually developed into the Socialist Workers Party.

Among the national leaders of the party the faction led by Jim Cannon included John G.Wright, Felix Morrow, Albert Goldman, George Breitman, Arne Swabeck, Morris Stein, Murray Weiss, George Clarke, Bert Cochran, Ted Selander and George Novack as well as Farrell Dobbs, Vincent Dunne and the other leaders of the Minneapolis teamsters union. In Boston, those whom I held in highest esteem supported Trotsky and this undoubtedly strongly influenced my own views. Larry Trainor, Kim Dolson, George Weissman, both the Konikows, and John Brooks Wheelwright were all strong supporters of the Trotsky position. Also, as the discussion went on for many months, it was evident that the seamen were unanimous in support of the Cannon faction.

The printed internal discussion filled several thick mimeographed bulletins with contributions from all the major party leaders as well as a number of rank and file members. The special discussion meetings of the Boston branch generally had capacity attendance, bringing out even the Konikows and Jack Wheelwright who didn't often come to regular branch meetings. Larry Trainor, tough, and bitingly incisive, led the attack on the Shachtmanite minority, seconded by eloquent Kim Dolson, voluble Willy Konikow and sometimes by Jack Wheelwight who delivered an erudite, well-structured and persuasive address. The minority defense was led by Larry's brother, Bill Trainor, who in sharp contrast to Larry, was gentle and almost courtly even in the heat of argument. Before the discussion period was over there were few who hadn't had their say in one of the meetings.

This dispute, reflecting the trauma of the awful events going on in the world, eventually led to a split in the party in which roughly a third of the membership departed the SWP. The remnants of the faction that split, under the leadership of Max Shachtman, went on to form the Workers Party which carried on for several years before disintegrating. Initially the Workers Party's principal difference with the SWP was in its analysis of the Soviet Union, but it moved gradually to the right over time. Jim Burnham wrote a book called *The Managerial Revolution,* and discovered he was really a conservative. Dwight Macdonald dropped out, and so eventually did Irving Howe and many, many others. While the main body of Shachtman's Workers Party drifted to the right and fell apart, some like Hal Draper held to the original left-wing socialist orientation and continued to publish their views.

Meanwhile, concurrent with the wide-open internal discussion and disagreement over questions we took to be fundamental, the work of the party went on as ever. After the split, we retained the party name but the name of our paper was changed from *The Socialist Appeal* back to its original name, *The Militant.*

15

Love and Marriage

In November of 1939 the organization received a letter from Nina Tucker asking for more information about the YPSL and its programs. I called her and we made an appointment to meet in a cafeteria on Dartmouth Street near the central library. Nina was attending the Boston University School of Music which was located right behind the library.

Arriving at the cafeteria, I met a pretty blonde woman of my age. She was soft-spoken and modest, but from the questions she asked and her comments I concluded she was also very bright. She played the violin and was working toward a degree in music. Her father was a teacher and her parents had little money. Though Nina lived at home with them, she was paying her tuition by working as a waitress. I liked her immediately, and we talked for a couple of hours before I walked with her back to the School of Music and made a date to meet her again soon.

She joined the YPSL and we saw more and more of one another. Nina would come to the party headquarters on Lagrange Street after class and help me with whatever I was doing. She typed lists and labels, went out with me to visit prospective subscribers or members. I came to rely on her and miss her when she didn't come around. I missed her gentle good humor, her willingness to participate in whatever I was doing. I valued her sound judgement about the people we met. I guess I'd known her for about three weeks when she invited me to her parents' home for dinner.

We took the rapid transit out to Watertown Square, then bussed to Waltham. I liked Mr. and Mrs. Tucker immediately. Erie was a jovial, rotund, humorous man and his wife, Nina, was motherly and down-to-earth. They welcomed me without reserve. As I sat in the living room discussing books with Erie, I could see and hear Nina and her mother in the kitchen. I liked the easy camaraderie with which they worked together getting the meal, discussed the dietary value of some foods they were preparing, laughing together over some minor mishap.

Before we sat down to eat, Nina took me upstairs with her to bring a tray to her bedridden grandmother. I was introduced to Grandma and was pleased to see how kind and considerate Nina was toward the old lady. Grandma, skinny and wraithlike, was very gracious to me, but had some criticism of the meal though she hadn't yet tasted it. I was to learn that Grandma was a pain to everyone in the family, not just because she whined and complained about everything, but because they knew she was not nearly as sick as she pretended. Though presumably bedridden, she came downstairs to the refrigerator when no one else was at home.

The meal the Tucker women served was delicious. It was also my introduction to the concept of health food. Mrs. Tucker was an ardent advocate of healthy diet, she made her own whole wheat bread and was the kind of cook who gives "health food" a good name. Years later, Nina was to have a career as a nutritionist. After dinner Erie asked his daughter if she felt like playing, then accompanied her on the piano as she performed a couple of light classical pieces on her violin. Then they did a jazzy little number that Erie called the "bulldog song," that caused, Wendy, their little Boston terrier to jump about and yap. They didn't know why Wendy reacted that way to that piece, but she always did.

Later in the evening Nina's younger brother, Donald, dropped in. A slender, enthusiastic youth, he managed a cooperative grocery store in a nearby neighborhood. I was impressed by the familial warmth in their greetings and especially by the strong bond of affection obvious between Nina and her kid brother. Having known very little of this kind of family life as I was growing up, I found the evening with the Tuckers heartwarming.

After this pleasant evening with her folks, Nina and I started spending all of our spare time together. We soon knew we were in love and when we had nothing more pressing to do, we did a lot of necking at the office. Then we'd go out to the movies and do more of the same. In February, not wanting to be guilty of lewd and lascivious conduct in the eyes of the law, we went to City Hall and took out a marriage license, which cost two dollars. We had blood tests and waited the statutory three days, then went before a justice of peace to be married. Kim and Mary Dolson stood up with us for the ceremony, after which we went to a Chinese restaurant for a celebratory meal.

I now left Konikows and my full-time position as YPSL organizer. The Konikows had been willing to give me room and board but that didn't include a wife, and my pittance from the branch barely covered carfares and cigarettes. I continued as organizer on a part time basis, but now I had to look for a job. Nina and I moved into a small apartment on Tremont Street in the south end, which we shared with Jane Huntington, my former roommate from East Dedham Street. Nina still had her waitress job but I had to find something.

Finding work was not easy. In spite of the New Deal, millions were still unemployed, most of them with more skills and experience than I had. The type of jobs previously held had enabled me to survive in a furnished room on an austerity diet or getting my meals as part of my pay, but that was not good enough now. Erie Tucker tried to help me find a job, but it was soon evident that I was not qualified for any work paying more than mere subsistence wage. Undeterred, I kept trying.

I did land a job as counterman and short order cook in a diner. It was in an out-of-the way place in Winchester and required lengthy travel to and from work. The job called for ten hours a day and I found that very tiring. Perhaps I wasn't wholly recovered from the accident. Worse, it paid only $14 a week and the long hours made doing anything else practically impossible. After a few weeks of this, I quit and went back to driving a taxi. This time I got hired by Town Taxi, the second biggest company. Town was also non-union but had a lock on a few good stands in town, so it was better than the independent had been, but not much. Also, driving a cab my hours of work were flexible and this gave me time for my work as branch organizer.

However, now my expenses were much greater than when living with the Dolsons, so Nina and I just got by from week to week, living very frugally, eating little better than I had in my early days in Boston, except that she got some meals at work. For a while we slept on a single bed belonging to Jane, the same cot she had occupied at the East Dedham Street flat. We didn't have the money to buy a larger one.

In April the Tuckers invited us to stay with them in Waltham. They were hospitable and made us feel at home, even though it was a small house and Mrs. Tucker's invalid mother occupied one of the three bedrooms. While they made us welcome, I was not pleased with this arrangement. We much preferred being on our own but we weren't making enough money to support ourselves in Boston, and Nina had been forced to drop out of school. Living in Waltham, Nina continued to wait on tables while I drove cab and looked for a better job.

One day there was an ad in the Boston Globe for a butcher at the Brighton Abattoir, a fancy name for a slaughterhouse. It was in Watertown which was close to home. I wasn't exactly a butcher, but I had helped killing and dressing hogs, cattle and poultry, both at home on the farm and at Good Will. I had no principled objections to killing animals for food. The job paid $18 a week, which was more than I had been making, so I applied. When I walked into the place the first day I almost walked right out again. I was assailed by steam, noise and the smell of blood and ordure, and by the scene of dozens of living, screaming creatures being systematically reduced under garish lights to hanging carcasses. But other men were doing it and I needed the job. I could stand it if they could. I applied for the job and was hired.

The place specialized in killing pigs and processing the meat. It was a production line operation with the hogs, hundreds of them, held in a basement pen. To this basement enclosure a continuous chain-conveyor with projecting hooks came down from the floor above, passed through the basement and went back up through a three-foot-square hole in the floor. A man stood under this hole and grabbed the pigs, one by one, slipped a short chain over one hind leg and attached the chain to a conveyor hook. The pig was yanked, kicking and squealing up through the hole.

As the pig ascended to the main floor, the basement man would slit his throat. At the rate of about 15 an hour the pigs rose, hind foot first, screaking and bleeding, through the hole in the floor. They then passed over a huge tank of hot water into which they were dropped. After an interval in the water, another conveyor moved them onto a big table where four men scraped off their bristles before inserting a gambrel stick into their slit hind hocks and hooking them to still another conveyor. On this conveyor line, their innards were removed and passed on to another line for processing. The eviscerated carcasses went on into a cool room.

Nothing was wasted except the blood and the proverbial squeal. In addition to the usual pork products we had produced on the farm, here they stripped and cleaned the guts for sausage casings, and everything that wasn't used directly went next door to a processing plant where it — was reduced still further. I was generally assigned to scraping bristles or stripping guts, two of the least skilled jobs. I hated the work and didn't stay there too long — only a couple of weeks. I quit the slaughterhouse job, thinking to go back to cab driving, but Town was laying off and none of the independents needed anyone at the time.

When I couldn't find anything else, I started hanging around the Seafarers International Union (SIU) hall. Though I had made only that one trip on the SS HARPOON, the life and work of a seaman held great attraction for me, and my SUP trip card gave me some entree at the SIU hall. I think it had been in the back of my mind all along that this was where I belonged and what I would go back to when there was an opportunity. But now I had a lovely and loving wife, and had every reason to stay in port to be with her. I also enjoyed the work I was doing for the party. But I couldn't find a job ashore so I kept going back to the Seafarers' hall.

Shipping was very slow, but the port agent told me that if I waited long enough I'd probably get a ship. So I stuck it out and finally got a job. And then another. As a permit man, I was pretty much restricted to relief work, often only a few days at a time, mostly on the overnight passenger ships running daily between New York and Boston, or Boston to Nova Scotia. I didn't like being away from Nina, but at least I liked what I was doing and was making more money than I had been ashore.

As the union agent and the ship personnel got to know me, I was working fairly regularly on one or another of these ships, either as assistant bartender or ordinary seaman. The New York/Boston ships were in Boston on alternate days, docking at the Atlantic Avenue pier at 8 a.m. and sailing again at 5:30 p.m. When in port I tried to see Nina if she was off and I didn't have to work myself. Sometimes she'd come down to the ship but this was very unsatisfactory to both of us. However, there were still no better jobs ashore and I was intent on becoming a regularly employed seaman.

Nina and I talked about this wholly unsatisfactory situation. She wanted a place of our own and for me to be at home with her. I did too, but I had to have a job and I wanted to be a seaman. The issue remained unresolved.

16

Call of the Sea—Marriage on the Rocks

Finally, in June of 1940, when I had put in the requisite amount of time aboard ships as a permit man, I applied and became a full member of the Seafarer's International Union. Now I had an equal chance at any jobs that came along if I held papers of certification for that rating.

Early in July, I shipped as second cook and baker on the SS FRANCES SALMAN, one of three ships of a small company specializing in hauling cargoes of bulk sulphur between Galveston, Texas, and various east coast fertilizer plants. I liked the FRANCES SALMAN crew and worked well with the chief cook and steward. Luckily, I didn't mind too much having the air filled and all surfaces covered with sulphur dust whenever we were loading or unloading in port.

The only part I didn't like was that the ship rarely went to Boston so I never got to see Nina. We wrote and I sent money but I missed her. While I was working I didn't have much time to think about it, but at night in my lonely bunk I'd think of her and how much I was missing. I wanted to talk with her, to hold her, to lie with her. But I also wanted to become a seaman, doing the thing I seemed best qualified to do. It was a conflict without resolution. I thought that perhaps in time it would work out.

It was on August 21, 1940, near the end of my third or fourth trip out of Galveston and headed for Portland, Maine, that

I went into the crew's mess thinking to have a talk with an able seaman we all knew as "Kentucky." Kentucky, a droll sort, was one of my best friends aboard. With him I could discuss unionism or politics and he knew my views in a general way. Kentucky had a good radio and he knew more about what was going on in the world than most of our shipmates. He was by himself, sitting with his back against the bulkhead, earphones clamped to his head, listening intently.

Kentucky motioned me to sit and be quiet. I watched as he listened to the news, his face grave and concerned. Then he removed the earphones, letting them hang from his neck

"Trotsky has been murdered in Mexico City," he said. "Someone split his head open with an axe."

I stared at him, incredulous. "You sure?"

"No doubt about it. Biggest thing on the news."

I continued to stare, unbelieving.

"Want to listen?' Kentucky asked, pushing the radio across the table toward me.

'No...thanks." I couldn't say anything more. I left the mess room and went to my cabin which I shared with the chief cook.

Leon Trotsky murdered. Hounded out of the Soviet Union by Stalin, then out of France and Norway, Trotsky had been given asylum in Mexico. There he and his wife, Natalia, lived in Coyoacán, a Mexico City suburb, in a house provided by artists Diego Rivera and Frida Kahlo. He was protected by an armed guard provided by the Socialist Workers Party.

In an earlier attack on May 24th, a gang of Stalinist thugs masquerading as Mexican police and armed with machine guns had stormed the house in the night, overpowered the guards and riddled Trotsky's bedroom with gunfire. Miraculously, Trotsky and Natalia survived by rolling off the bed and lying still in the dark. One of the guards, Sheldon Harte, was kidnapped and murdered.

Following this attack, the defenses of the compound had been strengthened and the vigilance of the guards increased. But they'd found a way to murder him, to silence forever the greatest revolutionary tribune of our time.

Shocked and saddened by this final piece of viciousness, I went about my work, cooking and baking for the crew, unable to share my feelings with any of them. Though some knew I had socialist views, none could have appreciated what the murder of Trotsky meant to me.

When the ship arrived at the dock in South Portland and started discharging a partial load of sulphur, I made arrangements with the steward for the afternoon off. When I went ashore at noon, the ship was slated to leave again that same evening at 7 p.m. I walked around Portland for an hour or two, then decided to take a trip out to Belfort Street to see my sister Anne and my Uncle Harold and Aunt May. They had cared for Anne since she was an infant, and it had been almost three years since I had seen any of them. In the fall of 1937, I had stayed with them while looking for a job in Portland, leaving there to go on that bootless venture into door-to-door magazine subscription sales. As always, the Pledgers were welcoming and it was nice seeing my little sister, a pretty blonde now ten years old.

Being with them helped take my mind off the tragedy in Mexico City. But when I got back to the harbor, I found the FRANCES SALMAN had left the dock an hour before the scheduled departure time. I had missed the ship, my gear was aboard, and I had nothing with me but the clothes I wore and a few dollars in my pocket. Of course the ship would pick up another cook in Galveston, the next port of call, so I took the Greyhound bus home to Boston. Later the company mailed me the wages due and the chief cook shipped my seabag to the union hall in Boston.

Back in Boston, disappointed and angry with myself for having missed my ship, I registered at the union hall where they told me shipping was very slow. We held a memorial meeting for Leon Trotsky at the SWP headquarters on Lagrange Street and about 200 people turned out to hear James P. Cannon, the party's national secretary. In his memorial address, Cannon reviewed Trotsky's lifelong devotion to the cause of socialism, his outstanding leadership in both the 1905 and 1917 revolutions in Russia, his unswerving commitment to follow the truth wherever it led, his long fight against the Stalin usurpation, standing for what he believed was right even when he had to stand alone. Jim Cannon told how a GPU agent, Ramon Mercader, posing as a sympathizer had managed to see Trotsky alone on the pretext of seeking some editorial advice and struck him from the rear with a mountaineer's axe, piercing his brain. The assassin was captured by Trotsky's guards, but Trotsky died of his wounds. This murderer was later tried in Mexican courts, proven to be an agent of Stalin's secret police, convicted and spent 20 years in prison before returning to his masters in the Kremlin.

Cannon was one of the most eloquent orators I have ever heard and this was an inspiring tribute to our fallen leader. Bishop Huntington and his wife attended the meeting on the invitation of their daughters. Afterwards, I heard the bishop comment that it was one of the finest sermons he had ever listened to. Though he well knew that Cannon was an atheist, I believe the bishop's comment was sincere praise and he meant exactly what he said.

During this time, Hitler — emboldened by his success in Poland and with the Soviet Union immobilized by the Stalin-Hitler Pact — invaded Scandinavia, The Netherlands, Belgium and France. In August he started bombing London. President Roosevelt leaned strongly toward joining the war on the side of the Allies but was restrained by a strong isolationist sentiment widespread throughout the country. Isolationism was also promoted by the German-American Bund and others who favored the Nazis. The Communist Party, following the dictates of Stalin's foreign policy, chanted that the Yanks were not coming and made apologies for the Nazis.

Seemingly as preparation for dealing with political dissent in the coming war, Congress passed and Roosevelt signed legislation known as the Smith Act. Essentially, the Smith Act made it a crime to advocate any radical political change. It was assailed as a "Gag Act" by a wide spectrum of labor and civil liberties organizations, but to no avail. The Smith Act became the law of the land. We had joined all the other liberal and labor organizations in opposing this legislation, never thinking that our party leaders would become its first victims.

The Trotskyists generally held the position that the workers had a legitimate interest in defeating fascism, but that we could not rely on the other capitalist nations to do the job. We believed that fascism was the last desperate convulsion of the capitalist system and that our capitalist rulers had more in common with the Nazis than with their own exploited workers. Believing that the socialist reconstruction of society was the only way to defeat fascism finally and decisively, our first priority was for the working class, each in its own country, to overthrow its own ruling class. We urged the German and Italian workers to overthrow their fascist rulers and the Russian workers to do the same with the Stalinist bureaucrats.

The fact that we were entirely ignored by the workers of every country did not persuade us of the impracticality of this proposal. We were largely ignorant of the real extent of Nazi bestiality as were most people in the democratic countries at that time, and we did not anticipate the determination of the bourgeois democracies to wipe out Nazism, since their initial reaction to Hitler was to appease and make excuses for him.

Though we did not resist the draft or in any way defy or hinder the war effort, we continued to preach the pure doctrine of democratic socialism, to publish anti-imperialist propaganda, and to defend union workers' interests against all encroachments by employers operating under the cloak of war hysteria. We continued to defend the rights of workers and the civil liberties of minorities (e.g., Japanese-Americans), even in wartime.

I stayed in Boston working occasionally on one of the New York to Boston passenger ships and waiting for a better berth. Less than a month after Trotsky was murdered my good friend, Jack Wheelwright, was killed crossing Massachusetts Avenue. He was struck by a car driven by a drunken driver. John Brooks Wheelwright, Harvard-educated scion of one of Boston's oldest and proudest families, was a talented, nationally-known poet. He was also a committed revolutionary socialist. We used to laugh at his eccentricities. Who else would mount a soapbox to deliver a socialist lecture in Boston Public Gardens clad in tuxedo, spats and a racoon coat? I think these things only endeared Jack to us because we knew he was 100 percent sincere. He would be sorely missed by his Boston comrades.

Nina and I had been married nearly a year but things were not going well for us as a couple. We didn't have a lot of fights. She didn't reproach me. But Nina, naturally a very cheerful person, was not happy, and I was insensitive to her feelings and to her needs. I didn't like being away from her so much but thought that a seaman's work was what I was best suited for and the place where I could be of the most use to the movement.

Nina minded my absence a great deal and couldn't see much future for us the way we were going. She knew what family life was like, and it wasn't like this. I refused to think about the future, hoping it would take care of itself. And perhaps I was afraid to make that kind of commitment. I have known many men for whom going to sea has been a mode of escape from responsibility. There may have been an element of that in all of us who followed the sea, and I've sometimes wondered how much of a factor that was in our marriage.

Shortly before I shipped on the FRANCES SALMAN, Nina found a good job as waitress in a fancy restaurant on the south shore and rented a furnished room nearby. She was very good at her work and the tips were excellent. She was now making enough money so we could have gotten our own apartment again, and I could have stayed ashore and looked for a job where I would be at home every night. On the other hand, I wanted to continue as I was, returning home occasionally and expecting her to be there waiting for me.

When I returned to port, I'd stay with her at her rooming house in Hingham, or at her parents' house. Our reunions were joyous. She would run into my arms and I'd hold her tight, both of us so happy to be together again. We would make love and talk about everything that had happened while I was gone, then make love again. We'd go to an Italian tavern in the south end and sit for hours over a glass of beer and a pizza, talking, holding hands and just looking at one another.

But then I'd leave again. She was increasingly unhappy with the situation. I knew this but was unable to take the only action that would change it. Then while I was at sea and away from home for several weeks, she entered into an affair with the pastry baker at the restaurant. When I came home she asked me to quit the sea and I refused. Then she told me she wanted a divorce. I told her if that's what she wanted, I wouldn't try to stop her.

Nina was very upset by all this. She was a very loving and loyal person, but became convinced there was no future in being married to me. She told me that she had been warned before she married me. A couple of older party men had told her that because of my rustic Maine background and general lack of sophistication, I would lack appreciation of a woman's needs and aspirations. At the time I put this down to jealousy on their part, but today I think they were probably right, whatever their motivation. I shipped out again and Nina went to live with the baker. I remained on good terms with Nina's parents who seemed to assign to her most of the blame for our breakup. For a while they were cool toward her. However I may have felt then, I have long since come to the conclusion that I was much more at fault than Nina. My immaturity and selfishness were the major contributing factors to the failure of our marriage. Her affair with the baker lasted only a few weeks, and he went home to his wife and children.

Nina got an uncontested divorce in 1941. It was the best thing she could have done for herself, and I didn't blame her then, or now. However insensitive I had been when I still had Nina and she was trying to make our marriage work, once I lost her irretrievably I was assailed with grief. But by the end of 1940 I realized it was too late to save what had gone forever and I wanted to get far away from Boston.

17

Men Who Go Down to the Sea in Ships

For some time I had thought I would change from the steward's department to the engine department, and in February, 1941, I had my chance. The SS MILLINOCKET needed a wiper and I took the job. Wiper is the lowest rating in the engine room, equivalent to laborer. The wiper works days directly under the supervision of the first assistant engineer. He cleans bilges, paints, polishes brass, handles stores and does everything else the engineer tells him to do. As it turned out, I didn't stay wiper long on that first trip. The 8-12 fireman had gone ashore, got drunk and missed the ship, so I was promoted after being aboard about two hours. Prior to the MILLINOCKET, I had always been on day work aboard ship, either in the steward's department or as an ordinary seaman on the overnight passenger liners.

This is a good place to explain, for those who do not already know, the organizational structure of a ship's crew and the watch system on which it operates. Though new technologies have changed and reduced manning requirements on some modern ships, the basic structures remain the same today as they were sixty years ago.

The primary division in the ship's company is between licensed and unlicensed crew members. Ship's officers sit for examinations and receive licenses qualifying them to serve as master or mate, engineer or assistant engineer aboard ship. Other crew members receive only certificates of identification and of service, which attest their qualifications to perform as able seaman, fireman, oiler, etc. These are known as the unlicensed crew.

Each of the three departments aboard ship has its own clearly defined responsibilities. The deck department is headed by the captain who is assisted by his three mates (a larger ship might have more mates and/or cadet officers). These officers, directing a crew of unlicensed able-bodied and ordinary seamen, operate the ship, navigate and steer it, and maintain the vessel itself. The bosun (a contraction of boatswain) is a straw boss who directs the work of the deck crew, and the ship's carpenter is also attached to the deck department.

The engine department, under the direction of the chief engineer and his three (or more) assistant engineers, supervise a crew of firemen, oilers, watertenders and wipers who operate and maintain the ship's power plant, engine and all auxiliary mechanical equipment wherever located. A larger ship might also carry an electrician and a deck engineer who has responsibility for maintaining cargo winches, steering engine and all other deck mechanical equipment.

The steward's department supplies, prepares and serves all food and beverages used aboard ship, provides mattresses, linens and towels and has responsibility for housekeeping duties in cabins of officers and passengers, if any are carried. All members of the steward's crew on cargo vessels are on day work, though hours may be adjusted to the mealtime requirements. In port, the deck and engine departments generally go on a daytime schedule except as needed to operate the boilers. At sea, watches are set and most of the operating crew stand around-the-clock watches.

Watches are established by law as of four-hour duration, twice daily. Thus the 12 to 4 watch works from midnight to 4 a.m. and from noon to 4 p.m. The 8-12 watch is on duty from 8 a.m. to noon and from 8 p.m. to midnight. The 4-8 watch works those hours both in the morning and the evening. Some men have strong preferences about which watch they work. I have stood all three, but where I had a choice took the 4-8.

The ship was already under way when I went down into the boiler room at 7:45 p.m. on that first day aboard the MILLINOCKET. I had no idea what a fireman did on watch. The boiler room seemed immense to me. It was an awesome place with flaming hot oil forced under pressure into fire boxes. The air was hot and seemed to pulsate with the blast from the fires. Steam-driven pumps chugged and hissed in the offing. It was like nothing I had ever seen before.

There was a clear area running athwartships in front of the boilers about 35 feet long and 12 or 14 wide. The cylindrical boilers themselves, two of them towering above me, were perhaps 14 feet in diameter. Each had three fire doors roaring in their business ends, facing into the boiler room. Besides the boilers, the bulkheads and ship-side areas at both ends were filled with pumps and other auxiliary equipment and festooned with gauges and other instruments. Entrance to and exit from this inferno was through a narrow passageway between the boilers leading into the engine room.

The fireman I was relieving, a Puerto Rican named Jesus, wore only short pants and a singlet. His brown skin glistened with sweat which he mopped at with a wiping rag. He knew I was green and explained everything patiently. After about ten minutes of instruction he judged I was ready to take over the boiler room.

The routines were simple enough. I had to watch the steam gauges and adjust the fires to keep the steam in working range but not let it go high enough to blow the safety valve. I had to watch the water in the glass-tube water gauges on the end of each boiler and if the water level dropped below a certain point, open the intake valve a little; if it rose too much, close the valve a bit. Jesus showed me how to operate and lubricate the fuel oil pumps and how to clean burners, install them and light them. And that was it.

I was on my own but if I got in any serious difficulty I could call the oiler or the engineer, both working only a few yards away in the engine room. My watch partner, oiler Manuel Vasquez, who was to became one of my best friends on the ship, looked in several times during the watch to chat and perhaps to see if I was getting along all right. But I got through that first four-hour watch without any problems or needing to ask anyone anything.

This one watch was enough to complete my conversion from kitchen/galley to the engine/boiler room. It wasn't that the work was easier, but since I had been drafted as cook at age 12, I had been trying to get out of the kitchen. From that time forward I have cooked only as an avocation and done other scullery work only as a volunteer. Now I can enjoy cooking as a creative activity, something not possible for me during the years I had to do it for a living.

The MILLINOCKET was a smallish freighter, just over 3,000 tons. She was one of a fleet belonging to Bull Line, a company running primarily between Puerto Rico and east coast ports. They brought general cargo down to the island and cargoes of raw sugar back to various refineries in the states. Our first port of call was San Juan where we stayed three days to discharge cargo.

Puerto Rico was to me an exotic land. The trees and foliage were tropical, the architecture was Spanish tropical, the colorful streets teemed with people of every hue, buying and selling products such as I had never seen before, and speaking a spirited language I did not yet understand against a background of lively Hispanic music. It was very exciting for a young man only recently from the backwoods of Maine. I was tempted to pinch myself as a reality check, that I should be so far from home in this alien and fascinating clime.

Typically, the deck and engine crews of Bull Line ships were about half Puerto Rican, the rest white Americans with a sprinkling of Filipinos and an occasional Hawaiian. The steward's department crews were black Americans. Those who became my closest friends aboard ship were Puerto Rican. They were among the staunchest of unionists and very loyal friends. On the MILLINOCKET I made several friends with whom I later sailed on other ships, always good companions. I especially remember Juan Rios, Manuel Vasquez and Hernando Sanchez.

All the Puerto Rican seamen spoke English, but I tried to learn Spanish and they helped me. They would speak Spanish more slowly when I was with them and explain if there was something I didn't understand. I got a book on learning Spanish the quick and easy way. I used to study it on watch, learning grammar and memorizing long lists of vocabulary. After a couple of months working on this ship, I could converse in Spanish about simple things and understand most of what I heard. Being a good mimic, I could even pass as Puerto Rican if I confined myself to the phrases I knew best.

I also picked up a lot of expressions that had to be used with care in some places. There were those who might take umbrage at being called a cuckold, a pimp or a fag. And in some circles it was not good form to say "fuck you and fuck your mother!" Even in Spanish. But aboard ship these were common forms of address.

On all SIU ships, regular meetings of the ship's unlicensed crew members were held in the crews' mess room. At these meetings delegates would be elected for each department, grievances and complaints aired and discussed. The quality and variety of the meals served to the crew were always major topics of discussion, the steward and his crew receiving a lot of admonition and advice. I always took an active part in these discussions and generally served as recording secretary of meetings after it became known I was willing. Though nominated, I declined to serve as engine-room delegate while I was still only a wiper. Later, when I was a duly certified fireman, oiler, watertender or deck engineer, I would often be elected and serve as delegate.

Individual grievances reported to these meetings were generally on a departmental level, involving perceived discrimination in work assignments or in awarding overtime work. Sometimes personal slights or offenses by officers were cited. Occasionally, an aggrieved member was considered off-base by his fellow crewmen and a discussion in the meeting could resolve the problem. Much of the discussion of food revolved around personal likes and dislikes, but issues of corner-cutting and penny-pinching by the steward were a constant. Sometimes meetings would pass resolutions concerning the number and variety of meats to be served at each meal, or the quality of the lunch to be left out for the night watches. These were all dutifully recorded by the secretary.

After the ship's meeting adjourned, the delegates would call on the captain, and if necessary the other department heads, and present any demands or adjudicate grievances as required. In my experience on many ships, I recall few instances where the crews made what I would consider unreasonable demands, or cases where the ships' officers responded other than sensibly, and generally in a conciliatory fashion. Disputes that couldn't be resolved aboard ship would require the intervention of the union's port agent or his representative at the next port of call, and sometimes they'd involve the company's shoreside officials as well.

Things seemed to have come a long way since the bad old days before union organization was accepted, however reluctantly, by the shipowners and their representatives. Seamen of my day were beneficiaries of the brave men who fought, got beaten and sometimes killed to establish the right of the merchant sailor to first class citizenship and decent working/living conditions. As I remember, the MILLINOCKET was a good ship in that regard. A suggestion by the ship's meeting was usually enough to bring a quick adjustment of whatever problem was presented.

In addition to San Juan, each trip included one or more of the ports around the island — Fajardo, Ponce, Mayaguez, Arecibo or Aguadilla . Each had its own special flavor but I liked them all and had a good time in every one. A good time then consisted of going to a nightclub/bar with my friends and shipmates, ordering a bottle of rum and some Coca Colas. The bar provided bowls of ice and cut limes at no cost. The rum from the bar cost $1.35 for a fifth and the Cokes were a nickel. At a liquor store, the fifth of rum was 65¢ for Palo Viejo, but 85¢ for Boca Chica or one of the better brands. Rum was a nickel a shot at various stand-up counter bars along the street.

It was very uncommon to find a seaman who didn't drink. In fact, a man risked being looked upon with suspicion if he persisted in such anti-social behavior. There were some who drank more than others — more at a sitting and more persistently. But if you had asked any of them whether they thought they had a drinking problem, the probable answer would be, "You bet! There's plenty of times I can't raise the price of a drink." They'd all admit to an occasional hangover, but seamen whenever in port, wherever they were, drank whatever they could get. They got drunk, sometimes raised a lot of hell, and thought they were having a lot of fun. At sea, where they couldn't get it, they didn't miss it. They just sobered up and did their work until the next port.

I guess I was a fairly typical seaman in this regard during those years. How many of us ended up chronic alcoholics, it would be hard to guess. I know some who did, but I know more that didn't. Anyway, when I was in New York or Boston, I went to a bar once in a while. When I was in some port where there was little else to do and where all my shipmates were carousing, I went along with them.

I estimate that party members in the merchant marine, on average, drank less than the usual seaman. Some were just naturally abstemious and some had more serious things on their minds when they got in port, such as visiting the public library or otherwise improving their minds. Perhaps this was especially true of those who came to the merchant marine when they were a bit older and more mature. Some of my closest friends and best drinking companions were comrades like John Keeley and Ed Costello, both from Boston and at one time both patrolmen (elected port officials) for the National Maritime Union in the Port of New York. Others, whom I held in equally high esteem, rarely drank more than a glass or two.

It was generally true that a seaman could be drunk and miss his watch, putting the burden on someone else, and be forgiven — if he didn't make a habit of it. It was assumed that a drunk couldn't help it, and there any of us might stray. A sober shipmate, on the other hand, was not excused so easily.

Morris Chertov was a New York City comrade in his early thirties when he first shipped as crew messman, the only job available to him while he was still a permit man. His first ship made a couple of stops in the states, then went to South America where it also made a couple of calls before arriving in Buenos Aires. Morris was a studious fellow who was more interested in exploring the culture of the places he visited than in getting drunk with shipmates. In the states he went to the library or the party headquarters, in foreign countries to museums and cultural or historical attractions. I think he was relatively abstemious, though I have often gone out with Morris for a drink.

By the time his ship got to Buenos Aires, Morris was well thought of as a messman because he was pleasant, hard-working and conscientious. He was also an object of good-natured derision because he never went to the bars with shipmates, and always came back to the ship sober. Off duty, he was rarely seen without a book in his hands. As a permit man, he was on sort of probation with his shipmates but thus far he hadn't done badly, despite his intellectualism and suspicious sobriety.

But in Buenos Aires he went ashore one afternoon, either misjudged the time or was delayed, returning to the ship a half hour late for supper. In the absence of their messman, the crew had to serve themselves as best they could. Their indignation at being so neglected turned to outrage, their ill temper aggravated by the fact that their messman was this high-brow non-drinker.

Coming on board late, Morris was hurrying to his post. He told me years later that he was wondering if there was any way he could make amends for this dereliction. He said that through the open messroom porthole he heard irate shouts and hesitated, listening. He could tell by their voices that most if not all of them had been drinking. He heard his name mentioned and stopped. Some crewman loudly expressed the opinion, concurred in by several others, that Morris thought he was better than his ordinary shipmates, never getting drunk, never going to the whorehouses.

Morris made a quick decision. Mussing his hair and disarranging his clothes, he completed his way to the messroom door where he stood reeling. Mumbling unintelligible words, he lurched into the messroom and fell onto a bench. Looking around at his startled shipmates he struggled to get them into focus, then said, "Nishe mornin."

This his shipmates could understand. Their wrath dissipated like snow in the summer sun, and they laughed and slapped Morris on the back.

"Ol' Mess got drunk! Ho, ho, ho!"

"Guess he's not so bad after all!"

Someone helped him back to his bunk. He was one of them now. They accepted, liked and trusted him, no longer considering him a suspicious alien presence. He, too, had feet of clay. If he had been guilty simply of staying too long at the museum, they could not have forgiven him. But being a drunk, all was forgotten. His crew recommended him for a book as a full member of the SIU and he served at sea for many years as able seaman.

When forty or more men are required to live together in close quarters, isolated from the rest of the world, sleeping in crowded fo'c'sles, eating all their meals together, performing work that requires constant cooperation and is vital to the safety of all, then the morale of the entire crew is dependent on each member doing his share and showing consideration for the feelings of others. This is true on any ship, but especially so on long trips which can become trying under the best of circumstances.

Most men adjust to these conditions, some more easily than others. Those who will not or cannot adjust to living and working harmoniously with others will become miserable themselves, and be a thorn in the sides of their fellows and a source of dissension among their associates. I have sailed with men who shirked their share of the work to be done, who consistently came on watch a few minutes late, sometimes so late the man they were relieving had to do part of their work—especially oiling the engine, which cannot wait. A good shipmate will always relieve the watch a few minutes early.

There are many ways of being inconsiderate, such as turning up the volume on a radio or creating other disturbances so others can't sleep. Even personal hygiene can become a matter of general concern if a shipmate will not keep himself clean enough not to offend the nostrils of these who must share his fo'c'sle.

I remember one young fellow who shipped out of Baltimore as ordinary seaman on a Bull Line ship. He seemed a likeable young man, but after he'd been aboard a week or ten days I heard some rumblings from the deck crew about his odor. Unlike some later ships where the crew occupies two-man cabins, on this ship the entire deck crew bunked together on the starboard side forward, with the engine crew on the port side, with toilet facilities between. This boy's fo'c'sle mates said he hadn't had a shower since coming aboard and smelled so bad it upset all who slept near him. Soon other crewmen who did not share his quarters were made aware of his stench in the messroom.

A couple of the older men took the lad aside and advised him in a friendly way to clean himself up. He agreed to do so, but it was soon evident he had no such intention. A couple more days went by, the boy smelling riper all the time, his condition a matter of general concern and open comment. Then, one afternoon, a delegation of shipmates told him he had to take a shower and wash his clothes. He was given a deadline — clean himself up by tomorrow noon, or else.

Tomorrow noon arrived and the lad had still made no move toward the shower. By prearrangement, after the noon meal the pump was started to furnish sea water to the fire hoses on deck. The young man was seized by a group of his shipmates, stripped, thrown to the deck and scrubbed with long-handled deck brooms under a stream of brine from the nozzle of a fire hose. He was then shoved into a shower stall with a cake of soap to finish the job. He was not allowed to dress himself until he'd scrubbed all his clothes and hung them up to dry. The ship's officers made themselves scarce while all this was going on. They knew it was happening and didn't want to interfere, but couldn't openly approve.

This fellow had to learn the hard way and he left the ship at the next mainland port. Most such misfits do not last long aboard ship, or they lead very lonely lives, shunned by their mates. To be a "good shipmate" is considered a primary virtue among seamen. I was fortunate that adjusting to life aboard ship came easily to me, perhaps because of the five years I spent living in a boarding school dormitory. I have fond memories of many good shipmates, men who would share their last dollar with a friend, who would risk injury or death to save their ship or the life of a comrade. It was men like this that I sailed with on the MILLIN-OCKET and with whom I visited the garish attractions of the waterfront watering holes.

In Puerto Rico each of the big waterfront bars had its contingent of girls. Young women of every complexion, size and shape, mostly in their late teens and all pretty in a Latin way. The bar didn't pay them but permitted them to hang around because they attracted business. They sat with the customer, even sat on his lap if they liked him, and maybe drank a little.

I guess you would call them free-lance prostitutes but they didn't work very hard at it. And they had little in common with the B-girls who haunted many of the waterfront bars in the states, urging patrons to buy them high-priced drinks consisting mostly of colored water. In collaboration with the bartender, the B-girl would stay sober until the seaman was drunk (or sometimes drugged) then they'd roll him for whatever he had left from his payday. This was a common experience of seamen in mainland American ports. I have had several shipmates robbed in this fashion but I can recall no such instance involving a Puerto Rican bar girl.

These girls were fun-loving and affectionate, they didn't order any drinks, and if they really liked you, they didn't want any pay for more intimate services. All of them I talked with lived at home with their parents and brought money into the house. The parents knew how they spent their afternoons and evenings. The girls told me their parents didn't mind and hoped they would find a nice man who would marry them, maybe take them to the States. Many of them found just that.

At one time or another over my Puerto Rican years, I had such a friend in several of the ports. In San Juan, at different times, there were three of them. I gave them gifts but for the most part these were not commercial relationships, and perhaps they thought I was a good matrimonial prospect. For me they were good company and the only source of affection available. Remembering them today I can call up most of their faces and many of their names, each a distinct personality but all lively, loving, passionate and generous. I can only hope they all found what they were looking for.

It was on the MILLINOCKET that I first tried trolling for game fish. I never would have initiated this, but the carpenter talked about fishing and I was the only one aboard who was interested enough to do anything about it. I had the interest, but without help I wouldn't have known how to start.

The carpenter and the bosun supplied all the equipment, and with the carpenter's help, I attached a two-by-four outrigger about 16 feet long to the poop deck rail. It was hinged so it would swing aft along the rail when a guy line was released. From the end of the projecting spar I attached 200 feet of heaving line followed by a 20-foot length of smaller line and a five-foot wire leader. At the end of the leader I attached a long-shanked hook with about a one-inch throat. For a lure I fashioned a piece of white sail canvas in a cone shape and lashed it tightly around the line just above the shank of the hook. It had to be dressed so smoothly and securely it would pull through the water for days without coming loose.

Needless to say, I had a lot of help getting it done right. But when the lure and its lashing were complete, they would last for several days in the water before the canvas itself would start to fray and have to be replaced. The MILLINOCKET was an old ship and not very fast, maybe clocking nine or ten knots per hour. This was faster than anyone would choose to troll, but we didn't have a choice. The ship's principal business was not fishing. Once the line was in the water, I'd pull the outrigger into position straight out from the ship's side, so the line would ride as far as possible out of the wake.

Though I was the only one interested enough to rig the line, everyone on the ship kept watch and wherever I was they'd would let me know if a fish took the lure. No one ever bothered my line, but through the engine room gratings if I was on watch or through the fo'c'sle hatchway if I was in my bunk I'd hear a yell.

"Fish ahoy! Fish on the line!"

I'd drop whatever I was doing and rush to the poop deck. By the time I arrived there would usually be several shipmates standing there, watching the fish in the water. Releasing the guy line so the outrigger would swing in alongside the after rail, I'd pull the line in by hand. I always had plenty of volunteers to help pulling in the fish.

I didn't catch many fish but surprisingly few were lost once they were hooked, because with the speed of the ship combined with the speed at which we pulled it in, the fish was out of the water a good part of the way to the ship.

Whatever I caught, I'd carry it forward to the galley and present it to the chief cook, whose name was George but whom almost everyone called "El Bicho Grande." This epithet had been bestowed on him by San Juan bar girls who would have no traffic with him due to the extraordinary size of his organ. George, of ebony complexion, was a very nice guy, a good cook and a good shipmate. He never seemed to mind the constant reference to his most personal attribute but I usually called him by his right name or his title.

"Here, George. I brought something for you."

"Ahh! Bonito! They're good! And I was wondering what I'd give you guys for supper."

Actually he wasn't wondering. The fish was always extra. And the bonito, a small tuna, was very good when George got through with it. And the kingfish was good eating too, though not as tasty as the bonito as I remember it.

Once I brought in a long ferocious-looking pike-like fish, the likes of which I had never seen before. This one had more fight in him than anything else I'd ever caught and it took a sharp rap from the carpenter's hammer to subdue him.

"Got something for you, cook," I told George.

"Take it away. Barracuda is no good. Not fit to eat."

I had to take George's word for it and tossed it overboard. That was the only fish George refused to cook, but whether my catch was edible or not, I enjoyed the fishing as it broke the monotony of the week-long voyages between the island and the mainland ports.

18

On the Beach in San Juan, Mobile, New Orleans

On the MILLINOCKET I worked part of the time as wiper but most of the time as fireman because the ship was often shorthanded. According to Maritime Commission regulations, a man had to work for six months in the engine room before he could take the examination for a fireman's certificate. When I paid off the MILLINOCKET I was lacking only 16 days for my six months.

I spent a couple of weeks beachcombing around San Juan and visiting with a party member, a Puerto Rican lawyer, who lived in Santurce, a San Juan suburb. The lawyer, Garcia, was a former associate of Luis Muños Marin who had been a socialist before he founded the Popular Democratic Party and won big in the 1940 elections campaigning under the slogan "Bread, Land and Liberty."

In Puerto Rico I also visited Irving Geldman, an American school teacher from Minneapolis who lived in Mayaguez and had married a Puerto Rican woman, also a teacher. I enjoyed talking with them, I read their newspapers and their file of *The Militant*, and got caught up on what was going on in the world whenever the ship was in San Juan or Mayaguez.

It was from Irving Geldman, while I was still with the MILLINOCKET, that I learned that leaders of the Socialist Workers Party and of Minneapolis Teamsters Union Local 544 had been indicted on July 15, 1941, under the Smith Act and were to be tried on charges of conspiring to overthrow the United States government by force and violence. Irving's brother, Max Geldman, a Minneapolis SWP leader who had been an organizer of a WPA union affiliated with the Local 544, was among those indicted.

The Minneapolis teamsters had set an example for the entire American labor movement. In a hard-fought strike in 1934 they had transformed Minneapolis from a notorious open-shop town into a stronghold of unionism, increasing the membership of the teamsters local union from a few hundred to more than 6,000. They had spearheaded union organization in the whole area and were especially influential in the Mid-West Teamsters Conference, challenging the iron control of Dan Tobin, the corrupt boss of the International Brotherhood of Teamsters. Tobin, who was also head of the Democratic Party Labor Committee, wanted to get rid of the militant Trotskyist leaders of the Mid-West Conference. Roosevelt, who wanted no opposition to his war plans, saw eye-to-eye with Tobin. If they could railroad these militant socialists to jail, both would achieve their purposes.

Tobin's first move was to appoint a receiver with absolute power over Local 544. The membership responded by voting to affiliate with the CIO. A couple of weeks later the FBI had raided the headquarters of the SWP in Minneapolis and St. Paul confiscating piles of socialist books and pamphlets. They arrested the officers of the local union, and indictments were handed down by a federal grand jury. Irving told me a committee had been set up to organize support for the accused and raise money for the defense.

Also, during the time I was on the MILLINOCKET, Mussolini's fascist troops were trying to subdue Greece, Hitler's forces had overrun Yugoslavia, and in June Hitler had invaded the Soviet Union. All Stalin's concessions to Hitler had done him no good and the American Stalinists overnight had become the most frenzied of warriors. They campaigned night and day for American entry into the war. In the unions they pressed for a no-strike pledge, calling upon American workers to forget all their grievances and join forces with their bosses to combat Nazism. The bosses loved it and whittled away at union working conditions, while making billions in profits.

In September I shipped on the SS EDITH for a trip around the island and then to Pensacola, Florida, where I quit because I now had served my requisite six months time in the engine room. At that time there was no union hall in Pensacola, so Mobile seemed to be the best bet for getting my fireman's certificate and a ship. The Waterman Lines, under contract with the SIU, was headquartered there and operated several ships running to South America. So I took a Greyhound bus to Mobile.

I found a cheap room in a rooming house not far from the union hall, then had a set of passport photos made and went to the Maritime Commission office. I filled out an application and took my fireman's examination. I had been working as a fireman most of the past six months and had studied a book on steam-power theory and practice, so the examination was not hard for me. But before I could get the certificate, I had to have a physical examination.

I had long known that one of the requirements for a rating higher than wiper called for 20/20 vision in both eyes. This could be corrected vision, but no known eyeglasses would do anything for a glass eye. The physical examinations were regularly taken at the Marine Hospital where everything was free to seamen. I had never heard of any seaman going anywhere else, but the fine print on the form stated that the physical could be performed by any licensed physician. This was probably because there are places where Marine Hospitals are not readily accessible. However, I knew that if I went to the Marine Hospital, I didn't have a chance of passing the eye test.

Pondering this, I decided I might be able to fool a private doctor or talk him into something. I found a doctor who practiced out of his home with a shingle hanging by the front gate, an elderly gent who didn't seem to have much of a practice. He was a pleasant old man who liked to talk, so we chatted for a half hour before he started the exam.

He wanted to know what I was doing in Mobile and where I came from. Learning I was from Maine, he told me he had been there in the army during the World War (the first and only one at that time) and had taken advantage of some leave to see part of the state, strange to him since he was a native of Mobile. We talked about the places he'd visited, some of which I remembered with some sense of nostalgia.

As we talked I studied his eye-test chart, but doubted I'd be able to memorize it well enough to pass the test that way. Only a perfunctory examination was required to complete the rest of the form. The doctor asked me a few questions, checked for hernia, tested my hearing and looked to see that I had two arms and two legs, then came the eye test.

"Cover your left eye and read the chart down as far as you can," he told me.

Placing my left hand over my left eye, I read the chart quickly.

"Now cover the other one"

But I changed hands instead of eyes. Placing my right hand over my left eye, I again read the chart and the doctor started to enter the test results. Then I was stricken by conscience. This old doc was too nice a guy. He might get into some serious trouble if he attested that I had 20/20 vision in my blind eye.

"I'm sorry, doctor," I told him. "I fooled you. My left eye is glass and I cheated."

"Why did you do that?"

I explained that if I didn't have good corrected vision in both eyes they wouldn't give me the certificate. I said there was nothing about the job I couldn't do with one eye, and in fact I had been doing it for the past six months as a substitute. I told him I hadn't seen anything out of the left eye since I was a small child, but that the limited vision had never limited my life in any way. I told him it meant a lot to me to get the certificate, but not enough so I could hoodwink him and risk getting him into trouble.

The doctor asked me some more questions about how I'd lost my eye and what I'd been doing since I got out of school.

"Well," he said, "I can't lie about it and put down here that you have good vision in both eyes."

"I know."

"But I'll do what I can." He wrote on the form in the place provided for eye-examination results, signed the paper and gave it to me.

I read what he had written. "Patient has excellent unocular vision."

"Perhaps that will do it," he told me. "Let me know how you make out."

I assured him I would. I knew now it all depended on how careless or ignorant the official at the Maritime Commission would be. I thanked the doctor, paid him a three-dollar fee, and went back to the Commission offices hoping for the best.

The man who was making out certificates was suspicious.

"How come you went to a private doctor? You're supposed to go to the Marine Hospital."

"No. The regulations say the examination can be done by any physician." I pointed out the place on the form. It seemed to be news to him but he didn't deny it. Nor did he give up.

"Everybody goes to the Marine Hospital. Why do you have to be different?"

"This doctor is just around the corner so I preferred going there instead of taking the bus out to the hospital and waiting on line for half a day. That's what I had to do the last time I was out there."

I don't know whether he was so put out about my going to a private doctor he forgot to look at the physical exam results, or whether he didn't know the meaning of unocular. In any case he filed the report and made out my fireman's certificate.

I had passed the hurdle that had worried me for months. From now on I didn't have to worry about my vision being substandard according to Maritime Commission rules. Future upgrades would not require an eye examination, and I later went on to get certified as oiler, watertender and deck engineer without any problems. Now that I was no longer an apprentice (wiper), I could play a more active role in influencing union policy aboard ship and in port meetings. I could be more open in expressing my political beliefs and trying to recruit fellow seamen to the party, and in every way be more effective in my primary mission — acquiring a following among my fellow seamen as a way of advancing the cause of socialism, creating a more just social order.

I went back to the doctor's house, showed him my certificate and thanked him for his help. He seemed almost as pleased as I was with my success. I now went to the union hall to register as a fireman.

I walked into the SIU hall in Mobile which was in a ground floor store, with a big plate-glass window fronting on one of the main streets. The place wasn't very big, maybe 20 x 40 feet, but it was clean and bright with lots of light from the street. It was furnished with the usual folding chairs, benches and tables, but there didn't seem to be much going on. Three or four guys playing cards and a couple reading. I looked around to see who was in charge. There was the usual blackboard for posting jobs, but nothing on it. One corner of the hall had been fitted out as an office and there, behind a desk, sat a small, portly fellow.

I approached the desk. "How's shipping?" I asked.

He looked me over. I don't know what he was hoping to see, but he didn't seem too disappointed. He smiled. "It's tough," he said. "Needed two AB's and an oiler yesterday, but there's a lot of men on the beach."

"Well, I'll register anyway. Who's the dispatcher?"

"I am. Port agent, too."

I handed him my new fireman's certificate and my union card. He looked them over and duly registered me as of 8:15 a.m. on October 15, 1941. He told me there were 19 men with fireman's credentials ahead of me.

Nothing to do now but wait and hope some ship would call in for a lot of men. There was no one in the hall I'd ever sailed with or seen before. I drew up a chair and watched the card game for a while. They were playing penny-ante poker and none of them seemed very good at it. But I was too broke to join the game, so I struck up a conversation with the newspaper readers.

Each morning I'd go to the union hall and look around for the new friends I'd made here in Mobile. If there was some kind of discussion going on, I would join in, often finding opportunities to inject some of my political views. One or two, Red Murray and Shorty Davis, would generally agree with me, but most were not political. However, most were militant unionists and in that we had common ground.

Bobby Frye was almost always in the hall. An ordinary seaman about my age, slightly built with dark complexion and pointy nose, Bobby didn't seem to have fixed opinions about anything, except country music of which he was a great fan. He had a small radio on which he could raise the local country station and, having nothing better to do, I listened to a lot of doleful ballads about love unrequited or lost. Some of those tunes and lyrics stick with me to this day.

By afternoon the crowd at the hall had generally thinned out, but I hung on with the hope a job would turn up while I was the only fireman around. I'd collect all the discarded newspapers, settle into the most comfortable chair I could find, then glance through the news and cull out all the crossword puzzles. Doing the crosswords passed the time, and sharpened my mind. Or so I liked to believe.

I had a little money left from the EDITH but if it was to last I'd have to be very careful. I ate sparingly and after the hall closed spent my evenings reading at the public library. Between the union hall and my rooming house was an orange juice stand where I could get a large glass of fresh-squeezed juice for a nickel. They also had big bowls of peanuts sitting on the bar. I went there at least a couple of times each day for a glass of juice and several handfuls of peanuts. It was the cheapest meal in town, satisfied the appetite, and I could have done worse nutritionally.

Just as the port agent had said, shipping was very slow and after about a week I was thinking of moving on. I had been lucky enough to get a couple of days work as standby fireman on one of the Waterman ships in port. I'd earned a few dollars but it was not a regular job. I was still far from the top of the firemen's list and my savings were dwindling. My room rent was falling due and I decided to hitchhike to New Orleans.

Then at the end of the day as I was leaving the union hall, Bobby Frye hailed me from a bar a few doors down the street. I hadn't seen him in the hall all afternoon and wondered where he'd gone. I joined him at his table.

"Sit down," he told me. "I've got a live one here." He gestured at a man making his way toward us from the direction of the men's room. A "live one" on seaman's parlance was someone with money and willing to spend it.

The man was walking unsteadily. Arriving at the table, he sat down and Bobby introduced us. Henry was all the name he gave the man. Henry, about forty years old, was a bland looking fellow, a countryman, but dressed for town in an ill-fitting suit and already considerably under the influence. I sat with them and drank a couple of beers. Henry was talkative and I learned that he had a farm somewhere in the country outside Mobile. He had come to town to sell some livestock, pigs I think it was. His business was completed and he'd go home tomorrow, but now he was enjoying his visit to the city.

This bar was a pretty dull place, nothing to do but drink, and then drink some more. There was no entertainment, no girls, no life, and Henry wanted to go someplace with more going on. Bobby was game to go with him but I declined. So they departed in a taxi looking for night life and I walked back to my room.

The union hall opened at eight o'clock the next morning and I got there a few minutes past. Bobby was already there and he seemed to be waiting for me.

"You should have gone with us last night," he told me.

"Yeah? What did you do?"

"The cabby took us to a private nightclub and we had some drinks. There were lots of girls there and they were available. I had one and Henry paid. Too drunk to do it himself. Then I got him back to his hotel room and he passed out."

"Sounds like you had a big night of it."

"Better than you know," he told me. "After he passed out I went through his pockets and took his wad." He showed me a roll of bills, maybe about $50.

"You robbed him?"

"Yeah. Well, we were both drunk."

"That's no excuse. It was a lousy thing to do. Henry's a nice guy and he was treating you all evening. That's a helluva way to repay him."

"I guess you're right about that."

"You don't have to keep it. Go back to the hotel and give him his money."

"I wouldn't dare do that. When Henry wakes up he's goin' to be mad as hell. Maybe he's already called the cops. We're in Alabama and they put you in the chain gang for less than this."

"Henry seems like a nice guy. If he gets his money back he'll be all right. Come on. I'll go with you?"

"Henry was so drunk last night and the way he was throwing his money around, he won't remember where it all went. He spent most of his pig money himself, but he'll accuse us of stealing it."

"Us? I didn't have anything to do with it."

"Henry doesn't know that. And he remembers you. He was talking about you just before he passed out, so it wouldn't surprise me if the cops came looking for you too."

I didn't know whether to believe Bobby or not, or how much of a threat this actually was, but it was worth considering. "I'm planning to leave town, anyway," I told Bobby. I'm going to New Orleans."

"Good! I'll go with you and I'll buy your ticket."

"I was figuring on hitchhiking," I said. I didn't really want to hang around with Bobby.

"They're tough on hitchhikers down here too, you know."

"Yeah," I said. "I know." And I did know. Ed Costello's sister, Florence, had told me just before I left Boston that she had a letter from Eddie. He had been picked up hitchhiking and sentenced to 60 days on an Alabama chain gang for vagrancy. So I could either risk that or take the train or bus. But if I paid for a ticket, I'd arrive in New Orleans broke.

"Come on," said Bobby. "Let's take the train. I'll pay."

"Okay." I agreed, and an hour later we were at the depot boarding a New Orleans bound train.

In New Orleans, Bobby registered with me at the union hall but then disappeared. Maybe he thought I might ask him to share his stolen money, but he needn't have feared that. I wanted nothing more to do with him.

Shipping was a little better here, but there were a lot more men on the beach waiting for work. As I had in Mobile, I spent my time hanging out in the union hall, reading and talking with mates about the war in Europe or union problems. This hall occupied the entire second floor of an ancient building on Royal Street in the heart of the French Quarter. The place was huge, cavernous and dark compared to the hall in Mobile, and the office space was nearly as large as the entire store in Mobile. All day long there were scores of men lounging, playing cards, sleeping on benches, coming and going.

The weekly port meetings of the union were attended by all the unemployed seamen in port, with generally between 100 and 150 present. The meeting would be opened by the Port Agent, an old SUP militant whose face I can still see clearly and whose name was Armstrong if memory serves me. The meeting would then elect a chairman, a recording secretary and an auditing committee. I often served in one capacity or another, as I was getting to be known to a lot of the men on the beach.

Since New Orleans was a busy port with several ships arriving or departing every day, I occasionally saw an ex-shipmate or a party member who happened to be in port and who would let me have a couple of dollars. After my money from the EDITH was gone, I lived in a series of flop houses, the last one costing only 25 cents a night. This was a huge loft of a commercial building divided into about 40 cubicles, each eight foot square. The solid partitions, made of rough lumber, rose only about six feet from the floor, and above that was chicken wire up to a height of ten feet. Each cubicle had a door that could be locked with a padlock, and each contained a cot and a blanket. There were evil-smelling toilet and shower facilities near the entrance. The principal advantage over sleeping on the street was that I could lock my seabag in the cubicle during the day and it would be reasonably secure. Some overhead lights stayed on all night, and there was a constant traffic of drunks staggering in, fumbling for their locks and falling onto their cots to snore, gargle and mumble for the rest of the night. It was hard to get any rest there and I stayed only three or four nights before shipping out.

In New Orleans I wasn't eating very regularly either, but I learned which bars near the union hall were best to hang around. You looked for a place frequented by seamen, with a nickel beer and good free lunch for customers. One of the best was directly across the street from the union hall.

Sailors with their pay in their pockets are generally liberal spenders and many, after they had known you for a few minutes, would freely ply you with beer. Don't ask for food. They don't spend their money on food. Plenty of beer, but no food, so the free lunch is important. It may not be very good, running heavily to salt herring, cheese, salami, hard bread and pickles. But that's better than nothing, and that's mostly how I survived during my time in New Orleans.

I did, near the end of my stay, find a restaurant that would give me a filling meal once a day on the cuff. The owner sometimes did this for a seaman, someone he knew, and I ran up a little bill with him. When I came in about 11 months later, he didn't seem surprised to see me. I paid the bill and he told me my credit was always good at his place, but I never had another occasion to avail myself of it.

19

Yugoslav Preview on a U.S. Army Transport

The war in Europe went on. Though the United States wasn't in it yet, our country had made many military preparations and was helping supply the Allies. Among other preparations, some Yugoslav ships that had fled their country when the Germans invaded, or were out of the country and didn't go back, were being refitted here for war duty in the service of the Allies. One of these ships was a combination passenger/freighter of the Zetzka Plovidba line which had spent several months in the shipyard at Mobile where she was renamed the U.S. Army Transport (USAT) SS COLUMBIA. And one day the union dispatcher chalked up on the board about ten jobs for the USAT COLUMBIA. They were mostly stewards department, but they also wanted a fireman/watertender.

I talked with the Port Agent about the ship and he told me she had a civilian crew picked up from wherever they could find men, but they had kept most of the original Yugoslav crew. He said they were paying union scale, but that I could expect conditions that wouldn't be tolerated on a union ship. I asked his opinion on the possibilities of organizing the ship. He said it would be great if it could be done, and a couple of union men would be shipping in the steward's department. I think he would have enjoyed a showdown with the U.S. Army Transport Service. By this time I had been living on handouts, barroom free lunch and hope for nearly a month, and I had to get out of that flophouse cage. So I took the fireman job.

The COLUMBIA was a sorry old tub below decks. There was no sign the shipyard had done anything in the engine or boiler rooms. They should have overhauled those old boilers, or at least cleaned them. But they hadn't. When underway, we belched fire from our stack. The crank bearings on the old quadruple-expansion reciprocating engine ran hot and required constant attention.

Above decks she looked pretty good, though they had converted a lot of space into a huge kitchen big enough to provide meals for the thousands of troops they expected to carry. They had also built thousands of bunks in the cargo holds. Ladders led down from the well deck through the cargo hatches to the cavernous holds where these soldiers were to sleep. The United States wasn't in the war yet, but the government must have figured it was just a question of time. The U.S. Army had established bases in the Caribbean, not only in Panama but in Trinidad, and in British and Dutch Guiana.

Most of the COLUMBIA's crew were Yugoslavs — Croats, Serbs, Dalmatians, Bosnians and Montenegrans. Most of them spoke little or no English, and I spoke no Slavonic language. Fortunately, my watch partner was Maté Glavan, a tall, powerfully-built Dalmatian, in his early thirties, with blond hair, blue eyes and square, but rather flat, Slavic features. Maté, some years prior, had jumped ship and lived in New York for several months before being deported as an illegal alien. He spoke English very well and became my best friend on the ship. He also spoke Spanish, Italian and Greek.

Of the remainder of the crew, two or three others came from the union hall with me. The two I remember were black guys who shipped as saloon messman and salad man. The rest had been rounded up from somewhere. Most were Hispanic, most spoke no English, and many had never been on a ship before. The

Transport Service must have rounded up a bunch of unemployed culinary workers and herded them to the Maritime Commission offices to outfit them with seaman's papers. They were all in the stewards department trying to cook and serve meals for people who spoke no Spanish.

Before signing articles, we all had to swear an oath. I don't remember the exact terminology, but the gist was that we were not planning to overthrow the government by force and violence. I was offended by this, more by the stupidity of it than the content. If someone were determined to overthrow the government by force and violence and could do so by signing onto this misbegotten ship, would he hesitate to swear such an oath?

The issue of violence has often plagued the labor and socialist movements. In innumerable instances, peaceable striking workers have been attacked by goons and police. If they have defended themselves they have been accused and often convicted of illegal violence while the employers' armed thugs are almost never prosecuted. Historically, ruling oligarchies reluctant to relinquish power have often resorted to violent means to hang on — as in Spain in the thirties when the legally elected republican government was overthrown by General Franco with the support of fascist regimes of Italy and Germany. Socialists would agree that a democratically elected and legally constituted socialist regime has the right and duty to defend itself against counter-revolutionary violence.

People today will recall that in the sixties a few so-called "new leftists" not only advocated violence but occasionally practiced it. And for a few years the illegal American Communist Party, driven underground by the Palmer raids of 1919-21, preached "violent overthrow of the government." But they did nothing but talk, and then only to themselves, and perhaps the occasional police spy. At no time have I or any socialist of my acquaintance ever *advocated* the violent overthrow of the government or conspired to change the government by other than constitutional means. Of course that was the charge against the leaders of my party indicted under the Smith Act. But this was a frame-up, probably not even believed by those who brought the indictment. I have always objected to such loyalty oaths on principle. However, I needed the job so I suffered the indignity, signed the articles and went on watch, glad that I was still a civilian even if I was working for the army.

The USAT COLUMBIA was not a happy ship. Speaking with the Yugoslav crewmen I sensed that the Croats hated the Serbs, and the Serbs despised the Croats, Dalmatians and Bosnians. Maté and a few others were notable exceptions. Though I became aware of it only years later, I was getting a preview of the archaic tribal, ethnic and religious animosities that would plague this Balkan nation and provide the fertile soil in which vicious nationalist demagogues would sow the seeds of its eventual destruction. Neither the Americans nor Yugoslavs on board the COLUMBIA seemed to like or respect the Cubans and other Latins, but most of the Hispanics didn't give a damn and clearly showed it by their attitude.

The officers were of the original Yugoslav crew, and they seemed to have a feudal attitude toward the unlicensed crew. Maté told me most of them were Serbian. They kept strictly to their own part of the ship where we were not permitted to go, and they associated only with each other and the few American army officers aboard.

Quarters for the unlicensed deck and engine crew were forward. The main deck, the well deck and the shelter deck were crowded with soldiers, troops being distributed around to the new army bases in the Caribbean. This made it hard to move from fo'c'sle to the engine room or messroom amidships, but the poor soldiers had nowhere else to go except to stay in the sweltering holds where their bunks were ranked row on row and tier on tier.

I talked with a few of the soldiers; they were mostly homesick youngsters who would much rather have been somewhere else. Almost anywhere else. Most of the time they sat despondently on deck, looking at the water and talking among themselves. Fortunately, for the two months I was aboard we had mostly fair weather and calm seas, so few of them were seasick.

We sailed the same day I came aboard, November 24, 1941. The next day the galley crew discovered at sea that most of the new range tops and ovens installed at the shipyard didn't work. Either they didn't work or the green crew didn't know how to work them. I never found out which. The only equipment they could use were the steam vats, so they steamed everything — meat, vegetables, eggs, desserts. They had laid in a prodigious supply of Wonder Bread, making me suspect the army knew about the equipment problems before we sailed. To make meals more interesting, the Hispanic messboys didn't understand the Yugoslavs or the American seamen. Maté and I were among the few who could communicate with the Hispanics, though I couldn't make myself understood to the few Yugoslav messboys. Meal time on the COLUMBIA made me wish to be back at the free lunch counter of a Bourbon Street bar.

The passage between New Orleans and Panama was not unpleasant except for the fouled-up commissary department. The weather was sunny, and off-watch I spent most of my time in the fo'c'sle or on the forepeak which was a restricted area for the soldiers who covered nearly every square foot of space on the well decks and hatch covers. On watch I became better acquainted with my partner, Maté Glavan, native of the small island of Lukoran near Split off the Dalmatian coast. From his account, most of the men of the island were sailors or fishermen.

Maté was a member of the Yugoslav Communist Party and intensely interested in the European war and especially as it affected Yugoslavia. At that time the Chetniks under General

Drazha Mihajlovic had been getting a lot of favorable publicity for their resistance to the German occupation. Maté was scornful of Mihajlovic and the "heroic Chetniks." He said Mihajlovic was a Serbian nationalist more intent on fighting the partisans of Croatia and Bosnia than the occupying forces of Germany and Italy. I later learned that his analysis was correct, and Mihajlovic was eventually abandoned by his British sponsors. Maté had a lot of faith in the Communist Party of Yugoslavia and praised Tito. I had heard of this leader of the Yugoslav Communist Party but knew little about him.

I told Maté my views on Stalinism and he didn't disagree. But he assured me Tito was different, that the Yugoslav party was genuinely revolutionary and would establish a democratic socialist republic. I warned him that Stalin would never allow such a thing, but he assured me that Tito and the Yugoslav party would never submit to dictation from Stalin. I was dubious, but as it turned out, he was surprisingly prescient about the submission part, and tragically wrong about the democratic republic part of his vision.

In any case, Maté and I had much in common and discussed all manner of topics during the long engine room watches. He lent me an English/Serbo-Croat dictionary and a self study book, then helped me learn a few fundamentals of the Slavic language. During the time I was aboard the USAT Columbia I acquired enough words and phrases to communicate on a primitive level with the Yugoslav messboys.

A couple of days out of New Orleans I went below to relieve the 12-4 fireman ten minutes early, thinking to sound him out on union organization. This fellow, Willis, was a big slob of a man, about 30 years old, who seemed to spend most of his time on watch standing under a wind-scoop ventilator, hanging from a ventilator wheel, fast asleep. Though I admired his ability to relax, I wondered if he was aware of what was going on in the boiler room. But I noticed the engineer on his watch kept a sharp eye on Willis, and he always turned over the watch with everything in good shape.

When I went into the boiler room, Willis opened his eyes and peered at me, showing no signs of surprise that I was early. Maybe he didn't even know what time it was. Detaching himself from the ventilator wheel, he start to lurch toward the passageway to the engine room.

"Wait a minute, Willis. I want to talk with you."

He stopped, grunted and stepped back under the ventilator, holding onto the wheel with one hand.

I asked, "What do you think of conditions on this ship?"

He looked at me sleepily for a few beats, then said, "Lousy."

"I agree," I told him. "Do you belong to any union?"

"Nope."

"Where you been sailing?"

"United Fruit." This was a notoriously anti-union outfit.

"I see. Well, if we were to start organization on this ship, would you be interested?"

"Nope." Releasing his grip on the ventilator wheel, he slouched again toward the exit passageway.

After checking all my gauges, pumps and burners and finding everything in top shape, I went into the engine room where Maté was just finishing his four-o'clock round on the main engine. After he finished checking the generator and auxiliary pumps, he joined me and I told him of my talk with Willis.

"I think you're wasting your time, Mark," he told me.

"I certainly was with Willis."

"The rest of them, too. Vladic and I have sounded out most of the deck and engine people. They're all hopeless." Vladic was an able seaman, an older man and a Dalmatian like Maté.

"I'd guess the steward's bunch aren't much better, from what I've seen of them."

"Worse," said Maté. "Kimmy has talked to some of them and he says they're no good." Kimmy was a Yugoslav messman.

"We were a union ship, you know," Maté continued. "All that changed after the war started and we went on the run. The officers stopped dealing with the crew and we had no place to go. Then the army took over and they had a meeting where they warned us. Told us there would be no bolshevik unionism on any army transport."

"What about the guys who used to be active in the union? Wouldn't they like to see the union come back?"

"They might like it, some of them. But they won't stick their necks out. I'd take a chance and Vladic would. Maybe two or three others. But what good would it do? We'd just get fired, and probably locked up."

I had to agree that there were no prospects for unionization of the USAT COLUMBIA. I have been on many ships, before and since, including a couple that were non-union, but I have never seen a crew so uncongenial and unpromising. And from what I'd seen of the officers, I didn't doubt they'd cracked down on the Yugoslav seamen's union at the first opportunity. No doubt they'd welcome the chance to have another go at it.

Our first port of call was Colon where we landed some of the troops and unloaded cargo for the American base in Panama. We lay at the dock for a few days before leaving for Trinidad. It wasn't bad shore time in Colon where everything was neat and clean, American style. We were able to get some good food and drink beer in pleasant surroundings. Maté and I and a few other shipmates took the train to Panama City for a change of pace. This was more like Puerto Rico, except dirtier and more raucous, and we had a good time sampling the night life.

20

Wartime in the Caribbean

When we left the bright lights of Colon on December 6th and headed for Trinidad, none of us realized that our Panama City expedition would be our last peacetime carousal for many years to come.

The ship was loaded with fresh troops and supplies for the American army base at Port-of-Spain. Prior to joining the COLUMBIA I had not known the U.S. Army had all these Caribbean bases. From reading the newspapers, I was aware of the tensions building between the United States and Japan but had no inkling of the imminence of attack.

The next afternoon word spread quickly through the ship that the Japanese had bombed Pearl Harbor in Hawaii and destroyed most of the American fleet lying at anchor there. Our country was now in the war and I like everyone else I was stunned by this news. The war, which had been something happening in Europe, suddenly became real and close to home. My brother, Tex, was stationed at Schofield Barracks not far from Honolulu and the word was that all those bases had been bombed and strafed. And we all knew German submarines were operating in the Atlantic and might now be lying in wait along our course.

We were ordered to black out all ports; smoking or any other lights on deck were prohibited. We knew we had to do it, but it was a bit ludicrous because we constantly belched fire from our smoke stack, whether due to bad fuel, faulty combustion, filthy fire tubes or a combination of all three. We tried to keep it under control, but it was a losing game. In the months that followed, the U.S. lost hundreds of ships in the Caribbean, the Gulf of Mexico and the west Atlantic. I never knew whether the USAT COLUMBIA was one of them, but she was a prime candidate.

Only smaller, shallow-draft vessels could dock at Port-of-Spain at that time, so we lay at anchor in the large sheltered harbor and shifted cargo to open flat-bottomed barges. Small naval vessels ferried the troops ashore, and the crew members traveled by bumboat if they wanted to get to town. Port-of-Spain is the capital and major city of Trinidad, and a trading crossroads for the whole Caribbean area. The downtown was a clean British sort of place with modern stores and hotels and other establishments mingling with the more Trinidadian shops. After dark the tempo picked up and night spots throbbed with calypso music.

I didn't experience a lot of this as I was saving my money, hoping to find a way to get out of the army transport business and back to the States. I had taken the COLUMBIA only as a way of getting off the beach in New Orleans and had no intention of making a career of it. The ambience aboard was too depressing and the situation too dangerous for my taste.

Whether the military had planned it from the start, or whether they were making it up as they went along, I never knew. Anyway, we were informed that the transport COLUMBIA had found a regular niche. She was to be used for the duration of the war to shuttle troops and army supplies about the Caribbean, using Port-of-Spain as home port. Our first trip was to Paramaribo, capital of what is now called Surinam but was then Dutch Guiana.

Paramaribo at that time was a sleepy colonial port town on the left bank of the Suriname River about 17 miles up from the Atlantic Ocean. Along the river we could see some cleared land, probably plantations of some sort, but the impression was mostly of jungle. Paramaribo's main street, running parallel to the river, had two or three ancient two-story brick buildings and some wood-frame, white-painted houses for the Dutch residents. Beyond that was a rambling shanty town where the less privileged lived. The bulk of the population were Creoles, descendants of African slaves freed in 1863, Javanese, Asian Indians and some Amerindians.

Even the main street of Paramaribo was unpaved, hard-packed dirt, with cows and sheep wandering freely, grazing along the roadside, fertilizing the street and the landscape. Paramaribo was and still is the only large town in the country and it seemed to exist principally for shipping. A long pier ran along the river bank and whenever we were in the port other ships lay along the pier, taking on or discharging cargo. Alcoa Steamship Company ships frequently docked here on their way to load bauxite ore at Paranam a few miles upstream.

The ALCOA SHIPPER, an ore carrier of about 5,000 gross tons, was in port and we tied up just astern of her alongside the same pier. I visited the SHIPPER, which carried an SIU crew, and talked with the men. There wasn't anyone aboard I knew, but they were all friendly and I ate one meal with them, wishing I worked that ship instead of the COLUMBIA. I didn't learn about it until months later, but the ALCOA SHIPPER was torpedoed by a German submarine on May 30th en route to New York with a load of bauxite. Two of the 32-man crew were killed by an explosion in the engine room and five others went down with the ship.

A hundred yards from the dock was a place called The Icehouse, a two-story, unpainted, square wood-frame building which was the only place in town where liquor and cold beer were available to take out. Closer to the dock was a rambling weatherbeaten structure, the cathouse where some Javanese girls were available. The women were reasonably priced and some very pretty; the beer was overpriced and not cold. The large crew of the COLUMBIA and the men off the ALCOA SHIPPER and a couple of smaller ships also in port overwhelmed the amenities of Paramaribo. I don't think they were used to hosting that many seamen at one time.

We stayed in Paramaribo only a couple of days. We off-loaded some supplies and a few soldiers disembarked. Exactly where those soldiers and supplies went in Dutch Guiana I never did know. Then, having done what we came to do, we returned to Trinidad and loaded more troops and canned beer for Georgetown, British Guiana. Though they called our destination Georgetown, we didn't actually stop at the city which lies at the mouth of the Demerara River. Instead we went up the river a few miles to dock at a pier built as part of the U.S. army base. There was nothing to be seen there but army barracks, some tufted reeds and mangrove along the riverbank and the surrounding jungle. The whole area appeared to be a malarial swamp, and it rained all the time we were there. We didn't even leave the ship during our short stay. Then it was back to Port of Spain to load for another trip to Paramaribo. When we arrived back in Port-of-Spain, several of the crew who had shipped in New Orleans, including my fellow SIU members, wanted to quit. I was among them. I didn't like the ship. Aside from Maté, and a few others, I couldn't communicate with the rest of the crew, and I didn't much like them either. The food situation had not improved and showed no promise that it ever would. The ship was scheduled to stay on this run until the end of the war or until she was sunk, whichever came first. The implicit assumption was that the crew was scheduled to do likewise.

The more I thought about it, the less I liked the idea of sailing down the sea lanes of the Caribbean, where ships were sunk every day, in a poorly-armed rust-bucket with a stack that went off like a Roman candle. From my observation, there wouldn't be enough life boats and rafts for half the crew and soldiers when we were fully loaded. And even if there were enough room for everyone, there had been no lifeboat drills and I could picture the pandemonium that would break out if the ship were attacked. Panic would seem inevitable, with little chance the crew would be able to perform their function of launching and manning the lifeboats. We had two overlapping authorities aboard, the ship's officers and the army command, and I could communicate with neither. There was nothing I could do to decrease the danger and I felt under no obligation to stay.

Three of us went to the captain and told him we wanted our money. We quit. The captain turned us over to the military commander of the ship, representing the U.S. Army. He made explicit what had been only implied: we had, he told us, enlisted for the duration and nobody could quit. We replied that we had not enlisted in anything; that we were free American merchant seamen and could quit any time we wanted to. He said we were under army jurisdiction and would do what the army told us to do. Furthermore, we were in Trinidad, a British territory, and the British would allow us ashore only in our capacity as employees of the U.S. Army.

We thought this over and discussed it. By the time we got back from our third expedition to Paramaribo we had decided to test it out. Maté would have liked to quit, but as a Yugoslav he was stuck. As an employee of the U.S. Army, he could go ashore wherever the ship docked and be treated like an American citizen. But if he walked off the ship, he was an alien, possibly an enemy alien, and the best he could expect would be internment.

But three of us again went to the captain and told him we were quitting and demanded our money. Receiving the same answer as before, we packed our seabags and threw them into the first bumboat that came alongside. We were met at the pier by U.S. military police and escorted to the U.S. Army military reservation on the outskirts of Port-of-Spain, and there put in the army guardhouse.

We were told we would be tried by court-martial. We asked how we could be court-martialed when we were not members of the military. We got no answer to that. I figured it was because they didn't know the answer. We settled down to await developments.

The guardhouse wasn't bad. Looking temporary and flimsily built like all the other barracks structures on the base, but smaller than the others, the guardhouse was adequate shelter for that climate, but couldn't have held anyone who wanted to escape. But once out, there was no place to go and the casual guard posted at the entrance was enough to keep us from straying about the base. The quarters were better than those on the USAT COLUMBIA and the food much better, and we were soon joined by four or five other men from the COLUMBIA. These new guys were mostly drunks and fuck-ups of one sort or another — men too disorderly even for the U.S. Army Transport Service.

Accompanied by prison guards, we all went out on little working parties, mostly picking up trash. There didn't seem to be anything urgent or even necessary about the work we did, so I don't know whether it was to keep us amused or to show us who was boss. But nobody minded. A couple of the guys on such a working party figured out a way to smuggle in some rum. We were treated well enough by the guards and spent most of the time reading or playing cards, and waiting to see what the army would do next.

Finally, after a couple of weeks, the army decided we were right after all. They couldn't court-martial us, and they couldn't march us aboard the ship and make us stand watches. They could keep us in custody and make us do these odd jobs of work because they had the upper hand and we were in a foreign country. But they must have decided they were legally on thin ice, and there was no point in keeping us indefinitely. We might someday make some kind of claim if they did. So they decided to ship us back to the States on the next transport going that way. We received our discharges and our pay from the COLUMBIA as of the day we quit her, and boarded an American passenger ship the army had converted to its purposes.

This ship, The USAT CLAREMONT, had been a passenger cruise ship before she became an army transport, and I never knew her original name. She had been fitted out, as the COLUMBIA had, with a large number of steel-stanchion bunks, both above and below decks. But on this trip there were no troops aboard, only wives and children of military personnel who had been stationed in the Caribbean area. They were now being sent back to the States while their men were shipped off to other military posts. There must have been a couple hundred of these passengers but we didn't see much of them. They occupied the cruise ship's cabins while we slept in the bunks and used the toilet facilities built for soldiers on the after deck.

When they marched us aboard we found that our contingent of seven or eight men from the COLUMBIA was to be joined by about 15 civilian construction workers who had either completed their contract time or outstayed their welcome on the island. They had been part of a much larger group hired to build the barracks and other military facilities in Trinidad. At least some of this bunch were chronic drunks who had been fired by the military contractors. These guys came aboard ship with duffel bags full of local rum which sold for about $1 a bottle. For the most part, however, they just stayed quietly stewed during the voyage and didn't create any disturbances.

The army officer in command of the CLAREMONT, a colonel, called us all together as soon as we were underway, Port-of-Spain still visible over the after rail. A tall, slim man of about 45, he had the air of one used to exercising authority, but otherwise appeared amiable. He introduced himself and told us that he was in charge of all passengers on the ship. He said he'd heard there had been some trouble ashore, but he didn't know why each of us was aboard and didn't want to know. He said as far as he was concerned we were all just passengers going to New Orleans, and that's how he'd treat us unless we forced him to do otherwise. He said he had the authority to make us eat on deck from mess kits, but had decided we would dine in the main dining room with the other passengers and eat the same meals they got. He ended up saying he trusted we'd merit his confidence and hoped we'd have a pleasant voyage.

I was quite impressed with this colonel, and I guess the others were too. At any rate, there was no trouble, and as I got to know them, I realized that some of these guys were misfits with a long record of boozing, fighting and run-ins with the law. I wondered how things would have been if the officer in charge had been a prick like the one on the COLUMBIA. We had very good meals in the passenger dining room, there were plenty of good books in the ship's library, and the weather was good, though increasingly cooler as we went further north. After five uneventful days at sea, the USAT CLAREMONT landed us in New Orleans the 10th of February, 1942, at the same pier we'd left in November.

New Orleans was miserably cold and wet, much different from when we left there in November. In Trinidad I had worn only shorts, T-shirts and sandals. For most of the past nine months I hadn't needed warm clothes, and consequently had few.

I checked in at the union hall and found the situation hadn't changed much since I left. I had some money left from my COLUMBIA payoff but it wouldn't last long in New Orleans, especially if I spent it for clothes. If I didn't, I wouldn't last long myself. I did have some winter clothing I'd left behind in Boston at Jane Huntington's apartment. She was now married to Manny

Wiener and they had a place on Tremont Street. I had enough cash for the Greyhound bus, so decided to go back.

It was good to be back in Boston among old friends and visiting the familiar scenes. I found things were much the same as when I left. Several of the comrades had been drafted and three or four had gone into the merchant marine. I was able to borrow some recent books, a new novel of James T. Farrell and one by Dos Passos I hadn't read. Books I had been able to get on shipboard had been mostly classics or well-thumbed mysteries and suspense stories.

I had a pleasant visit with Nina. She seemed to have gotten over any bitterness she felt about our breakup and we didn't discuss our past difficulties. I was still very fond of her, but we both knew there was no going back. She was being wooed by several of the eligible men in the party, among them Dave Udell, an old friend who had gone to sea since I last saw him. She showed me a letter Dave had sent from Argentina where his ship had gone to pick up a cargo of flax seed. He was on the Waterman Lines' SS AZALEA CITY.

Shipping was slow in Boston, though maybe a little better than in New Orleans. But I felt at home here and had some contacts, so I soon found a job as fireman on a lighter in the harbor. The big flat-bottomed barge with a huge steam-powered crane used for loading and unloading ships was anchored in East Boston. I had the midnight shift and it was an easy job, paying enough to live on while I waited for a ship. The quarters aboard the lighter were poor — a dark narrow fo'c'sle with barely room to walk between the bunks. But I only slept there and the mattress was comfortable. Night work gave me a chance to engage in some party activities as well as attend union meetings and spend part of each day at the hall talking with my fellow seamen. After three or four weeks on the lighter, I shipped as oiler on another Bull Line ship, the SS ELIZABETH bound for Puerto Rico.

I was glad to be back on a familiar run with crews I enjoyed being with. On almost any Bull Line ship I'd find someone I'd sailed with before. Aboard the ELIZABETH I found two old friends from the MILLINOCKET, Sanchez and Juan Rios. They were congenial shipmates and good union men, and I could talk politics with them, though neither ever joined the party. And I always enjoyed time spent with them in port, whether in Puerto Rico or the States. That summer I worked on different Bull Line ships, making San Juan my home port, and at times acting as assistant port agent.

The agent, Dan Butts, was a black man and reputed to be an old-time SUP man. If this was true, he was something of a rarity. Very few blacks worked in the deck department aboard SIU ships, and no other that I know of on the West Coast. The SUP was well-known for the racist attitudes of many of its members. I don't know and never asked how Dan fared aboard west coast ships, but I know he was held in high esteem by everyone in the SIU.

Dan was a giant of a man, about six-foot-six inches and weighing over 200 pounds. As port agent in San Juan he was responsible for supplying crews and negotiating grievances on ships around the entire island. His work load was heavy at all times, so he was pleased with any help he could get. And I was glad to help, though I never got any pay except necessary expenses.

Mostly I helped in the San Juan office, but occasionally I'd go to one of the other ports to meet with a ship's crew and try to adjust problems aboard the ship. In a couple of instances, at Dan's request, I joined a ship just for the duration of its stay in the island ports. I could discuss politics with Dan, and he generally agreed with my views, though I never raised the question of party membership.

For the next couple of years I worked on various ships, more Bull Line than any other. As soon as I was eligible I had upgraded my certificates so that I was qualified for any unlicensed rating in the engine department. If I had a choice I generally shipped as oiler.

I now had many friends in the union who expressed their confidence by nominating and electing me to represent them aboard ship, to chair port meetings, and to serve on the strike committee in an action involving rates of bonus pay for working in war zones. We rarely encountered members of the Communist Party in our work in the Seafarers union. They were all in the National Maritime Union (NMU), affiliated with the Congress of Industrial Organizations (CIO). In the maritime unions, the conflict between the American Federation of Labor (AFL) and the CIO had nothing to do with industrial vs craft unionism.

The CIO, founded by John L. Lewis in a bitter break with the most of the leaders of the AFL, was generally regarded as more progressive, organizing workers by industry rather than craft. But the SIU, though affiliated with the AFL, was organized along industrial lines just as the NMU was. Harry Lundeburg, leader of the SUP, had wanted CIO affiliation for the SUP, but John L. Lewis gave it to the NMU, causing Lundeburg to turn to the AFL for protection against his enemies, the Stalinist leaders of the NMU. The differences between the competing unions all centered around the domination of the NMU by Stalinists who followed every twist and turn dictated by Russia's foreign policy interests. The SUP/SIU, on the other hand, engaged in militant struggles to preserve and extend the gains won by seafarers.

That is how it was with the issue of the government attempts to institute the fink book. It was the same thing with fink halls. The Maritime Commission, in an obvious attempt to undermine the union hiring halls, set up government hiring halls in New York, Baltimore and Seattle in 1938/39. The NMU refused to fight them because they wouldn't oppose the Roosevelt administration, but the SUP/SIU threw picket lines around any ships involved as well as at the government hiring halls. These picket lines were respected by all seamen and were joined by men from all the unions, though the Stalinist leadership of the NMU never supported the picket lines. These fink halls were closed because of the militant action of the AFL seamen.

And so it went. Joe Curran, President of the NMU, who had refused to back the SIU picket lines, came out strongly against government hiring halls right after the Stalin/Hitler pact. Then after the Nazis invaded Russia he reversed himself again.

Once the war spirit moved him, Curran supported a whole series of employer-inspired government proposals that would have taken the seaman back to the days of company-operated fink halls and fink books. He declared for a tri-partite arbitration board to settle all disputes. This proposal of the Maritime War Emergency Board (MWEB), with Captain Edward Macauley of the Maritime Commission as its chairman, would make the government representatives the final arbiter at all times.

Next there was a proposal by Colonel Frank Knox, Secretary of the Navy, that the U.S. Navy absorb the merchant marine. Only the SIU-SUP opposed it. Then the War Shipping Board (WSB) tried to establish an authority that would handle all shipping in all American ports and start issuing new credentials. It was the fink book and the fink hall all over again, with the WSB acting to charter and operate the entire American Merchant Marine under open-shop conditions. Joe Curran, spokesman for the NMU, was all in favor.

The Seafarers International Union stated its position unequivocally and published it in its official organ, the *Seafarers' Log:*

> The time has arrived to fight! The time has arrived to serve notice upon our enemies that the SIU has no intention of folding up shop and returning the seamen to the days of the Fink Hall and slavery! In 1939, 13,000 men banded together in the SIU to protect themselves against the avaricious shipowners and the reactionary — politicians they will not disband now! Let the shipowners mark these words! Let the Maritime Commission mark them! Let Knox and Macauley and Admiral Land and Joe Curran mark them!

These were the sort of issues upon which we, in alliance with the non-political leaders of the SUP-SIU, conducted a continuous warfare with the Stalinists who were leading the supposedly progressive CIO union for seamen, the NMU. Though we never had any great numerical strength in SIU ranks, we had some very able people. Joe Hansen, who later became a national party leader and editor of *The Militant*, sailed as an able seaman. Sam Gordon was editor of the *Seafarers' Log*, the monthly SIU paper, and many of us, myself included, contributed articles. Whenever I was in the port of New York, I always met with Sam. He would bring me up to date on what was going on in the SIU headquarters and he asked a lot of questions about the mood of the men aboard ship, and suggested subjects for articles for the *Seafarers'Log.* Sam left the SIU when the party sent him to Paris as SWP representative on the board of the Fourth International. Tom Kerry, who had advised me when I was in California after being paid off the SS HARPOON, was also a seaman and editor of the west coast MFOW paper, *The Marine Fireman.* I didn't see much of Tom during those years as he was active in the west and I was working out of the Atlantic and Gulf ports. Tom, too, became a national leader of the party.

These men are but a few of the eloquent voices from our party who led the fight to keep seamen free from the government regimentation sought by Washington and promoted by the Stalinists in the NMU. In these controversies we were overwhelmingly supported by the militant rank and file seamen, with even members of the NMU joining our picket lines. However, this support on issues, unfortunately, never translated into any significant influx of seafarers to the party. We had started with too little, and too late.

The Communist Party on the other hand entered the era of labor upsurge with an experienced cadre of militant fighters from the days (1928-33) of their Marine Workers Industrial Union (MWIU) and its predecessors. Though this organization was ill-conceived and had no real future, the militants of the MWIU, through personal sacrifices and heroic work against brutal repression, won a following for their "red" union among seamen and longshoremen, especially in Philadelphia and New Orleans. They also had the considerable prestige of the Soviet Union which still exerted a great influence on advanced workers everywhere.

The men in their ranks were, to give them the credit that is their due, for the most part skilled untiring union organizers, earnest fighters for union rights, and sincere and unflagging in their opposition to racial discrimination. I have no doubt that they were largely responsible for the NMU having, in contrast to the SUP-SIU, a policy of racial integration in all departments. The tragedy is that these militants were used, manipulated and deceived by a few leaders who misled them into positions which had only one purpose — that of serving Stalin's foreign policy. Despite all this they have left a legacy, in unions such as the International Longshoremen's and Warehousemen's Union (ILWU), of militant unionism, brotherhood, and a certain class consciousness that endures to this day.

I regretted then as I do today the deception and abuse to which these honest working class militants were subjected. But I came into little personal contact with them during my days in the SIU. They were elsewhere and conditioned to be hostile toward me and what I represented. Many, perhaps most of them, really believed Trotsky and his followers were a dire threat to their spiritual homeland, the Russian soviet paradise-in-the-making. So they referred to us as "traitors," "counter-revolutionaries," "running dogs of American imperialism" and other choice epithets. We were opposed to the class-collaborationist scabby policies their leaders put forth for seamen, and we called Stalin's crimes by their proper name. This left little margin for rational exchange of ideas and it is of no relevance today that history has proven us right in our estimation of Stalinism.

The day-to-day pressures of standing watches, the dangers of sailing in war zones, and the constant interactions with shipmates didn't allow much time for introspection. But if I paused to consider where I was trending, what I was doing and why I was doing it, I was satisfied with my lot. I was earning my way in the world, doing work that I enjoyed, associating with men I liked and respected. And more than this, I was working toward the goals I had when I became a seaman, a socialist seaman. I had a vision of a world without poverty, exploitation, depression and war, and I felt I was doing my share to bring it about. So I went about my work with enthusiasm, deriving pleasure from each modest success.

I have been asked why I moved around so much. Why didn't I get a steady job and stick with it? I should explain that very few seamen ever considered any ship a steady job. If a seaman signed articles, which amounts to a contract for a trip, he was obligated to complete that trip unless illness or other unavoidable circumstances prevented it. If you signed on for a trip to Africa or Java, you were required to complete that trip. If, for any reason, the ship did not return you to the port of embarkation, the company was required to pay your transportation back to that port. When the ship had completed its scheduled run and returned to the original port, the whole crew was paid off and very few of the unlicensed men elected to stay aboard.

On the other hand, in the intercoastal or coastwise trade, the ship could pay a man off, for cause, in any port or he could quit in any port if he so chose. If a man was fired, this could become a matter for union grievance procedures if he thought it was unjust. If a man quit, that was his own business.

I moved around a lot, from ship to ship, spending intervals between ships sometimes in San Juan, and sometimes in Boston or New York where I attended party meetings and caught up on events. Sometimes my reasons for quitting a ship were personal — illness or having something else I wanted to do. In a couple of instances I had joined the ship to perform a service for the union and quit when it was completed.

21

Men Who Went Down with their Ships at Sea

It was on my next visit to Boston that I learned the AZALEA CITY had been lost, disappeared at sea. I was to find out later that she was torpedoed on February 20, 1942, by a German submarine off the coast of Maryland while en route to Philadelphia from Bahia Blanca, Argentina, via Trinidad. She left Port-of-Spain on February 12th, sailing alone and unarmed. Neither the ship nor any of the 38 men aboard were ever heard from again. My friend Dave Udell was among those aboard, and he was already lost by the time Nina showed me his letter.

These were dangerous times to be on the water. The War Department had taken some steps to provide protection to merchant ships. Principally, this consisted of placing guns on some ships and giving naval escort to convoys of ships on some runs. The guns were manned by trained U.S. Navy personnel who lived and ate with the civilian crew. Their duties were to maintain and handle their guns in time of need. I have no idea how effective they were, but they might have given a small added sense of security to ships' crews. The escort vessels no doubt provided some protection to convoys, and they did sink a lot of submarines. But the U-Boats still sank hundreds of ships traveling in convoy.

Most of the ships running along the Atlantic coast and in the Caribbean sailed unarmed and unaccompanied, out there all alone. My first ship with a gun crew was the SS GREYLOCK, and it was the only one to come under attack while I was aboard. But it was not sunk at that time. The GREYLOCK was underway and sailing without convoy, en route from New York with general cargo bound for Halifax. The ship was about ten miles off Sambro Lightship outside Halifax Harbor and expected to make port before midnight. It was about 10:30 p.m. and I was off watch, in my bunk reading. I felt the ship make a sudden port turn, heard the engines stop, then reverse. These sudden maneuvers in the open sea at night could mean only one thing. It was what I'd been dreading, maybe expecting, for months. But no matter how aware I'd been of the potential, it was a shock when it came. I leaped from my bunk, scrambled into pants and a shirt, grabbed a life jacket and hurried on deck wearing clogs on my feet.

Most of the crew were already there, looking out over the water. There had been a torpedo; it was seen from the bridge but it missed, perhaps due to the quick evasive action taken by Captain Whitmore. We were all awaiting a second torpedo. Our naval gun crew were at their posts, scanning the water for a periscope and a chance to strike back. The night was pitch dark with a moderate sea running and nothing to be seen on the water. The GREYLOCK was under way again, steaming at full speed ahead. It was probably only a few minutes, but it seemed a long time, before the captain concluded the ship was no longer under attack. We never knew why there was no further attack.

We arrived in Halifax on schedule and off-loaded our cargo, then set out again, unescorted for Boston. On the trip to Boston the Greylock developed some problems with steerage. It seemed she was no longer responding to the rudder as she should have done. Whether this problem had anything to do with the attack is unknown to me. But we did limp back to Boston harbor without further incident and went into dry dock in Charlestown.

The ship lay at that pier for three weeks while repairs were made. During that stay I was forced to quit by an illness, recurrence of a fever contracted in the tropics. This put me in the Boston marine hospital and I was still there when the GREYLOCK reloaded and headed for Murmansk with a convoy. Returning from Russia in ballast, she was sunk in the Berents Sea on February 3, 1943.

During those years, every time I went to the union hall I heard of other ships that had been sunk and friends who had been lost. Even so, I don't think any of us knew just how disastrous these submarine and raider attacks were to the American Merchant Marine. Nor did I know that the area where I was sailing was one of the most dangerous stretches of water in the world. Perhaps it was as well that we weren't fully aware at that time. After the war was over the losses were tabulated and the full picture became clear.

We are especially indebted to Captain Arthur Moore of Hallowell, Maine, for his book, *A Careless Word...a Needless Sinking*. Published by the American Merchant Marine Museum in 1983, it provides a definitive assessment and tabulation of merchant ships and crews lost in the war. He writes:

> Merchant ships were literally "sitting ducks" as they sailed the East Coast of America during the first six months of 1942. A former German submarine officer, now living and working in the United States, referred to an assignment to the East Coast of America as "shooting galley duty."
>
> When the war broke out most of the ships of the American Merchant Marine had been built prior to or around World War I. One torpedo was enough to blow most of them apart and they sank rapidly. The condition of the ships and their equipment was a major cause of the heavy loss of life during the war at sea. In the cold waters of the North Atlantic, lifesaving equipment was inadequate for those who had to abandon ship. A large percentage of

the men lost died from exposure in lifeboats or on rafts. The lifesaving equipment on most fishing boats today is far superior to the best available in those days.

As this is a reference book, it does not tell of the sufferings of men struggling to survive in crowded lifeboats or on flimsy rafts. Nor does it tell of the dust-dry throats, the parched lips and swollen tongues of those with no fresh water. Nor does it tell of the agony suffered from being cramped in crowded lifeboats for days on end, unable to stretch their legs, Neither does it describe the frozen limbs of those adrift in boats on the North Atlantic or the Berents Sea and the horror in engine rooms where men faced scalding steam from exploding boilers and ruptured steam lines. Nor does it tell of the cruel and abusive treatment merchant seamen received at the hands of the Japanese while prisoners of war.

What Captain Moore's book does record is the name of each of the more than 750 American merchant ships lost to enemy action during the war, and the names and ratings of every one of the 6,847 crew members lost as a result of these sinkings. The book also tells the date, location and circumstances of each sinking, and the name of the submarine or raider that attacked her.

It was from Moore's book that I learned the fate of the AZALEA CITY. There I also found what happened to the GREYLOCK and the fate of several other ships on which I served, and how many of them were sunk after I left them, all in 1942. They included:

the FRANCES SALMAN in January of 1942;

the MARGARET on April 14th, the day after I left her, the crew of 29 never seen or heard from again;

the PIPESTONE COUNTY on April 21st:

the ELIZABETH in May;

the MILLINOCKET and the EDITH in June;

the ARLYN in August.

Reading the crew rosters of these and other ships, I remember and mourn the many good friends who went down with them, always wondering at my own incredible good luck. The extent of the casualties among Merchant Marine sailors was little known to the general public and entirely unacknowledged officially, though the casualty rate among seamen was more that double that of the Navy and Coast Guard, higher than that of the Army and Air Force. The Merchant Marine casualty rate of 3.6 percent was exceeded only by the Marine Corps with a casualty rate of 3.7 percent. It was not until 1988 that the sacrifices of the men of the U.S. Merchant Marine in World War II were recognized and the U.S. government granted survivors full veteran status.

In those years, like many of my shipmates, I slept on deck in good weather. We thought a man had a better chance in a cot on the poop deck than in the foc's'le if the ship took a direct hit from a torpedo. Of course if you were on watch below, in the engine room or boiler room, all you could do was hope the torpedo didn't strike amidships and blow up the boiler. If the hit was in a cargo hold area, a man on watch might have a good chance of getting topside to a lifeboat or raft.

With so many seamen being killed, it's not surprising that we lost scores of party men to attacks on merchant ships, a big loss for a small organization. The party suffered many war casualties during this period, among those who had been drafted into the armed forces as well as in the merchant marine. There wasn't much that could be done about the soldiers and sailors. But in order to preserve what remained of our basic cadre in the merchant marine, it was proposed that our seamen transfer to ships on the Great Lakes. There hundreds of ore carriers and some passenger ships employed thousands of seamen, and there submarines could not go.

This proposal met with stubborn opposition among many of the comrades who felt that if they fled to the Great Lakes and abandoned their deep-water mates, they would lose any credibility they may have achieved in the ranks of the merchant sailors. It was persuasively argued that continuing to sail on deep-water ships, we risked losing much more than our credibility. As had Dave Udell and many others.

As this was debated, two or three of those men most adamantly opposed to the Great Lakes move were themselves killed when their ships were lost to enemy attack. These comrades had lost everything except their credibility, which could now help neither them nor the cause in which they had believed. I particularly remember Ed Parker whose ship, the SS ILLINOIS, was torpedoed on June 1, 1942 about 400 miles from Puerto Rico en route from India to Baltimore. Of the crew of 37 men, only six survived. Ed had been especially vocal in opposition to the Great Lakes move. He and all the others would be sorely missed.

The rest of us gradually moved toward the inland waters, at least for part of the time. In the fall of 1942 I went to Detroit and shipped for a couple of months on a passenger ship on Lake Erie. But when the lakes navigation season ended with the coming of ice, I went back to Boston and took the first fireman/oiler's job that came on the board at the union hall, a seagoing steam tug called the WINTHROP. She was bound for Port Arthur, Texas, which seemed like a good place to go with winter coming on.

The Steam Tug WINTHROP was non-union, belonging to a Port Arthur firm, Sabine Towing Company. Sabine had bought her in Boston, had her refitted and was bringing her back to the Gulf to become part of their towing fleet. The SIU agent in Boston thought if he could place some men on her, we might make some progress in organizing Sabine, long a non-union stronghold in the Gulf of Mexico. As it happened, however, I was the only SIU man to sign on the WINTHROP and the only other union men aboard were Charlie Rowley, an AB from the National Maritime Union (NMU), and the chief mate who was a member of the Masters, Mates and Pilots union. Charlie came aboard with the same idea of organizing Sabine Towing.

Both the captain and the chief engineer were outspokenly anti-union, to the point of making veiled threats against "union agitators." Charlie and I were undeterred and found several of the crew who were open to the idea of organization. Since Port Arthur was an NMU town and the NMU already had not only the oil tankers but the other tug companies in that area under contract, I agreed the NMU was the logical union to organize Sabine, and I would help do it.

Everything on the WINTHROP seemed miniature compared to the larger ships I'd been sailing on. The single boiler and tiny reciprocating engine looked like toys. The single fo'c'sle was below decks, forward of the engine room, and had bunks for the three fireman/oilers, three Ab's, one ordinary seaman and a messboy. Officers had cabins in the deck house. But the most important difference was the quality of the food.

The cook/steward had been a short order cook in a restaurant before he joined the WINTHROP and he had not bought enough stores for the trip. The second day out of Boston we ran out of fresh milk, and fresh vegetables were in short supply. Eggs were reserved for the officers' table and the crew was given oatmeal or cornmeal mush with canned milk for breakfast. The cook seemed to think he was giving us a treat when he sliced the cold leftover cornmeal mush and fried it for supper. Needless to say, he got plenty of flak from the crew, but the captain backed him 100 percent and we wondered if they were not in partnership to rob the crews' mess for their own benefit.

With the lousy food as a talking point, Charlie and I convinced several of the unlicensed crewmen of the need for organization. Since we made no attempt to conceal our agitation among the crew, the captain was well aware of it. Charlie and I were told that when we weren't around both he and the chief engineer would fulminate against "commie unionism" before a captive audience of crewmen in the messroom.

However, our activities did bear some fruit. The Tug WINTHROP made an unscheduled stop in the Port of Norfolk for the sole purpose of buying stewards' stores. Fresh milk, eggs, vegetables and meat were brought aboard and we continued our voyage toward Texas. The food situation was still not good, but improved noticeably, with eggs in the morning and a meat at each meal. Not good by union standards, it was acceptable to most of the crew.

Charlie and I pointed out that the reason we were eating better was that we had scared the skipper with the threat of unionization. Some accepted this and others thought that now we'd won we didn't need anything more. Any further discussion was cut short when the WINTHROP ran into a hurricane off Cape Hatteras.

It started with light rain, soon becoming a deluge accompanied by high winds and huge waves. As the storm increased in severity, the WINTHROP had increasing difficulty maintaining headway. To avoid turning our beam ends to the waves and being swamped in the trough, we finally dropped anchor to help the ship hold position. Then we spent the next three days dragging anchor and running at half speed ahead into the storm, just trying to stay in place and ride it out.

The tug was old but must have been well built. She plunged repeatedly into those mountainous waves, each time rising with a shudder, shrugging off the tons of green sea that slammed onto her decks, only to dive again. Every third or fourth wave would bring her stern high out of the water and send the screw racing out of control. This required the engineer on watch to close the throttle immediately to keep the free-spinning propellor from tearing the little ship apart. As the stern settled back into the water he would again supply steam to the engine to keep the ship steady and maintain headway. The strain was such that the engineer and I took turns at the throttle.

In normal seas the deck of the WINTHROP was only three or four feet above the water, so in this storm every wave was a torrent that swept the decks from stem to stern, wild water rushing between the deck house and the two-foot-high bulwark. To go from the fo'c'sle to the messroom, or from messroom to the engine room or forward to the bridge, one inevitably got soaked to the waist. I soon noticed that the biggest waves came in cycles, every third or fourth being strong enough to sweep you off your feet and wash you overboard. The trick was to let a big wave go by, then make a rush for it before the next big one came along. This way I avoided being battered by the worst waves but resigned myself to being soaked every time I had to venture onto the deck.

During the storm most of the crew were seasick, so those of us who weren't incapacitated had to stand double and triple watches. One of the fireman/oilers and one of the engineers never left their bunks through the whole storm. The cook/steward took to his bunk when the storm started and never got out of it. There was a blessing in this because, even with the fresh stores, he was a lousy cook and the crew fared better with him out of the way. For the most part Charlie Rowley took over the galley and he turned out to be a very good cook.

I was fortunate never to have been troubled with seasickness. It is a terrible affliction as evidenced by the people I've seen suffer from it. People gag and heave, long after there is anything left to vomit. Most of the WINTHROP's crewmen stayed in their bunks, moaning and heaving, too weak and miserable to get up or do anything for themselves. A couple of men, the messboy and an oiler, perhaps less severely afflicted, toughed it out and managed to stand their watches, however little they felt like it.

One poor fellow, the ordinary seaman, sat for the whole three days on the floor of a privy that opened onto the deck. He sat there in the open hatchway looking green and miserable, his head between his knees, raising it occasionally to gag and heave, while looking out at the wild seas rushing past him just outside the door of his toilet refuge. I stopped a couple of times and asked if there was anything I could do to help him. There wasn't.

I have been at sea in all kinds of weather. I have seen the sea blue and placid as a mill pond and I've seen green waves that towered 50 feet above the ship and crashed thunderously on the deck as the ship rose sluggishly from the trough. I've seen deck cargo swept away and seamen cling precariously to lifelines and struggle to maintain their footing. But somehow, however threatening the sea might become, I have never felt frightened.

Perhaps an element of fatalism made me concentrate on the immediate and trust to the ship to see me through. So this hurricane off Cape Hatteras did not scare me, but it was the worst storm I ever experienced at sea.

Finally this storm was over, we raised anchor and resumed our course toward the Gulf of Mexico. Blessed with good weather for the rest of the trip, we arrived in Port Arthur only a few days behind schedule. In Port Arthur the cook and half the crew quit, including many of those we had convinced to join the union. Charlie and I stuck it out for a while, despite the hostility of the captain and the chief.

Sailing out of Port Arthur, the WINTHROP plied the waters of the Gulf of Mexico pulling loaded barges from one port to another. We made a couple of trips to Port St. Joe, Florida, and one to New Orleans. Charlie and I continued to talk unionism, but found that most of the replacement crew members were Sabine Company stiffs who had long been inoculated against organization.

Spring was coming and we agreed there was little hope of organizing Sabine Towing, so we both quit the tug WINTHROP in Port Arthur. Charlie shipped on a tanker and I returned by train to New York. There I ran into two old friends from Boston, John Keeley and Eddie Costello, who were working as able seamen on the Motor Ship BADGER STATE. They told me their ship needed an oiler and was scheduled to go up the New York State Barge Canal to Oswego on Lake Ontario. This sounded like a fun trip, especially with my friends aboard, so I joined the MS BADGER STATE.

22

Fresh Water Interlude

The MS BADGER STATE left New York City, headed up the Hudson, then worked her way through the farmlands of upstate New York. The ship was about as big as the canal could accommodate and we went gingerly, careful not to run aground. It was a rainy spring in 1943, and we had to stop at every highway bridge to measure clearance. In a few instances we had to wait for the water to go down so we could pass under. As we got further upstate, the channel narrowed and for safety reasons we rarely ran at night.

Each evening the ship would tie up in whatever village or hamlet we had reached by sundown. A couple of these towns had no piers or docking facilities and we tethered the ship to a convenient tree like a cow put out to graze. Here the crew would go ashore to sample whatever the small town had to offer in the way of entertainment. Generally this would be a bar or two, sometimes with a few local girls in attendance. Or there might be a movie or dance. The month we spent on the canal was unlike any other voyage any of us had ever undertaken. It was like a leisurely tour of the countryside, watching the scenery go by and stopping at all those small towns. As we had expected, it was quite enjoyable.

The BADGER STATE paid us all off in Oswego and I took a bus to Detroit, along with John and Eddie.

Wartime Detroit, manufacturing center of the machinery of destruction, seemed to throb 24 hours of every day with a frenetic energy. Its streets and alleys teemed with off-shift workers, tens of thousands of whom were recent immigrants from the hills and farms of the South, lured here by the promise of good jobs at high wages. They crowded the city's streetcars and buses, thronged into its honky-tonk bars and taverns, and swelled the ranks of the city's union locals. Rednecks, hillbillies and black ex-sharecroppers from the Mississippi delta worked side by side in the plants, attended union meetings together, many of them learning to put aside age-old prejudices and call one another "brother" in the cause of solidarity in the face of corporate greed and arrogance.

As one might expect, the majority of the Detroit party branch were employed in the automobile factories and active in the United Automobile Workers (UAW-CIO). Though outside the area of our immediate concern, the affairs of the UAW were of great interest to me and the other seamen. At that time there was a power struggle going on between the UAW International President R.J. Thomas and the supporters of Walter Reuther, one of the vice presidents.

Thomas was inclined to support the no-strike pledge extracted from the labor movement at the outbreak of war, and he was strongly supported by the Stalinists. Reuther showed more enthusiasm for fighting to maintain the gains the union had won during the big strikes of the '30s. Though we generally considered Walter Reuther a consummate opportunist, most of our members favored supporting him in his fight against the conciliationism of Thomas. This issue was not finally resolved, and it remained a topic of discussion in the party until Reuther defeated Thomas decisively and permanently. These concerns were the source of much of the discussion and planning at meetings of the branch, both formal and informal.

Some of our people were popular leaders in the UAW. To name only two, Ernest Mazey and John Anderson both held leading local union positions, and each also had a following in the wider councils of the union. Bert Cochran was not only a national leader of the party, but he had become an auto worker and played a key role in all deliberations on party policy in the UAW.

Cochran's analyses were always thorough, cogently-reasoned, encompassing not only the local detail but the broadest perspective. His arguments were persuasively presented and, to me, he was the outstanding leader of our UAW fraction. I would work with Bert in later years on matters relating to the auto union.

The SWP branch organizer at that time was Arthur Burch, a dry scholarly fellow in his middle forties who was said to have a law degree, though I don't know whether he ever practiced law. Arthur was a good organizer, business-like, meticulous and tireless. His political analyses tended to be dry and precise, as were his social relationships. I got on well with Arthur though I never felt very close to him. His wife was the Kay who had welcomed me to the Washington Square house when I first went to New York City to ship out. She was a warm person and I remember her with affection.

The Seafarers' hall was near the waterfront, close to the passenger ship docks at the foot of Woodward Avenue. After a couple of weeks hanging around the union hall, I shipped as a fireman on the SS CITY OF DETROIT III. Ed Costello also joined the DETROIT as an able seaman.

The DETROIT was a big white ship carrying passengers and some deck freight between Detroit and Cleveland on the overnight run. She was propelled by huge side paddle wheels driven by a horizontal triple-expansion reciprocating engine. The engine was a spectacular sight with observation windows all the way around so the passengers could watch the three 18-foot-long highly polished steel rods, each weighing more than three tons, rocking back and forth as they pushed the huge 8-foot eccentric cranks that turned the paddle-wheel drive shaft. She didn't turn up very fast, maybe 15-18 rpm, but it was very impressive. The engineer, in a neat blue uniform, looking as splendid as a hotel doorman, stood importantly on a platform above the crank shafts close by the engine room telegraph and the valves he could manipulate to control the engine.

The oiler didn't wear a uniform but was expected to dress with the awareness that he, too, was on display. He moved about the engine on steel-grating catwalks, feeling the bearings with his fingertips as they plunged past to gauge how warm they were running. Then, with a squirt can, he would deftly shoot jets of oil into small oil receptacles attached to each bearing. Timing was the essence of the operation, and if he was good he never missed the oil cup as he stood inches from the plunging heads and threshing cranks, calmly shooting them with lubricant. Modern engines may do it better mechanically, but it isn't as good a show. I had worked as oiler on an identical ship the year before and would move up to the oiler's position on the DETROIT later, but for now I worked where the steam power came from to drive that engine. And we were out of sight in the boiler room where no passengers ever penetrated.

This boiler room had six boilers with a total of 18 fire doors and each fireman was required to serve three doors. So there were six of us firemen on a watch, plus a watertender who was in charge. This was my first experience with coal-fired boilers. We had coal passers to bring the coal in wheelbarrows from the bunkers between the boiler rooms and the ship's sides. I was on the 4-8, the least desirable watch. We had seven hours of steaming every day while the other two watches had only four each.

When we came on watch at four in the afternoon we had to start getting our fires ready for the five o'clock departure. That meant having a good clean, but thin, fire going over the entire 4x8-foot grate surface behind each fire door. We had to be ready at the call for steam to sprinkle shovelfuls of coal evenly over the fire surface for the roaring blaze that would maintain pressure to run the engine. From that time until the end of the watch we threw coal into the furnace, occasionally using the 12-foot-long steel slice bar to break up the fire, and sometimes a hook to pull out big red-hot clinkers. And when we came back on watch at four in the morning, it was to shovel coal to maintain roaring fires until we docked at 8 a.m.

We worked stripped to the waist with sweat welling from every pore. Within an hour into the watch we were black from the coal dust that stuck to the sweat. With all the doors fed and the fires burning clean, you could sit down under a ventilator for a breath of fresh air and drink some cold water or coffee. But in a minute or two, the watertender would rattle a shovel on the steel deck plates — his signal for more steam. On this signal, we'd all grab our shovels, throw open our fire doors and start sprinkling on the coal. This was one of the hardest jobs I'd ever had, but I stuck at it for some months until an oiler's job opened up and I went into the clean engine room.

Something that made a big difference in working on this ship was the amount of contact I had with other party members. There were many seaman members now working out of port of Detroit. Among them were oiler Larry Dolinski and watertender Rico Panicali, both on my watch on the SS CITY OF DETROIT III. Besides Larry and Rico, a couple of the firemen and three or four of our deck crew were also party members, including my old friend from Los Angeles, Abe Harkavy, now an able seaman. When we went ashore in either Cleveland or Detroit, we went to party headquarters and attended such meetings as we could. At least now I could keep up with world events, the war in Europe and in the Pacific.

Among my most vivid memories of that summer was an incident involving Abe Harkavy whom I first met in the summer of 1938 after being paid off my first ship, the SS HARPOON. He had shown me around Los Angeles and taken me to his parents' home. Abe was about my age, a quiet, studious young man, always well-dressed, serious but of gentle humor and very good company. He was of medium stature, clean-cut, with regular features and black wavy hair. Abe was still in school at that time and lived with his parents in a modest but respectable house in Boyle Heights, a quiet residential L.A. neighborhood.

Mr. Harkavy had been an agronomist but now ran some kind of small business. Both he and his wife were socialists by conviction but I don't think they belonged to any organization. Mrs. Harkavy made me welcome at their house and seemed happy to feed Abe's friends when they came around. Abe's older sister,

Ann, was a member of the SWP but was not living at home. As I knew Abe then, I would say that he had all the qualities that would have made a very good school teacher or social worker. And that is probably what his parents aspired to for him.

The next time I saw Abe was three years later in New York at the party headquarters on University Place when my ship was in port for a couple of days. Abe had been hanging around on the beach for several weeks, but I noticed he wore neat slacks, polished shoes and a suit jacket over his polo shirt. We were pleased to see one another and I found Abe the same gentle, considerate fellow I had remembered. We went out for a beer and talked. Abe had only one glass. He was genuinely abstemious for himself but not censorious about other peoples' habits. He told me he had left school — I think it was a community college in Los Angeles — and shipped out.

A resolution passed at the 1940 party convention had stated, "The entire party membership must be directed toward rooting itself in the factories, mills, etc., and towards integrating itself into the unions and workers' mass organizations" Thus all our members were under sometimes not too subtle pressure to join the working class, "proletarianization" as it was called. This policy found several New York intellectuals operating lathes in auto factories or doing similar work. Most were none the worse for it, but it was not what most people wanted for themselves or their children. But Abe, wanting to do his full share, had gone to sea and was now an able seaman. Being bright and conscientious, he had become an excellent seaman. When I sailed with him later I would learn he was highly regarded among his shipmates for his skills.

But in New York I also noticed something different about Abe. It was nothing major and I didn't give much thought to it at that time. He seemed less open, quieter, more introspective, perhaps a little wistful. I did learn, though Abe didn't say much about it to me, that he was in love with a young woman who worked in the national office of the party. Sylvia was a stenotypist, fair, shapely and a little older than Abe.

I was in port only briefly so I didn't have a chance to observe the progress of Abe's love affair. I was told later by others on the scene that Sylvia gave Abe some encouragement, just enough to keep him panting, but no satisfaction. Still, Abe kept mooning after Sylvia. Finally she put a stop to it, some said brutally. But what is brutal? What is simply definite for one could be brutal for another. In any case, Abe took it badly, so I was told, becoming morose, withdrawn and contemplative.

And that's about how Abe was when I next saw him at the union hall in Detroit where we were both looking for a ship. As it happened, we went to the same one, the SS CITY OF DETROIT. I saw little of him on board ship. On watch I was buried in the firehold and Abe was on deck. Off watch, I either slept or went ashore. But I did see him from time to time, and we'd go ashore together and have a beer or snack and talk.

Eddie Costello, who was also an AB on the DETROIT, told me Abe was having a hard time with the mate. Chief Mate McTavish was a foul-mouthed son-of-a-bitch who stuck in everyone's craw, everyone who had anything to do with him. He didn't bother me but I'd occasionally hear him raging at some of his crew. A guy like Eddie would either ignore him, or give him back as good as he received. So McTavish would lay off Eddie, but seemed to get great satisfaction out of riding Abe Harkavy. Abe was too meek and gentlemanly to speak up for himself and he cringed at the foul language used by McTavish, and that only encouraged the mate to further obscenity.

This went on through the spring and early summer. Then one afternoon in mid-August Abe went to the party headquarters on Woodward Avenue in Detroit. The only person he found there was Larry Dolinski, the oiler on my watch. I was off watch at the time but had stayed aboard ship to get some rest. So I heard all of this from Larry who was quite shaken by the experience.

Larry told me he was by himself reading the paper when Abe came in. The weather was very warm, but Larry noted that Abe wore a collar and tie under his tailored jacket. Abe greeted Larry and sat down. Then got up immediately and started pacing.

"Where's Arthur?" Abe asked. Arthur Burch was the organizer, hence the responsible party official in Detroit.

"I think he went to the post office," Larry told him.

"I have to talk to him. I have something very important to tell him." Abe was still pacing nervously.

"He should be back soon," said Larry. "You might as well sit down and wait for him."

"It's very important news. It's the most important thing in the world."

Interest piqued, Larry asked, "What is it? Can you tell me?"

"I guess I could tell you," said Abe. "But I really have to talk to Arthur."

"What is it, Abe? Sit down and tell me."

Abe sat nervously on the edge of a chair, fidgeted, then told Larry, "I am the Messiah."

Startled, Larry studied Abe to see whether he was joking. But obviously he was serious...nervous, but completely in earnest.

"Yes," Larry conceded, "you'd better tell Arthur about it." As Larry told me later, he didn't know what else to say. He couldn't quite bring himself to pretend he believed in Abe's revelation and carry on a discussion with this as its premise. On the other hand, it didn't appear to be a subject on which Abe was open to debate or persuasion.

Then Arthur Burch returned to the hall and greeted them both.

"Abe has something to tell you, Art," Larry told him.

Arthur went into the office which was small and opened off one corner of the hall. "Come in here," he said. "It's more comfortable." He settled himself behind his desk and waited while Abe and Larry joined him, sitting opposite.

"What is it, Abe?" asked Arthur.

"I already told Larry and I thought you should know as soon as possible."

"Yes?"

"I am the Messiah."

Arthur studied Abe for a long silence, carefully weighing this information in his legal mind. "And how long have you known about this, Abe?"

"Well, I've had some inkling of it for several weeks, but yesterday I knew for certain."

"You realize you're not the first to hold such a belief. Others have been mistaken, you know."

"I know that. I've studied it and weighed it. I'm 100 percent sure."

"And you found it out yesterday?"

"Yes, on the morning watch. Mr. McTavish was cursing at me and suddenly I knew. I was certain."

"McTavish?"

"The mate," Larry volunteered. "He's a bastard!"

Larry told me that Arthur went on talking with Abe for a while, maybe five or ten minutes, questioning him closely about his religious beliefs, or lack thereof. Abe had considered himself an atheist, though he still had vivid memories of some Temple rites to which he had been exposed. Larry seemed unsure whether this exposure was from someone in his family or other religious Jews. Maybe Abe didn't say, but he had been haunted by these memories, and the belief that the Redeemer was on His way. Abe didn't seem to think Jesus of Nazareth was the real thing, maybe a major prophet. But he was convinced he himself was the Promised Messiah.

Arthur asked him what he intended to do about it, now that he had received this revelation. Abe wasn't too specific but he thought he had an obligation to let the world know. These tidings were too important to keep secret. He was a little unclear about how the party fitted into this picture, but he found no conflict between his new beliefs and his old. Finally Arthur seemed satisfied that Abe was not to be reached by reason, that his conviction was unshakable.

"Well, you were right to let me know as soon as you could, Abe," Arthur told him. "There are some other people who must be informed. Stay here with Larry while I make a phone call."

Larry said he couldn't think of anything to talk about while they waited. But Arthur made his phone call and soon returned to the office.

"I've talked with these people and they want you to come right out and see them."

"Who are they?" asked Abe.

"Some theologians," lied Arthur. "They're very interested in what you have to say and want us to come right away. You too, Larry."

Arthur closed the office and led the way with Abe obediently following. Bewildered, Larry went along behind. Arthur hailed a cab on Woodward Avenue, gave the driver instructions and they all got aboard. The cab headed west through Dearborn, past Willow Run, then through a couple miles of farm country. They turned through a gate and went up a long drive past grassy lawns bordered by shrubbery, dotted with stately shade trees. Here and there people wandered about the grounds. Ahead, set well back from the highway, was a long three-story red brick building. Larry noticed that the windows on all three floors were discreetly barred and though he had never been there before, he now realized where they were going.

Driving past the front of the building they arrived at an imposing concrete facade with five huge Doric pillars and three steps leading up to an entrance with a heavy glass door looking out on the expanse of greenery. They left the cab and Arthur led the way into the building where he spoke a few words to a receptionist. Soon an impressive looking gentleman in a three-piece suit came out and shook hands with all three, then invited them into his office.

In the office the man questioned Abe, briefly covering about the same ground Arthur had in the party office. Having completed his interrogation, he picked up his phone, pressed a button and spoke a few indistinguishable words. Soon a nurse in white uniform appeared in the doorway, followed by two husky orderlies in green uniforms.

"We have a room ready for you now, Mr. Harkavy. If you'll just come with us," the nurse told him.

Then, for the first time, Abe seemed to realize where he was and what was happening to him. He looked at the doctor, at Arthur, then Larry. Larry's face told him all he needed to know.

Suddenly, Abe bolted past the nurse, between the orderlies, through the lobby and out the front door. Recovering from their surprise, the orderlies went after him. The rest of them followed and watched as the orderlies chased Abe around the grounds. Abe was fast, dodging behind trees, running through shrubbery, leaping benches, eluding his pursuers and trying to make it to the front gate which stood open.

But the orderlies were also young, fast and persistent. They outnumbered Abe and were on their home turf. Finally, they cornered him, threw him to the ground and subdued him, then led him back to where the others were waiting. Abe tried to struggle, but they had his arms twisted behind his back and controlled him easily. By the time they reached the front door again, Abe was coming peaceably, his jacket ripped, shirt open and tie under one ear, a look of resignation on his face.

Coming up to those waiting by the steps, Abe looked at the nurse, looked at Larry and shook his head in sorrow. Then he stopped and looked at Arthur, his chin trembled, and he wet his lips with his tongue. Composing his features, he drew himself up and assumed an air of great dignity.

"Arthur Burch," he said, "You're a contemptible cad!"

Gentle Abe. Even to one he thought had betrayed him, these were the harshest words in his vocabulary. With that, he turned his face from them and allowed himself to be led inside the Michigan State Mental Hospital at Ypsilanti.

That evening when Larry told me about this extraordinary event, he said he hadn't known where Arthur was taking Abe or that he was going to commit him to an insane asylum, as they were then called. He also said if he had been aware he didn't know what else he might have done. We agreed that Arthur was doing what he thought best for Abe's protection, but I never could bring myself to talk about it with Arthur. Tears rolled down Larry's cheeks as he told me about Abe, but there was nothing else we could do, only grieve for him.

We learned only later that the Sylvia for whom Abe had carried the torch in New York was an agent of the Soviet Secret Police. She had been planted as a GPU spy in the SWP national office by Louis Budenz, a Communist Party official who defected in 1945. Sylvia Caldwell, also known as Sylvia Franklin, testified as an unindicted co-conspirator in the espionage trial of her two GPU handlers and associates, Jack Soble and Robert Soblen. To my knowledge, Abe was never aware of Sylvia's perfidy.

Abe Harkavy was then 26 years old and we never saw him again. Over the years I tried to find out what happened to him after that commitment but always ran into dead ends. Only recently I learned from his sister, Ann, that Abe died in the Ypsilanti hospital after being held there about two years. The report was that he never returned to reason, went into severe depression, declined food and just withered away.

I've pondered this tragic event often in the years since and I believe Abe was another victim of our violent times. He should never have gone to sea to start with and was as much a casualty of the war as those who went down with their ships or died in the front lines on the battlefront. As seamen, we were all under considerable pressure imposed by the war, the constant threat of submarine attack when at sea, and the loss of life among our close friends. Some of the pressure was self-imposed, resulting from our iconoclastic convictions and determination to actively support an unpopular cause. I think all of us showed some kind of reaction to these pressures, whether physical, mental or both. I developed symptoms of peptic ulcers, and I don't know today whether I actually had the ulcers the doctors treated me for or if my symptoms were largely brought on by stress. I knew other seamen, not necessarily party members, who acquired unaccustomed personality traits—unprovoked belligerence, sullen gloomy disposition, depression, profligacy, and other quirks which seemed to me stress-related.

Abe was not the only one I knew who cracked up under the pressure. But I was closer to him...an old friend and shipmate. From what I knew of others who buckled under the strain, they too came from sheltered childhoods as Abe had. I have always felt that Abe Harkavy would have done all right, perhaps brilliantly, if he'd never heard of proletarianization, never been exposed to the war and the Sylvias and McTavishes of this world. I guess most of us had had earlier conditioning which made us resistant if not impervious to the pressures of the times.

When the Great Lakes ships stopped running for the winter, they laid off their crews and had only a ship-keeper or two aboard until spring when they were ready to crew up for the next season. The ship-keeper jobs meant winter-long employment and light duty, so they were coveted by many. Deep-water men were not even considered for these positions, so when the SS Detroit made her last run on December 1, we all got laid off.

At the union hall I learned that Marty Polaner, SIU port agent, had wangled an agreement with the Riggers local of the Ironworkers Union to use unemployed seamen when extra men were needed. This made sense because of the related skills involved in the two trades. I went to the riggers hall to inquire and they sent me out on a job immediately. On the strength of this, I found a room just off Woodward Avenue, conveniently close to public transportation.

That first job involved dismantling and removing an unused stack that towered above the roof of one of the automobile plants. The men I worked with were old hands at this sort of thing, but I caught on quickly and was able to hold up my end. These guys recommended me to the Riggers' business manager who told me there was plenty of work that should keep me busy all winter. I found the work was congenial and rigger's pay was good, better than I had ever made before. I worked for a series of small rigging contractors who hired a crew from the union hall for whatever job they had in hand.

With this prospect, I decided to stay in Detroit rather than go back to the coast and look for a ship as I had the year before. Working as a rigger would give me the opportunity of living ashore, keeping regular hours and attending meetings on a regular basis. I welcomed this change. Having decided to stay in town, I rented a small efficiency apartment with Larry Dolinski. Larry had a stationary fireman's license and planned to find a fireman's job for the winter.

Another reason for staying in Detroit was that I had a girl friend of sorts and wanted to stick around on that account. Pat Walsh was a tall, slim colleen with black hair, pale complexion, a beautiful body and amiable disposition. I had known her slightly in Boston, attended a couple of parties where she was present but never spent much time with her. Her closest friend was Eddie Costello's sister, Louise, and they had come to Detroit together to look for jobs.

Pat and I had been to bed together and seemed to be compatible. For a while, I thought this might lead to a continuing relationship but things didn't work out that way. Though we were affectionate with one another, passionate when we were alone together, I think we were miles apart in what we wanted or expected from the relationship. She didn't say so precisely but I think she was looking for a husband and steady breadwinner. I wasn't explicit either, but knew I wasn't ready for that role. After a few weeks we agreed to break it off, though we remained good friends.

It was in December of 1943 that we learned the appeals of the SWP and Minneapolis union leaders had been denied and they must surrender to federal marshals and go to prison. Indicted under the Smith Act they had been convicted in federal court after a lengthy trial. The jury found them not guilty of the first charge of conspiracy, but found them guilty of advocating the overthrow of the government by force and violence. Albert Goldman, both a defendant and defense attorney, had used the forum of the trial to expound the fundamental principles of socialist theory and to prove that our program was far from being a conspiracy. His defense strategy was to make the strongest possible educational presentation to the jury, showing that our entire effort was to persuade a majority of Americans of the correctness of our ideas.

The government's case was primarily based on the dangers of labor unrest and the specter of the Russian Revolution. The defense enjoyed wide public support, with the Communist Party conspicuously on the side of the prosecution. Little did the Stalinists dream then that they would be the next victims of the Smith Act, which would later be declared unconstitutional.

Sentenced on December 8, 1941, the day the U.S. declared war against Japan, the Trotskyist leaders were given sentences of 16 months in federal prison. There would follow two years of appeals organized by the Civil Rights Defense Committee which rallied support from a wide spectrum of labor and liberal circles. This was the first peacetime prosecution for sedition in American history and the case became the most important civil liberties cause during World War II. Among the labor leaders who supported the Defense Committee were the top officers of the ILGWU, the Auto Workers, Textile Workers, Marine and Shipbuilding Workers and the state CIO Councils of New Jersey and Michigan. Support came in from 150 local unions representing more than five million workers and the case was featured in many labor and liberal publications. Three times the Supreme Court would refuse to hear their case and now they would enter prison in January 1944. The men went to Sandstone federal prison (Minnesota) and the single woman, Grace Carlson, was sent to West Virginia. They were to serve 13 months before being released from prison in February, 1945.

By the time the socialist leaders surrendered to the U.S. Marshall in January, 1944, the party had published two new pamphlets on the trial. One, *Socialism on Trial,* was a transcript from the trial proceedings, the testimony of James P. Cannon, SWP National Secretary, questioned by Al Goldman about the party's political beliefs and activities. The second, entitled *In Defense of Socialism*, contained Goldman's masterful summary for the defense. These two publications would prove to be the most popular ever issued by the party, convincing hundreds of the correctness of our socialist ideas.

Work out of the riggers' hall held up through December and January. T0he jobs were mostly moving heavy machinery, but occasionally there was a job rigging a hoist for taking down a stack or chimney. It was good work, paid well, well enough so I could afford to buy some new clothes. I hadn't owned a good suit since I wore out my high school graduation suit from 1936.

Larry Dolinski went with me to a store he recommended. He was brought up in the city and had some style sense, which I lacked. I might have bought the first thing the salesman showed me, but not with Larry along. I kept trying on suits and Larry kept them bringing out more styles and fabrics. Finally, we found two that we both agreed were right. One was a blue pinstripe and the other a rich tan gabardine. They were expensive, but when I looked in the mirror and saw how good they looked on me I didn't mind the expense. We also picked out a good overcoat, some new shoes and several shirts and ties. This was more good clothes than I had ever owned in my life. Mark Walker, fashion plate! The people back in New Portland should see me now.

After moving around so much, I found I enjoyed living in one place. And I enjoyed participating in the party affairs and discussions on a regular basis, something I had not been able to do for some time. And, predictably, when I stopped shipping the draft board sent me a notice to appear for induction into the army.

I appeared along with several hundred others for the physical examination and for a while I thought they might take me. First everyone had to strip, then stand naked in lines moving slowly from one doctor to another. They were processing the draftees as fast as they could. A psychiatrist asked me a couple of questions and passed me along. The next doc was hardly looking up at the people he questioned. I arrived at his desk, handed him my papers and waited.

"Did you ever have any accidents, injuries or operations?" he asked.

I didn't answer right away, thinking about where to start. Not hearing anything from me, he wrote "no" on the form and I guess he expected me to move on. I just stood there and he looked up and saw the 10-inch slash down my abdomen from the operation. Though the operation had been three years prior, the scar was still red and obvious.

"What's that?" he asked.

"That's where I had half my liver removed in 1939. It was from an automobile accident where I had my back broken. Compression fracture, first and second lumbar."

He made some notation on the sheet and passed me along to the next line. I had the impression he was offended somehow. The next doc asked if I was being treated for anything at the present time. I told him the Detroit Marine Hospital was treating me for a peptic ulcer, but the doctors there didn't seem to think it was serious.

At the end of the next line was an eye doctor. But he wasn't conducting any kind of eye examination. When I arrived at his desk, he asked, "How are your eyes?" Without waiting for an answer, he made some notation, as near as I could make out he granted me 20/20 vision in both eyes.

"They don't give me much trouble," I told him. "But the left one is glass and I have to take it out every night and put it in a box so it doesn't discolor."

He made some additional notation and I moved on to the next desk. There I was told to get out of line and put on my clothes. Then I was to wait in a small room where two or three other men were sitting. After I had waited there about an hour, an attendant came and gave me a paper saying I was rejected as a psychoneurotic hypochondriac and classed 4F in the draft. Meaning that I didn't have to worry about being drafted.

I have often wondered what would have happened if I had just gone through saying nothing. Would I have ended up in the army? Did they have many one-eyed soldiers?

23

Mission in Toledo

As the war went on, many employers, while reaping huge profits on war contracts and preaching patriotism, steadily chiseled away at the working conditions won by the unions. They used the cover of the no-strike pledge exacted at the beginning of the war. Workers who resisted were called unpatriotic, though the workers generally were very patriotic and fully supported the war against the Nazis and Japanese warlords. But many were also determined to defend themselves and their unions. The Stalinists, now super-patriots, tried to enforce the no-strike pledge. The Trotskyists, preaching class struggle and the need for a socialist solution to put an end to both war and capitalism, gained new adherents and new influence in the more militant unions.

Then, early in the spring, too soon for the ships to be brought out of winter hibernation for a new season, the party leaders in the area asked me to go to Toledo, Ohio. There, two or three old-timers and a few new converts were meeting on an informal basis. They wanted to establish an active party branch, but none of them had the know-how or the time to get it started. I was to go to Toledo, get some kind of job to maintain myself and turn this informal group into a functioning organization which could recruit new members and take advantage of the rising militancy among the workers resisting employer encroachments.

I was flattered to have been chosen for this important assignment and concerned about whether I was qualified for it. At the same time I would regret leaving my life as a seaman, and in effect canceling all the time and effort I had put into Seafarers Union affairs. I was assured that this new work was more important, that my work as a seaman had been good training for it, and that I would be more valuable as a leader of the party than as a union activist. With some reluctance I agreed. The more I thought about it, the better I liked the idea of immersing myself again in party work, of a future as a political leader, perhaps a full-time professional revolutionist — to me the most important career I could aspire to.

I first made an exploratory visit to Toledo along with Arthur Burch. Because of the proximity of Toledo, 60 miles southwest of Detroit, Arthur had been acting as an advisor to the group, in addition to his work as Detroit organizer. But the best Arthur could do was offer encouragement from time to time. They needed someone on the scene with enough experience and drive to pull the group together and focus its energies on some achievable goals.

So one Sunday Arthur and I went down on the bus and were met at the station by one of the Toledo people with a car. We had an afternoon meeting at the home of Basil McDonald who had been a mainstay of the group and done much to spark the revival. Also present were Tim McCormick, a railroad union leader and veteran socialist, as well as three or four auto workers, activists in United Automobile Workers (UAW) Local 12.

After some general discussion about the situation in Toledo and the prospects for building a branch, we relaxed with refreshments, chatting and laughing together. I liked all of these people and was impressed by the potential for a viable party branch in Toledo. I sensed that they liked me too, and they assured me they wanted me to work with them, so I accepted the assignment and moved down to Toledo around the middle of March.

I had now been in the movement for six years, engaged in many phases of party activity. My biggest responsibility had been as YPSL organizer in Boston, but there I had worked under the tutelage of the party branch organizer and with a committee of older, more experienced people. Pleased as I was by this mark of confidence in me, I knew I would now be on my own. I embarked on this new venture with a keen sense of anticipation. And some trepidation.

Toledo, a lively industrial city of about 280,000 at that time, is located on Maumee Bay, the southwestern tip of Lake Erie, at the mouth of the Maumee River. An important freshwater port and railroad junction point, Toledo was a major shipping center for the Great Lakes area, annually handling millions of tons of iron ore, grain, pig iron, coal, petroleum products, automobiles and auto parts. Its industrial output included automobile parts, industrial furnaces, glass, weighing equipment and machine tools.

Toledoans were also proud of their 2000-acre city park system, the WPA-built municipal zoo, the city university and a fine well-endowed art museum. I knew little about the city before I went there but was very well impressed by what I found. The workers of Toledo had played an active role in the organizing drives of the 1930's, bringing many thousands into the young unions of the CIO. The UAW was especially strong in Toledo and the hard-fought and bloody Autolite strike of 1934 was still a vivid memory for union-conscious Toledo workers. Many would remember that this strike was led by Trotskyists, among them Ted Selander, now branch organizer in Cleveland.

Arriving in Toledo, I first found a furnished room with cooking facilities in a seedy hotel on Monroe Street at the corner of Ontario. This was an ancient ramshackle building and most of the ground floor was occupied by a raucous barroom, hangout for construction workers. But it was a good central location and my room was large, clean, quite inexpensive, and fortunately at the back of the building so I heard little of the racket from the bar.

Next I had to find a job. I went first to the Central Labor Union offices, headquarters of the American Federation of Labor (AFL) downtown on Adams Street. There, I looked up an old social democrat to whom Tim McCormick referred me. The man was business manager for the stationary firemen's union. He let me know right away that he was retired from the political wars but was nonetheless pleased to see me and wished me well. And because Tim had sent me, he was glad to place me on a job. So

I went to work that night on the midnight shift tending the boilers at the Buckeye Brewery.

The boiler room was set apart from the main brewery in a small separate building across an alley or roadway. In the main building I reported to the engineer who was to be my boss and he took me to the boiler room to introduce me to the evening-shift fireman whom I would relieve. There were two medium-sized boilers generating steam for the brewing process. The boilers burned coal, but had mechanical stokers to feed the fires. I had to shovel coal to fill the hoppers, keep the fires in condition and wheel out the slag and ashes once each shift. I was glad to see the mechanical stokers. They made it a lot easier than hand firing.

It took about three minutes to show me everything I needed to know about the boiler room, and another ten minutes to fill me in on the major fringe benefit that went with working for a brewery — free beer on the job. The boiler room was furnished with a two-quart covered copper tankard with pouring spout, and the boss took me across to the cold storage room of the brewery and showed me where to fill it with beer. He also showed me how to breach a new keg if that should become necessary. He told me I could refill the growler with fresh beer at any time and as often as I wanted during the watch. Of course he expected me not to get drunk. He was very mild and matter-of-fact about it, just saying that any employee who couldn't handle the free beer got fired. Buckeye brew wasn't the best beer I ever had, but when I was shoveling coal in temperatures over 100 degrees, it was a very welcome beverage.

The brewery job was union so it paid fairly well. I was alone in the boiler room with plenty of time for reading. Sometimes a week would go by without seeing my boss. He'd stop by to bring me my check and chat a few minutes, otherwise I wouldn't see him or any other supervisors unless I ran into them in the cold storage rooms. Under the circumstances, the night hours were good for me so I stayed there for several months. Since I was off during the day, I could visit both day workers and those on the second shift, and many of the auto workers were on shift work. My evenings were free for meetings. My biggest problem was getting enough sleep.

I entered into my work as Socialist Workers Party organizer with great enthusiasm. At the start, I formally enrolled the members of that core group, about ten in all, and set up a Toledo branch. The first meeting was held, branch officers elected, and a program of activities formulated. They were an excellent group, enthusiastic, eager to learn and willing to work.

The basic activities of the branch were planned and conducted by several standing committees, each assigned to some aspect of the party's work. First there was the branch Executive Committee with overall responsibility. Other important committees were Agit/Prop Committee (agitation/propaganda) charged with sales of the party's pamphlets, and our weekly newspaper, *The Militant*; the Education Committee which planned and conducted classes for the members and such friends as we could attract; and the Social Committee that arranged parties, picnics, etc. As we grew, we would try to involve as many members as possible in the activities of one committee or another. As organizer I was ex-officio member of all committees and wherever practical I tried to attend all committee meetings to lend encouragement and support. This was an ambitious organizational structure for so few but we planned to grow rapidly.

In addition to the many meetings I attended, each member of our new branch wanted me to talk with his friends and fellow workers. I found the workers we contacted receptive to our message of the need for a militant struggle against employer efforts to weaken the unions. I found many receptive to the idea of a socialist reorganization of society and eager to learn more about it.

We started classes on socialist theory, using Karl Marx's *Communist Manifesto* and *Value, Price and Profit* and Lenin's pamphlets *State and Revolution* and *Imperialism, the Highest Stage of Capitalism* as class texts. The attendance was good from the beginning. The sales of party pamphlets and *The Militant* were good and every member participated. Within two months we had more than doubled our original membership.

A major part of our party activity and discussions at meetings revolved around the affairs of the unions to which our members belonged, in which they were active, and in many cases holding elective office. The biggest union in the city and most influential in the region was the UAW, so not surprisingly this was where we had the largest contingent of party members.

The UAW in Toledo had evolved a structure unlike that in any other place I am aware of. Instead of having a separate local union for each plant, there was one huge local which encompassed all the plants and auto workers of the city. The separate units of Local 12 elected their own negotiating teams, and all members participated in Local 12 elections. The biggest plant in town was Willys-Overland which at that time had more than 15,000 union employees, engaged in building the military "Jeep". The overwhelming size of the unit could allow a well-organized machine at Willys to dominate the affairs of the entire local.

Local 12 had such a machine headed by Richard Gosser who started his career as a shop steward in the electrical maintenance department at Willys and went on to become, eventually, an international vice-president. At the time I was in Toledo, Gosser was a very effective local boss with whom every UAW member had to reckon. He was UAW regional director and all the international representatives were appointed by and reported to Gosser. Even a plant unit as large as Spicer Manufacturing with 3,500 members had a constant struggle to retain some measure of independence from the Gosser machine.

When I first arrived in Toledo we had a couple of members at Willys. With them as a nucleus, we eventually added several more members in the plant but they never played a major role in the Willys unit affairs. This was partially due to the iron control of the Gosser machine, but another factor may have been that our Willys people were low-key types who functioned well as departmental stewards but could not challenge the leadership of the local. Our biggest contingent of auto workers was to be at

Spicer, a plant that produced the torque converter (automatic) transmission. It came about this way. Very early on, probably in my first week, I visited a man who was said to be an old member of the socialist party and who worked as an international representative for Gosser. Clayton Rusch wasn't that old, but he had been a socialist for a long time and was sympathetic toward our efforts to establish a branch of the SWP in Toledo. However, for himself, he wanted to keep his job with the UAW and that meant not unduly antagonizing Dick Gosser. So Clayton subscribed to *The Militant,* made some small financial contributions, and otherwise laid low.

But he made a major contribution when he advised me to go see Robert Burkart who had recently resigned as an international rep because of major principled differences with Gosser. Burkart had gone back to work at Spicer rather than take orders from Gosser who he felt was selling out the interests of the membership of the union to further his own ambitions. Clayton admired Bob, even agreed with him, but didn't have the courage to do likewise. He practically told me just that, but he did send me to Bob Burkart.

I visited Bob at the first opportunity in his home at West Toledo out near the Spicer plant. After a couple of long evenings of discussions, Bob joined the party, as did his wife, Margaret. This was the beginning of a close friendship and collaboration that lasted as long as I stayed in Toledo and played a major role in building up the party organization there. Tall, blond, handsome, Bob was a charismatic individual with a wide following among the Spicer workers where he could be elected to any office he aspired to. Starting with Bob, we steadily recruited members from Spicer and established a much wider circle of sympathizers, readers of our papers and pamphlets.

Through Tim McCormick we recruited some railroad men, principally from the Brotherhood of Locomotive Firemen and Enginemen of which Tim was an official of the local lodge. A tall dark handsome Irishman, Tim had been in the socialist movement since boyhood and had spent most of his working life on the railroad. A powerful public speaker, Tim was well known and highly respected in Toledo labor circles. His closest associate in the lodge, Harry Richardson, was less flamboyant but just as well regarded.

We continued to gain confidence and converts. Each new member was a cause of rejoicing to me. I felt sure we were on the way to becoming a powerful force in this key industrial center. We were beginning to make our influence felt in the unions, especially among auto workers and railroad workers. As soon as we had enough pledge income from members to afford it, we rented space in the downtown Roy Davis building, at the corner of Michigan and Monroe Streets. Our new party headquarters had one large room doubling as office and meeting hall. We equipped the hall with folding chairs, other furniture from the Salvation Army, a used mimeograph machine and an equally old typewriter.

There we conducted a regular schedule of classes, both beginning and advanced, and held forums on topical subjects, attracting good audiences. The only drawback was that during the first few months I was the only class instructor and, apart from an occasional guest speaker from Cleveland or Detroit, usually the forum lecturer.

But we were doing well. We were no longer a group of six or eight people meeting on an occasional Sunday afternoon to compare notes and reminisce. We had become an active organization, only a few score in number, but effective far beyond our actual membership strength. By the end of the first year we had several other members who would prepare and deliver a lecture at our regular forum meetings, or teach a class on the fundamentals of socialist thought.

With a headquarters for our meetings, we distributed mimeographed leaflets announcing all our public events at plant gates and in neighborhoods, especially in the two large black housing projects only a few blocks from our hall. As a result of these distributions, we got our first recruits from the projects. The first was Ed Hackley, a gentle giant of a man who had been a prize fighter, by his own account not a great one, and now a trainer and sometime fight promoter. Serious, thoughtful, known for sound judgment and unshakeable loyalty, Ed was from the start a pillar of our small society. He first brought around his best friend, Joe Magdleno, who worked as a bellman in one of the downtown hotels. In curious contrast to Ed Hackley, Joe was slightly built, quick and volatile where Ed was slow and deliberate. Joe stood about 5' 6" and tipped the scales at about 110, while Ed was 6' 8" and weighed 250 pounds. These two became the nucleus of our growing presence in the black community.

Essential to the life of any party branch were the social activities that were organized and run by the Social Committee elected by the membership. These parties, or socials as we called them, provided an opportunity for comrades to become better acquainted and relax in the company of like-minded friends. These were also occasions to which members could invite workers who were interested in our ideas, where they could meet in a comfortable relaxed atmosphere to discuss politics and union affairs. Here they could also dance, enjoy a drink and have a good time.

In the beginning we held socials at the Burkarts' home; then after we had rented a hall we held them at the headquarters. Usually these would be simple affairs, with music, dancing and an open bar. Sometimes there would be square dancing and small entertainments put together by the social committee. But on a couple of occasions we even had sit-down banquets where we served 60 people a lavish meal overseen by Joe Magdleno's wife who was a professional caterer. For those who joined the party, these social affairs became the major recreational outlets in their lives, and I have no doubt that our social programs provided a major cement binding our people to one another and to the party.

24

Falling in Love Again

During my time as a seaman and since Nina left me, I had known a number of women in the islands and in mainland ports, but there had been none that I took very seriously. Apart from the brief episode with Pat Walsh in Detroit, there had been none that I wanted to settle down with for more than a few days at a time. Since Pat, I hadn't formed any attachments, even fleeting. Though I don't recall being consciously aware of it, I was probably lonely for close companionship and the love of a good woman. This was something I hadn't really known since Nina left me in 1940.

I had been in Toledo about a month when I first met Bonnie Sponseller. Her parents had been in the Socialist Party in the early thirties. Her father, Sam, took part in the union organizing drives and went on to become a well-paid employee of a CIO union. But I was told that his ex-wife, Faye, whom he had abandoned along with their three daughters, might still be sympathetic to the socialist movement. Faye Sponseller and her daughters lived in a small house in West Toledo where I visited them at the suggestion of Bob Burkart who knew the family.

Faye made me welcome, brewed a pot of tea and introduced me to two of her girls. Rhoda was 17, a pretty redhead, and Lila, a blonde, was 15 and even prettier. Whether shy or uninterested, the girls didn't have much to say, leaving the conversation mostly to their mother and me, despite my attempts to involve them. Faye told me she was feeling old and tired, working full time to support her children since Sam left her. Any enthusiasms she might once have entertained had been ground out of her by her life as a single parent. But she said she still retained some of her socialist convictions and indicated she would be pleased to see at least one of her daughters so inclined.

Rhoda and Lila made no response and struck me as being rather giddy and interested only in whatever fad was current among teenagers. They soon took themselves off and left me with their mother. On further acquaintance, I learned that my first impressions of Rhoda and Lila were fairly accurate. They were good girls but typical teenagers.

I continued talking with Faye who was an interesting woman, even though not a prospect for recruitment to the party. Then the third, and eldest, daughter came into the living room. She had been in the shower and came out wearing a bathrobe. Introduced, she seemed delighted to meet me and perched crossed-legged beside me on the sofa.

Bonnie was a statuesque, sensual, flamboyant 19-year-old beauty, with a mass of wavy auburn hair worn long, falling about her shoulders. She was lovely to look upon and her scent was alluring. Furthermore, she was very interested in my socialist message, hung on my words and asked intelligent questions. Then I knew I'd come to the right place. I delighted in talking with her. But after a while Faye stood up, announcing it was her bedtime. Then I realized several hours had passed and it was nearly time for me to leave for work at the brewery. I said goodnight and left them, but not before Bonnie invited me to come back to continue our discussion.

That night at work I could think of little else than the beautiful, enchanting woman who seemed so receptive not only to my ideas but to me personally as well. At the first opportunity, perhaps the next evening, I was back at the Sponseller house, carrying on from where I had left off with Bonnie. On my next visit she was wearing not her bathrobe but casual attire, and I thought her more beautiful than ever. Striking in appearance, she dressed with the flair and distinction of a fashion model. As I soon learned, she modeled clothes at LaSalle & Kochs, a big downtown department store. I started out talking politics but soon our conversation moved on to more personal matters. She told me about her work, her love of music and her desire to become an artist. I told her about my work and she asked about my past, curious about my life as a seaman, the adventures and misadventures that had brought me here.

That evening, after a brief interval, Faye left us alone and our conversation became more intimate until at last I summoned the courage to embrace and kiss Bonnie. Her response told me she had been waiting and wanting this as much as I had. When I left her to go to work that night, my feet barely touched the ground. At work I spent the time, between filling the stoker hopper with coal and refilling my growler with beer, writing a lengthy poem about my love for Bonnie. Fortunately, the poem has been lost, but I can still recall the mood in which I wrote it.

From that time on, I went regularly to the Sponseller house, spending as much spare time with Bonnie as I could. Since Bonnie lived with her mother and sisters, one or more of them were almost always in attendance, or at least in the offing. So we couldn't feel entirely comfortable in their house. Though Faye never showed any signs of disapproval, the things we wanted to do called for some privacy, and Faye would certainly not have countenanced our staying in Bonnie's bedroom with the door closed. But spring was coming to Toledo and the weather turned nice, so we spent a lot of time among the shrubs in the back yard, rolling on the grassy lawn.

This went on for a week or two, and we became increasingly passionate and frustrated. Bonnie would have gone wherever I suggested, but I didn't want to take her to my room in the flophouse on Monroe Street. So one evening, on my day off, I took her out to dinner. It wasn't a fancy place, but better than I usually frequented. Then we checked into a good hotel downtown where we spent the night. The consummation of our love proved as exciting as I had dreamed it would, and we slept very little that night at the hotel.

The next day I rented a small furnished apartment on Collingwood Avenue, near the corner of Monroe Street. The apartment had only one living room with a kitchenette in the corner and a bathroom. At night a Murphy bed folded out of a closet and the living room became a bedroom. It wasn't much, but it was clean, affordable, and it was all ours, for Bonnie moved in with me. I continued to work at the brewery, and I kept up with my party work. On evenings when I had meetings or some one to call on, Bonnie would go along with me, participating in whatever I had to do, her warmth and personal charm making only friends.

Bonnie had told me some things about her father, about whom she had mixed feelings. She was proud of him and his role in the labor movement but resented what he had done to her mother, and she heartily disliked her father's new woman. She wanted me to meet him, so one day she invited him to the apartment. I suppose he was curious about this guy his daughter was living with.

Sam Sponseller was a stocky man with a florid complexion, a used-car-salesman personality and a reputation as a gifted stump speaker. I was quite willing to get on with Sam, because he was Bonnie's father if for no other reason. But I found his attitude arrogant and overbearing and, on reflection, he may have had the same complaint about me. At any rate, we didn't hit it off on this occasion, and that was the only time I ever saw him.

Sam started off telling me that he had "outgrown" his previous idealistic notions about socialism but thought the labor movement had a good future under its present leadership. He thought the CIO was doing just fine the way it was, and he wouldn't want to change a thing. I expressed the opinion that his was a good safe evaluation if he was primarily interested in holding onto his "pie card" with the union. He didn't appreciate that comment and advised me that we socialists would get nowhere lecturing the workers, trying to get them to think. They would ignore the socialist agitators as they always had and still continue to follow their "natural" leaders.

"By natural leaders, I suppose you mean people like you and Dick Gosser," I told him. He knew the contempt in which I held Gosser and took this to be offensive. And so it was intended. He was ready to fight and I don't know how it might have ended if Bonnie hadn't intervened and restored order if not peace. He left soon after that. Bonnie apologized for him, but her sympathy was with me in this dispute with her dad. I was sorry I hadn't tried a little harder for her sake, but we never referred to the incident again.

We stayed on together at the Collingwood apartment for the rest of the spring and into the summer. Bonnie worked at LaSalle & Kochs, but modeling was not a full time job with a regular salary. Still, she made enough to contribute to the expenses and spend a lot on clothes. Our home life was both delightful and frustrating to me. Bonnie was buoyant and fun-loving, usually affectionate and a pleasure to be with. In some ways she was surprisingly mature for a 19-year-old, but in other ways naive and childlike, even childish. Usually quite sensible, she could also be scatterbrained and impractical. In pursuit of her dream of an art career, she purchased an expensive art box with palette, oil paints, brushes, canvas and an easel, coming home one day just loaded down with art supplies. Appalled at how much all this stuff cost — enough for both of us to live on for a month — I was not very enthusiastic. However, now that she had the equipment I encouraged her to take art lessons. Nothing she did in class indicated she had any talent for this sort of thing, and after a few lessons she stored the art equipment in the closet and never looked at it again.

Bonnie was sensuous and exciting, but I found she could also be thoughtless and unreliable. She was passionate and loving, but in a different mood she was also capable of being insensitive and uncaring. So after the first few weeks, each day I would alternate between determination to cut loose my ties and despair at the thought of losing her. This went on for months. We would argue, and she'd go back to her mother's for a few days. Then she'd come to a meeting and we'd both know we had to go home together. Things would be fine for a while, then she'd come back to the apartment very late and with no word of explanation of where she'd been or why. I'd been expecting her since 5 p.m. and worrying about her. I would also imagine all sorts of things, jealous of whomever she was spending the time with. We'd fight and she'd go away again.

Things might have dragged on like this indefinitely, but a proposal from the party branch brought matters to a conclusion. For some time it had been evident that the party work would prosper if I could only devote more time to it. We had discussed this several times in executive committee meetings but there seemed to be no practical solution. Then, in late August or early September, Bob and Margaret Burkart volunteered to give me room and board if the branch could come up with sufficient money to provide for my other needs. Pledges were made to a special fund for this purpose. I would get $10 a week salary.

This seemed like a good solution to both my problems. I could quit my job at the brewery and devote full time to the party work. I could also give up the apartment and send Bonnie back to her mother. I thought we would probably get along much better if we didn't have the strain of living together. This turned out to be a correct assumption. I moved into an upstairs bedroom at the Burkarts, and Bonnie moved back to her mother's house.

The party work picked up and went more smoothly now that I could devote more time to it. Living at the Burkarts' was a pleasure. They were about my age, well-read and interested in everything. They had a good library and a fine collection of records, mostly classical. They lived in a big house in West Toledo near the street car line. Also in the house was their small son, Gordon, and a roomer, Art Kaminsky, whom I saw little of. Margaret was a good cook and they were both excellent company. And though they were relatively new members, they were enthusiastic about the party and its program. Bob was a leader at the Spicer plant as well as in UAW Local 12.

With all my days free to do party work, I felt the need of better transportation than the municipal public transport allowed. Though streetcars and buses would take me almost anywhere in the city, the long waits at car stops and transfer points meant half the day was wasted standing around. Because of the war, no new automobiles had been produced since 1941 and the old ones were wearing out, so any car in good shape was priced too high for me.

Then I learned that a friend, a fellow who considered himself a party member though he rarely came to any meetings, had a Model T Ford he wanted to get rid of. When he heard I was interested, he practically gave it to me. I think I paid him $10. This Model T was much like the one I abandoned in Boston. A year or two younger, it was a coupe without a top instead of a pickup without a top, and with a starter instead of a crank.

The Model T increased my mobility considerably, but due to wartime gas rationing I had to use public transport when the gas stamp supply ran low. Bonnie and I still got together often and she enjoyed driving around the city in my old open-air Ford, and sometimes we went into the countryside, though the gas rationing limited such excursions. Now that we no longer had the stress of living together we had a great relationship.

I often had to attend party regional conferences in Cleveland or Akron, and Bonnie would go with me. She also went with me to a national party convention in New York, and occasionally to a UAW fraction meeting in Detroit where our leading UAW members would develop strategies for our work in the union. Bonnie had no role to play in these meetings but she enjoyed them and I was proud to have her along.

At about this time our members in the railroad unions became involved in an extensive campaign to resolve a dual-union situation which had plagued railwaymen for decades and resulted in substandard wages for all the workers involved. At that time a railroad engineer operating a passenger train in the New York Central main line, responsible for millions of dollars worth of equipment and the life and safety of hundreds of people, was making a lower wage than a drill press operator in a UAW plant.

The reason for this wage disparity, our people were convinced, was that there were two unions competing for the dues and allegiance of the firemen and engineers. The International Brotherhood of Locomotive Firemen and Enginemen (BLF&E) was by far the largest and enrolled both crafts. The International Brotherhood of Locomotive Engineers (BLE) was for engineers only, but would accept as members those who qualified as engineers (had passed the tests) even though they were still employed as firemen. In practice a man moved up to an engineer's job after he had served anywhere from ten to twenty years as a fireman, depending on the need for more engineers in his division.

Tim McCormick had recently advanced to an engineer's job on the New York Central main line, running between Toledo and Elkhart, Indiana. He had been a member of the BLF&E all the 18 years he had been railroading, was an officer of his lodge and an influence in the International. His closest associate, Harry Richardson, was also an engineer on the Elkhart run and secretary of the lodge.

Tim and Harry agreed that the two unions were competing with one another for members instead of addressing the problems of the men who worked on the railroad. They had long urged the necessity of merging the two organizations and presenting a united front to the employers, just as Eugene V. Debs had urged a little over 50 years prior when he was Grand Secretary and Treasurer of the firemen's union. Debs had been unsuccessful, finally quitting his secure position with the Locomotive Firemen and founding the short-lived American Railway Union.

There was considerable rank and file sentiment in favor of amalgamation, but it was still bitterly opposed by the entrenched bureaucracies of both organizations. This was one thing on which the many well-paid officials of the BLF&E and BLE agreed.

Then a man named Russell Walker, based in Cleveland, set up an organization which he called the "Consolidation Committee" to work toward uniting the two unions. Russ Walker had been a high officer in one of these two unions and had seen at first hand how impossible it was to accomplish anything substantive for the workers under this dual-union setup. He was an energetic man, an accomplished orator with a charismatic personality, and he was willing to risk his time and enough money to get it started.

Tim and Harry joined Russ Walker's committee immediately and thereafter played a leading role in the nationwide campaign for consolidation of the two operating rail unions. For me it meant meeting often with Tim, Harry and our other railroad members, and with Russ Walker (who never became a member of the party) discussing strategy and ways of advancing the cause of consolidation.

This being a major development in the union movement and one of national scope, we received full support from the national party. Paul Rasmussen was sent in and became editor of the *Consolidator,* which was mailed to every member of both unions. At different times Farrell Dobbs and Vincent Dunne came to Toledo to meet with our local people and advise them. We held one conference in Chicago attended by party railroad workers from other states, including Henry Schultz from St. Paul. I learned a great deal from working with these veteran union strategists.

It was a bitterly fought campaign that went on for several years, with the paid officialdom of both unions, backed by the railroad companies' management, using every means to discredit the leaders of the committee and defeat consolidation.

I left Toledo before the issue was finally resolved, but the struggle for uniting the two unions went on through the years 1945 to 1948, and we were very much involved in it. Though I left before the issue was concluded, I learned later that the embattled bureaucrats made enough concessions to stave off consolidation and eventually to defeat it in conventions of the two organizations. The BLF&E did succeed in consolidating with some of the other operating unions in 1969 forming the United Transport Union. However, the Brotherhood of Engineers is still going it alone with a membership about one eighth that of the BLF&E.

25

Giving Matrimony Another Chance

Bob Burkart's house, close to the Spicer factory where he worked, had long been a popular gathering place for some of his friends among the militant unionists in the plant. They would come there after work to have a beer, listen to music and discuss union politics or working conditions in the shop. This became even more true after I went there to live. Bob and other members would invite fellow workers to stop in and join our conversations. And many of these workers became members of the party as a result of these meetings. Among those who often came to the house was Paul Schoenfelt, soft-spoken, very bright, and active in the union.

One evening a few weeks after I moved in with the Burkarts, Paul and I were on the way into town on the streetcar. As the car turned onto Ashland Avenue, Paul pointed to a passenger sitting a couple of seats ahead of us.

"That's my cousin there," he told me. "Would you like to meet her?"

I looked her over and saw a rather demure appearing, very pretty young woman with wavy light brown hair worn in a short cut. She was reading a book.

"Sure," I said. "Why not?"

We got up and went forward. She closed her book and a smile lit up her face. She greeted Paul affectionately and he introduced me.

"This is my cousin, Marjorie Smith. Marge, this is my friend, Mark Walker."

She gave me a nice smile, I shook her hand and she stood up. "This is my stop," she said. The streetcar was approaching Bancroft Street and she moved to the front of the car, debarking when it stopped. Paul and I continued on downtown.

Paul explained to me that she was his mother's brother's daughter, daughter of Dane and Dorothy Van Auken. She was, he said, a very bright student who had worked her way through the University of Toledo as an art major and was now employed as a commercial artist. She had been married but a short time when her husband, Graham Smith, was sent overseas. He was a radio operator in a B-17 bomber and was killed in the saturation bombing of Hanover, Germany, in the spring of that year. His cousin, Paul said, had been going through a hard time in consequence. He thought perhaps I could interest her in socialism. If I'd like to give it a shot, he'd see if he could set up a meeting.

A few days later Paul asked me to dinner at his house and said his cousin would be there. After this meeting, it would be up to me. It didn't occur to me that Paul and his wife might be indulging in a little matchmaking.

The dinner went off very nicely. Bernadine cooked a fine meal and we had a good wine with it. Dinner conversation was general and touched on politics only peripherally. Bernadine Schoenfelt was a strict Roman Catholic and had no use for the unorthodox ideas held by her husband. I was charmed by Paul's cousin. She was lively, interesting and an engaging conversationalist. She was very articulate, quick-witted and obviously very bright. I thought she'd make a great addition to the party. She was certainly a fine looking woman, too. But I still had Bonnie and wasn't looking for another.

The evening ended well. I escorted her home on the streetcar and she told me that her family called her Marge or Marnie, but she preferred to be Maggie. On the streetcar ride I opened up some political questions we hadn't discussed at Paul's. It was obvious she was in sharp disagreement with me about politics, but when I asked if we could get together for further discussion, she agreed. We set a date for the first evening that I had no other meeting scheduled.

Maggie Smith lived alone in a small apartment on Bancroft Street just off Ashland. I arrived at the appointed time bearing a bottle of wine, probably not very good and certainly not expensive. She greeted me cordially and urged me to make myself comfortable. I looked around the apartment. It had a large rectangular living room with a dining area in one corner. Two steps down at one end of the living room was a small hallway off which opened a smallish bedroom, long narrow bathroom and a kitchenette. The whole place was imaginatively decorated and furnished, very comfortable looking, with a floor-to-ceiling bookcase at one end of the living room. I liked her place very much and told her so.

She brought glasses and I opened the wine. I commented on the paintings on her walls, several of which she had signed. She told me she hadn't been painting for the past few months because her job took so much of her creative energy. She liked her work, which was designing "visual-front" store facades for promotional use by Libby-Owens-Ford Glass Company. A new concept in merchandising, the visual front opened up the whole inviting interior of a retail outlet to the passerby, presumably informing and welcoming prospective customers, and making it easier for them to enter the store. The aim of her department at L-O-F was to promote the use of Thermopane, a new insulating glass that allowed large structural uses in futuristic design for store fronts. Maggie showed me a few of her airbrush designs and I found them strikingly original.

We went on to discuss politics the rest of the evening. She had generally liberal views on social questions, such as race, unionism and religion, but when it came to larger political issues we were at opposite poles. She had been reading Edmund Burke, the late 18th century British statesman, essayist and political theorist. Maggie was very impressed by his philosophical and political viewpoints.

Though Burke was something of a liberal in his own way and had supported the American cause during our revolution, he was vehemently opposed to drastic or revolutionary changes, particularly those he regarded as abandonment of tradition or surrender of cultural heritage. These views were forcefully presented by Burke in his opposition to the French Revolution.

Maggie ably defended his viewpoints and the evening ended with neither of us having made a dent in the other's convictions. Toward midnight, she made delicious egg salad sandwiches and opened a couple of beers. When I went home I was as far from my objective of converting her as I'd been before I came. But it had been an enjoyable evening and when I suggested following it up with further discussion, she agreed.

When I went again to her apartment a few days later, I again brought a bottle of wine. Again we spent the whole evening disagreeing. But I enjoyed myself and I think she did too. At any rate, after the wine was gone, we had sandwiches and beer. We agreed to continue our talks sometime soon and, of course, I left behind our newspaper and some pamphlets for her to read.

This went on, with meetings at her apartment two or three times a week. In the heat of our arguments, one bottle of wine seemed to disappear rather early and I started bringing two bottles. We still had fundamental disagreements, but we enjoyed each other's company and agreed on continuing the discussions. In fact, I found that the more I talked with Maggie, the more attractive I found her and the more my interest became personal as well as political, but so far I made no romantic advances and her behavior had been quite proper. She had started reading the literature I brought and it seemed to me I should be making more headway than I was.

I told Bob Burkart about my progress, or lack of it, with Paul's cousin and told him I had enjoyable times, mentioning that we had shared one bottle of wine on my early visits and two bottles on later occasions. Bob was reminded of a story by Rabelais about a fellow whose experience in seduction had taught him that there are three kinds of women. There are one-bottle women, two-bottle women, and the occasional woman who cannot be seduced without plying her with three bottles of wine. He suggested I take a third bottle the next time I went to visit Maggie.

On my next visit I arrived with three bottles of wine and told Maggie the story. I told her I hoped the Rabelaisian theory would prove sound in the area of political seduction. We laughed about that and she told me she had been reading the materials I left for her and found them very convincing. This time, instead of arguing a contrary position, she asked questions. It seemed like hundreds of questions which I answered as best I could.

When I first met this woman I had thought she was reserved, shy and rather prim. As we got better acquainted, I realized she was none of these things. But her attire gave that impression. When I saw her, she was usually wearing her business costume. This was a well-cut, conservative business suit, worn with a tailored shirt and nylon hose. Respectable women then wore panty girdles and other undergarments that seemed designed to straighten out all the curves and give them, as nearly as possible, stick figures.

Perhaps these impressions of Maggie were colored by comparisons of her slim elegance with Bonnie who abroad dressed like a fashion model and around our apartment had worn nothing at all, or a flimsy wrapper prone to falling open to reveal her voluptuous attributes.

But late on that three-bottle evening, I found that Maggie was not only a beautiful woman who was a vivacious and spirited companion. When shucked out of that formal attire and released from her straitjacket undergarments, she had a lovely full-bodied figure which had been partially camouflaged. That night I didn't return to Burkarts' after we had our midnight sandwiches and beer. Now I had two girl friends because I still saw Bonnie from time to time. Even though Maggie was an entirely satisfactory lover, I couldn't seem to get Bonnie out of my bloodstream.

It wasn't that I preferred her to Maggie. I didn't. I just didn't want to give up either of them, not even after I left Burkart's and moved into Maggie's Bancroft Street apartment. I did not at that time think of the move as a permanent arrangement. It just seemed like a good thing to do, especially since I spent so much time there anyway. But I intended to continue as I had been.

Bonnie's reaction to my new living arrangements was unenthusiastic, but she never reproached me about them, and I'm not aware of any occasion when she was hostile or antagonistic toward Maggie. Bonnie and I both knew we couldn't live together, but we still liked being together and managed to meet occasionally as we had in the past. I think she was most hurt by the fact that I now took Maggie with me when I went out of town to a party conference or convention.

Maggie soon became a mainstay of the party branch, both through her financial support and her willingness to participate in any and all of the activities. Everyone appreciated her enthusiasm and eagerness to learn. She was outgoing and friendly, liked well by everyone, with one exception.

Wayne Decker was an older man, perhaps in his late forties. He worked at Spicer, was influential in the union and had been an active and useful member of the party. He was also an inveterate and incurable gossip. He liked nothing better than to retail scurrilous tidbits about other people. I had felt for some time that Wayne's constant intriguing and tale-bearing were a disruptive influence in the organization but hadn't mentioned it to anyone, hoping it might resolve itself. One day he came up to Maggie, within my hearing, and started telling her about one of our members, a married man, having an affair with a woman who worked in the Local 12 union office.

Maggie didn't hear him out. With some heat she said, "Wayne, he is my friend and I don't want to listen to that kind of gossip about him. If you can't tell me something good about my friends, don't talk to me about them."

Wayne Decker became Maggie's enemy from that moment forward, though she never changed toward him. Perhaps others had felt like telling Wayne the same thing Maggie had, but no one else ever did to my knowledge.

I had been living with Maggie for a while then, becoming more and more convinced that this was the woman I could spend my life with. Living with her was as peaceable as it had been stressful with Bonnie. She was constant and reliable, a stimulating intellectual companion, and our love life was exciting and delightful. And she had this outspoken honesty and steadfast integrity to a degree I had not encountered in any one before. I asked her to marry me and she said she'd think it over. Of course she knew about Bonnie and that may have given her pause.

We went on living together at the Bancroft Street apartment. It was as though we were married in all respects except the ceremony, and I didn't put any pressure on her or inquire about her reservations. But she knew it was a standing offer.

Then we attended a national convention of the party in New York City and at one session Morris Stein, one of the party leaders, made a major report, some two hours long. Morris, a short, courtly gentleman and a plumber by trade, was an eloquent orator and a brilliant theoretician. I had known and admired him for many years and I remember this report as an inspiring speech, one of the best I ever heard. After the speech, which ended the session, Maggie told me she'd like to meet the speaker. We went forward to the rostrum and I greeted Morris and introduced him to Maggie Smith.

Morris shook her hand and told her, "I've heard of you and I hear nothing but good things about what both of you are doing in Toledo."

"Thank you," Maggie said. "I thought your speech was wonderful and I wanted to tell you that it convinced me to accept a proposal of marriage to this guy."

Morris looked astonished, then very pleased. I must have looked the same way because this was her way of surprising me, letting me know she accepted my proposal. I was speechless.

"I'm delighted to hear it," said Morris, "but that isn't at all the effect I'd expected to have."

We laughed and Maggie told him, "I have been considering it for some while, but your speech removed all my residual doubts. I know now what I want."

"Congratulations to both of you!"

His wife, Sylvia, a charming woman whom I had also known and long admired, joined us and Morris told her about the unexpected consequence of his report to the convention. They were the first among many to wish us well in our future life together.

Back home, Maggie told her parents who lived in Toledo and with whom she had been on good terms, even though she saw them infrequently. They got very steamed up about it. Her father, who was Director of Publications for Willys-Overland Motors and who had been a Republican all his life and vociferously anti-union, went down to the Toledo office of the Federal Bureau of Investigation (FBI) to inquire about me.

The FBI chief showed him, so he reported, their voluminous dossier on this Mark Walker, a dangerous radical and labor agitator. The leaders of his party were already in federal prison and Walker was likely to end up there at any time. They said he should keep his daughter from marrying this man at all costs. He should forbid her to even see him again.

Poor Dane Van Auken knew that forbidding his daughter to do something was not going to get him anywhere. However, he could try to scare her and he did, describing the thick file he had been shown by the FBI — the file that documented and detailed all the nefarious activities of the man she proposed marrying! When he found out she wasn't scared, he threatened to disown her. She was still unmoved, so he did disown her and refused to speak to her for about five years. His wife, Dorothy, was also opposed to our marriage and, though appearing less distressed than her husband, she too cut off all contact with her daughter.

As to the FBI file, I assumed there was some exaggeration involved on the part of Dane Van Auken, and possibly the FBI. We, of course, knew the Bureau was interested in the activities of our party and we also took it for granted that we had at least one informer in our midst. We were also reasonably sure we knew the identity of one of them. However, it was more than 50 years later that I learned, through a Freedom of Information Act (FOIA) request for my file, the full extent of their surveillance.

When the FOIA office pulled my file they informed me it contained approximately 728 pages. This was later revised to 599 relevant pages of which 388 were considered suitable for release. Many were withheld on the grounds of potential violation of privacy, or the exposure of the identity of an informant. Many more pages, for no apparent reason, were blacked out almost in their entirety. In most reports by informants of meetings and other activities, all names except mine were expunged. But in some instances (by oversight perhaps?) lists of party members were left intact. For instance, names of some ten nominees for Toledo branch delegates to the party's national convention held in Chicago in November, 1946, escaped the FBI censor's black felt pen.

Whatever else may have been expunged, the FBI files did report my attendance at practically every party meeting in the period from 1944 through 1953. It recorded every post I ever held in the party from branch educational director to member of the National Committee of the Party. Numerous speeches and talks I delivered over those years are mentioned, with the content or words sometimes distorted by the "confidential informant" to cater to the sensational tastes of the FBI paymaster. However, on the whole, the voluminous file is made up of FBI boilerplate denial forms and boringly repetitious informant accounts of non-events, occasionally enlivened by the prosaic minutes of Toledo branch meetings.

Oversight of my activities seems to have constituted a cottage industry employing several confidential informants and a score of FBI agents. Frank Donner, in his book *The Age of Surveillance* (Knopf, 1980), writes that in a 16-year period the FBI paid out a total of $1,683,000 to 301 informers who joined the SWP and its youth affiliate and another 1,000 who provided information but didn't join.

The surveillance recorded in my dossier started at about the time our party leader's were indicted in Minneapolis. The only entries for the period prior to Detroit were some employment records from steamship companies. The 20-year FBI scrutiny continued until 1963 when the bureau finally concluded I was no longer a threat and removed my name from its "Security Index.". This index, as I also learned from Frank Donner, was J. Edgar Hoover's secret list of "agitators" and other dangerous individuals, subject to mass arrest under a master warrant, with suspension of habeas corpus and "custodial detention" (concentration camps) without judicial review.

The FBI notwithstanding, Maggie and I entered into matrimony without the blessings of either of our parents. Mine were far away in Maine and New Jersey, and I notified them by letter after the event. First we went down to Toledo City Hall to get married by the city clerk. But as we sat in the park before City Hall, Maggie told me she didn't like doing it this way. She wanted something with a little more ceremony and with friends present. So I called Tom Reahorn, a Baptist minister who was a good friend and a party sympathizer, despite his religious vocation. The Burkarts agreed to host the event and Maggie's best girl friend, Joanne Burke, agreed to be bridesmaid. The marriage took place in the Burkarts' home on February 9, 1945, with Bob and Margaret as witnesses. It was a small affair but much more pleasant and satisfactory than a City Hall ceremony would have been.

Being married made no noticeable difference in our life together. I continued to work for the party and was getting $15 a week now. Maggie stayed at her job with Libby-Owens-Ford designing visual-fronts, promoting the use of plate glass. That is, she kept on until she was fired for talking unionism in the lunchroom to a group of women from the L-O-F steno pool. This was quite a shock to her. She believed she had the right to talk to anybody about anything on a lunch break. But her immediate superior, who was very embarrassed by this turn of events, gave her a glowing recommendation and she went to work in the advertising department of LaSalle & Kochs, the same big Macy-owned downtown department store where Bonnie worked as a model.

My old Model T had always been unreliable, but I kept it going as best I could. Then one cold night the engine block froze solid and developed a big crack. I had the cracked block welded, but the car never ran well again.

I heard of a 1937 Dodge sedan that was for sale cheap. Paul Schoenfelt went with me to look at it in the back yard of a housing project. The car hadn't run for months and wouldn't start, but it seemed salvageable. I paid $30 and had it towed to a garage owned by a friend of Paul Schoenfelt's, where he was already rebuilding a 1934 Plymouth. There with some guidance from the garage owner and helping one another, Paul and I took our old cars' engines apart and completely rebuilt them. Engine blocks were re-bored, the heads planed, then fitted with oversize pistons and put back together with all new gaskets, main and crank bearings. We replaced or rebuilt all the auxiliary equipment under the hoods—carburetors, fuel pumps, distributors, spark plugs and wiring harnesses.

I got a lot of satisfaction out of the hours I spent in Mather's garage, and when I was finished my old car ran like new. As long as I kept the car I never had any trouble with anything under the hood.

Meanwhile our 18 party leaders convicted under the Smith Act had served their sentences, been released from prison and resumed the activities interrupted by their indictment. The war went on. The Soviet Union, having repulsed the German invasion, was now on the offensive along the entire eastern front. In western Europe the Allies had liberated Paris and were driving toward the German heartland. In the Pacific, the Japanese were being forced to yield one island stronghold after another.

At home there were shortages, but few complained about them. Meat and gasoline were rationed but the rationing created little hardship. The allowance was generally sufficient and there were always ways to finagle a little extra. Almost everyone seemed to have an angle — knew someone with a source of black market gas stamps, had a friend who worked behind the meat counter or at a gas station.

The party had set up a summer camp at Grass Lake in Michigan. It started by staying open only two or three weeks for people nearby but developed into an all-summer operation. Here was started the first "Trotsky School" which enrolled promising young members for a full summer of study under a faculty which was headed by George Novack and George Clarke. When the camp entered its third year Maggie was asked to act as assistant to Oscar Coover, the camp director. I would miss her, but we felt it was an important assignment and she should accept it.

As it turned out, I went up to camp every weekend, a drive of about 90 miles, to deliver supplies. Meat rationing was in full force and there were no provisions in the law to accommodate camps like ours, making it difficult to provide good meals for those attending, working or studying at Grass Lake. So through Sam Pollack who was an official of the butchers' union and a friendly meat market manager in East Toledo, I was able to secure a weekly supply of meat for the camp, which I packed with dry ice and hauled in my reconditioned '37 Dodge. Thus I got to spend the weekends at camp with Maggie and the camp got a regular supply of meat for the table.

Cigarettes were also scarce and we, along with most of our friends, were constant smokers. We not only thought we had to have them, we thought they were good for us, as the tobacco companies kept telling us. During the scarcity, a rumor that a store had received a cigarette shipment would bring a line extending around the block within minutes of the report. We had a neighborhood grocer who slipped his regular customers a few packs on the sly, and then cheated when adding up the bill. Addicted smokers had to choose between correcting his addition and cutting off their supply of cigarettes, or just considering the overcharges part of the price one paid for smoking regularly.

In the course of my regular activities, I still ran across

Bonnie, at meetings, at someone's house, at a party. Often Maggie was with me and on the surface things remained on a neutral plane. But I was always acutely aware of the strong attraction still between us. Once in a while I would see her alone, and on these occasions I would want her as badly as I ever had. Sometimes these encounters were accidental and sometimes they happened at my initiative. In every case, whatever went on between us was my doing.

Bonnie would protest, "No! We shouldn't do this. It isn't fair to Maggie."

This might give me pause momentarily, but the allurement was too strong and I would persist. So despite Bonnie's misgivings and my twinges of guilt, we'd do what we both so wanted to do. I could no longer tell myself I was in love with Bonnie as I had been in the early days of our relationship. But the sexual attraction was just as strong as ever, so on several occasions I did what I kept telling myself I must not do. And afterwards I'd tell myself I should not have done it, and wouldn't again. But placed again in temptation's way, I would succumb once more.

Maggie of course found out, either by intuition or someone telling her. I knew it would not have been difficult for her to learn about it. While Bonnie and I did not flaunt our relationship, neither did we go to any great lengths to conceal it. So finally Maggie confronted me.

I came home after spending part of an evening with Bonnie. I had told Maggie I would be seeing Phil Drake, an old seaman buddy who was then working at Autolite. I had dropped in on Phil, but gone on to Bonnie from there.

As I came in the door, she started, "You've been with Bonnie, haven't you?"

"I told you I was going to see Phil Drake."

"I know what you told me. But you've been with Bonnie, and this isn't the first time."

"Well, she is a party member."

"That's not what we're talking about, and that's not why you were there! You weren't just talking with her! I can smell her on you!"

I don't know whether she actually could or not, but it was possible. Chagrined at being found out and confronted, I reacted defensively. "I can't have you questioning me about where I've been every time I go out."

"And I won't have you lying around with other women! If that's what you want, get out!"

"All right, I will."

Saying nothing more, I hastily packed a bag while Maggie watched me in stony silence. I left the apartment without even saying goodbye. Outside, with nowhere else to go, I drove to 16th Street, a few blocks away, and rented a furnished room.

At first I was angry, but also knew that I was entirely in the wrong. However upset I was at being found out, I didn't have a good case. How could I plead that I wanted to be married to one woman but still be free to enjoy sex with another when the urge overtook me? Whatever my actions had been, I didn't really believe that this was a credible position to hold. So anger soon gave way to loneliness and remorse, considering how much I had lost with little to gain. I knew, and Maggie knew, that I would never leave her for Bonnie. I wouldn't go back to Bonnie even if Maggie were lost to me forever.

I stayed in the barely-furnished room for three days. I don't recall whether I had any meetings or other work to do, but I didn't see either Maggie or Bonnie during that time and spent most of it mulling over what had happened and considering my options. Though I wasn't aware of it until later, Maggie was also going though a bad three days, during which she spent some time with her sister, Dana, receiving comfort and counsel.

Finally, I realized what I had to do. I went back to the apartment prepared to beg for forgiveness. But Maggie met me, not with reproach or recrimination, but with a plea that I come home and not let this folly destroy our love. We embraced and cried.

I have asked myself since that time why I continued to have this fatal attraction for Bonnie. Was it just that I wanted to have it both ways? Have a wife at home and still behave like a single man? Was I influenced to some extent by the idea of sexual license implicit in some Marxist literature — that the marital bond is a bourgeois institution, a cultural unit of capitalism and an abridgement of individual freedom. Many radicals believed that and some acted on it. Or did I have trouble making a full commitment to the woman I loved? Was it something from my early conditioning, or my family history, that made me afraid of that kind of commitment? Had my failure with Nina resulted from the same weakness? Had that earlier failure cast its long shadow on my later marriage?

I'll never have definitive answers to these questions. I only know that through the combination of my three lonely days in a barren room, Maggie's patience and her sister's sound counsel, the most important relationship in my life was salvaged. And I was never again tempted to sow any more wild oats with Bonnie, though I saw her occasionally and she was just as sexy as ever.

Though Maggie's parents had disowned her when we were married, she maintained a warm relationship with her sister and brother. Dana, who was four years older, lived in Toledo with her husband, Norton Young, and their daughter, Gartha Ann. They later had a son, Rick. Dana had been in show business in New York City before she married, having appeared in several Broadway plays. I think she missed the bright lights and was bored with being a housewife in a little burg like Toledo. It was during this period that she took to drinking heavily, a problem that contributed to her early death. But she was a good sister and we visited her and her family as long as we stayed in Toledo. Maggie's brother Bob Van Auken and his wife Wanda lived on the family farm in Hudson, Michigan. We also visited the farm for an occasional weekend and were made welcome.

My father and his family were still in Maine, Dad working at a variety of jobs that offered him a chance to make a living. We exchanged letters from time to time. Mother and Earl were working on expensive estates in New Jersey where they hired out as cook and butler. Mother also wrote several times a year.

Tex was in the army in the South Pacific; Larry, classified 4F because of a back injury, was working around Portland, Maine; Norman was in the Army Air Force Medical Corps and Richard was in the Navy SeaBees. Anne was still with the Pledgers and going to high school. Marianne was at the Boston University School of Music, but no one had any other news about her. I knew where my siblings were from Dad's letters but never had any direct communication with them during this period.

On April 12, two months after Maggie and I were married, President Roosevelt died suddenly and was succeeded by Vice-President Harry Truman. On April 25th a conference to establish the United Nations took place in San Francisco and in May the German Army surrendered to the Allies at Reims, France. On August 6th an atom bomb was dropped on Hiroshima, and another hit Nagasaki on August 9th. This brought the Japanese surrender on September 2nd.

The end of wartime restraints brought a wave of labor unrest as pent-up resentments and grievances were allowed to surface. Strikes, slowdowns and sit-downs accompanied the changeover from war to peacetime production with attendant layoffs. Demobilized troops came home to enjoy the fruits of victory, but they returned to a shrinking job market. Wartime shortages, rationing and restrictions seemed no longer tolerable now that peace had come to the world.

We were active, trying to interpret these events and capitalize on them to build and strengthen our movement, and we were modestly successful. Through 1945 and 1946 we worked hard and rejoiced in small advances, while waiting and working toward the sweep of radicalization that would accompany the economic crisis we regarded as inevitable. Though there were many economic dislocations accompanying the changeover from wartime to peacetime production, the crisis we had long anticipated never occurred.

As we emerged from the war it became increasingly evident that our pre-war predictions were not coming true. Far from facing imminent crisis, U.S. capitalism was thriving; it was the new world economic powerhouse. The Stalin regime not only appeared stable, it was expanding into eastern Europe. The long-awaited wave of socialist revolutions in major western European countries did not arrive. And all these disappointments had their probably inevitable repercussions within our party. Al Goldman and Felix Morrow developed some differences while still in Sandstone prison serving time for their conviction under the Smith Act. Their criticisms did not seem unreasonable to me but, as the internal discussion continued, it appeared that Al and Felix were moving steadily to the right and they were indeed on their way out of the party. Both left in 1946, going first toward Shachtman's Workers Party, then continuing their rightward course, ending in ignominy. As our isolation continued and expectations were unfulfilled, there would be other factional disputes and defections, especially among intellectual leaders of the party.

In Toledo, and in the Ohio/Michigan area generally, we were somewhat insulated from the factional ferment that troubled intellectual circles in New York and some other areas. Our day-to-day concentration was primarily on building the party organization and confronting the immediate concerns of workers on the railroads and in the auto and steel plants who looked to us for leadership. We read the internal bulletins and discussed the differences, but without heat or rancor and without any notable defections.

In 1946 the party nominated me to run for U.S. Congress on the Socialist Workers Party ticket from the congressional district encompassing Toledo and Port Clinton. We worked hard to collect some 2,500 signatures required for a place on the ballot. We secured many more than the required number of signatures but were ruled off the ballot on a technicality by the elections board. The stated reason was that our petitions were filed in two batches on consecutive days instead of all at once. We had been assured by the clerk of the board that this had long been the common practice with both major parties, though the law did not specifically allow it. Though the technicality on which our petitions were ruled invalid was patently phony, there was no mechanism for appealing the decision of the elections board without hiring a lawyer and going to court which we were in no position to do.

One of our members, Wayne Decker, who had once been a Republican precinct worker in Toledo and still had contacts with local leaders, learned that the Democrats on the Board of Elections were afraid I would draw enough votes to affect the outcome and insisted that I be barred from the ballot. In any case, I was ruled off, so the party ran me as a write-in candidate for governor of Ohio. This was not as effective because no voter takes seriously a candidate whose name isn't on the ballot.

But I did campaign all over the state and we attracted some good crowds and recruited some new members. Our basic election platform called for replacing the disastrous boom-or-bust capitalist system with its exploitation, wars, and depressions, with a just and rational socialist society. Before primarily union audiences I stressed the need for strengthening the workers' organizations and fighting back against the employers' efforts to chisel on wages and scuttle hard-won working conditions.

The message was well received by those who attended our rallies — industrial workers in northern Ohio, coal miners in the south and university groups throughout the state. On election day I received a few thousand votes. Those were the ones that were counted, and many, perhaps most, precincts didn't even bother to tabulatc write-in votes.

Of course we realized we had no chance of winning and regarded the election campaign only as a vehicle for putting our program before the people at a time when there was maximum interest in issues. Viewed in that light, I guess our campaign was a success.

26

Change of Life

When Maggie first became pregnant I was shocked. Neither of us expected this and had not planned on it. Children at this time would be totally disruptive of our way of life. My first thought, and perhaps Maggie's too, was of how this would affect our party work, up to now the most important consideration in our lives. At no time did we think of abortion as an option but we must have expressed some of these misgivings to others, because Dana, Maggie's sister, volunteered that she would like to adopt our baby if we didn't want to keep him.

I think it was Dana's offer that jolted us into a realistic appraisal of our situation. Confronted with this reality, we both knew that we wanted our baby, that no one else should raise him. Whatever the consequences, our baby would be our responsibility and ours alone. Having decided that, we started preparing for his arrival which we eagerly awaited.

On February 24, 1947, Maggie went to the Flower Hospital and our first son, Michael Orrin, was born. When her labor started I called her doctor and took her to the hospital. But when I went later to visit, the nurses took one look at me and wouldn't let me in. I had come down with measles. As I was confined to the apartment for the next couple of weeks, Dana took Maggie from the hospital to her house to avoid exposing the baby to the disease. So I didn't see Mike until he was more than two weeks old.

I was delighted to have a son. We both were, and we spent hours every day holding him and playing with him. He was aware and alert right from the start, and we were endlessly fascinated with the things he did and his responses to us. We also read a lot of books on child rearing and consulted other parents to make sure we were doing things right. Mike might have had an easier time if we had consulted less and just followed our instincts.

The books at that time recommended setting up a feeding schedule and sticking to it. They advised feeding the baby every four hours and letting him yell if he got hungry before his feeding time. This was believed to be good for him. Mike was born hungry and has always had a remarkably good appetite. Most of the yelling he did as a baby was because he wanted to eat.

He was a much happier baby when we finally decided to hell with the experts and started to feed our baby when he was hungry. The others who came later were not subjected to any character-building hunger. In this as in many other things, they profited from our learning experiences with Mike and had an easier time.

Maggie had given up her job at LaSalle's during the final weeks of pregnancy and would not be able to start working again, at least for a while. We had been getting by on my $15 a week from the party, but now that we had a child I had to look for other work. I was proud of my new son and of his mother, and I knew that they were my responsibility. Up to now, Maggie and I had been partners and she made more money than I did, but that had never mattered. Now I had a family to support and this must be my first priority. Perhaps the fact that my father's family had broken up, with my brothers, sisters and I farmed out to relatives and strangers, steeled my resolve, though I recall no such thoughts at that time.

There weren't many jobs available in Toledo just then. Industrial employment was down; my friend in the fireman's union didn't have anything; construction was slow and many riggers were idle. Besides, I had achieved a certain notoriety through my political activities and many prospective employers recognized my name and shied away.

Though I did not think of it that way then, this marked the effective end of an era for me. In everything I had undertaken for the past decade, a primary concern for me had been the advancement of the cause. Party work had taken precedence over personal considerations; my personal affairs had been arranged so as not to conflict with the party's interests. I had been, and increasingly so over the years, a dedicated "true believer," totally devoted to the cause.

I did firmly believe that a socialist world was possible and that I could make an important contribution toward its achievement. I could picture a world without want, without wide disparities in income, without exploitation, a world where the advantages of education and culture would be available to all, where people of different races would live in harmony and nations would war no more.

This vision of a more just society had made my life worthwhile, my party work meaningful and I had faced each day with enthusiasm. Small victories — new recruits brought into the movement, a lecture series well received by a receptive audience, a trade union strategy well conceived and successfully executed, another class of students versed in the fundamental precepts of socialist thought — these had meant more to me than wealth to which I'd never aspired.

It had been ten years since I left Maine, a Down East farm boy, going to Boston to seek my fortune at a time when jobs of any kind were at a premium. My life would surely have been different had there been an opportunity for an education beyond high school or employment other than menial labor at subsistence wages.

I had found my fortune, but it was not just what I'd had in mind when I set out ten years before. It did not consist in material goods, but in a wealth of good friends and comrades, engaged in a common worthy cause. Above all, it now included a wife and a son. Over the coming months and years, the growing needs of the family occupied most of my time and gradually eroded first my availability, then my interest in political activism.

There was no definitive break with the party, either then or later. I agreed with the party's objectives, its analyses of political and economic trends, and with the strategies we had followed for advancing the cause of socialism in the post-war era. I continued to attend branch meetings, accepting assignments to teach classes or deliver lectures. But I had less and less time for it. I had to find a job and later that spring after Mike was born, I went to Cleveland looking for work. Through the fireman's union I got a job on a dredge working in Lorain harbor. It was a long way from home — about 80 miles. I slept aboard the dredge, and got home only on weekends. Otherwise it wasn't a bad job, but it didn't last. The channel dredging was finished and they laid off. the whole crew.

I then answered an ad for steeplejacks. A lot of this work required the same rigging skills I had used at sea and as a rigger. So I was hired. The work was mostly in Cleveland, and again I went home only on weekends. Maggie, who suffered from fear of heights, was not exactly thrilled.

The steeplejack outfit was run by two brothers, Paul and Frank Hriko. The business had been started by their father and at one time the old man and his five boys did the work. But one by one, over a period of years, they fell — the father and three of his sons. The father and two of his boys were killed, the third son injured so he would never work again. Only Paul and Frank carried on. I heard about these calamities after I had been working for them a few weeks. Had I known sooner, I might not have taken the job.

At the start I worked for Frank Hriko with a crew repairing an Episcopal church tower on the east side. The major part of the job was chipping out and replacing weather-damaged mortar between the stones of the granite tower. We worked from a swing stage some 80 feet in the air above Superior Avenue and got to the stage through the bell tower which was reached via inside ladders. The work wasn't too hard and it paid well.

After a couple of weeks, Frank told me he liked my style and gave me a big raise. Soon after, Paul Hriko took me off the church to do other jobs such as painting flagpoles, painting the highest steel smoke stack in the city, and finishing off the rebuilding of a brick tower above the roof of a Greek Orthodox church on the west side.

Painting a flagpole is a two-man job — one up the pole in a bosun's chair and the other on the ground to send up anything the painter needs. If a pole was more than 30 feet high, we took turns going up in the chair. I never minded the heights, but was glad I never was asked to climb a pole that didn't already have a pulley installed at the top.

The big smoke stack, about 12 feet in diameter, towered 75 feet above the boiler room of the huge Swift meat-packing plant on Cleveland's west side. Painting the stack took one man on the ground and four men up in bosun's chairs hanging from pulleys attached to the top rim of the stack. Each painter would cover a quarter of the stack's circumference as we worked our way down, applying paint with six-inch brushes. A man below, on the power plant roof, kept us all supplied with paint, drinking water and anything else we might need.

Even though they'd banked the fires the night before to let the thing cool down, that stack was still hot and we had to keep moving our feet to keep them from cooking. As we got closer to the bottom, the stack got hotter and the paint would smoke as it was brushed on and we were hopping around in our bosun's chairs like crickets on a hot stove. I was glad I didn't get any more stacks to paint.

When I got to the Greek church, the tower, six by six foot square and about 30 feet high, rising above the ridge of a very steep slate roof, was nearly finished. We still had to lay a few top courses of brick, install a cap, a weather vane and lightning rod. The job complete, we took everything down, sending load after load of leftover materials, tools, and scaffolding down to the ground, a hundred feet below, on a messenger cable.

Finally, the last man on the tower sent down the pulley serving the messenger before coming down himself. I was chosen to be last off the tower. All the equipment had been sent down and then it was just me, up there on the top of that tower. I was clinging to the top of a ladder which was lashed by ropes wound around the tower, and I had a light line attached to my belt to be used for lowering the ladder sections. Easing my way down the ladder, one four-foot section at a time, I would reach up and untie the lashing from the ladder section above me, flip the rope clear, then tie both ladder and rope to the messenger line on my belt and lower them to the ground. There were seven sections of ladder and I worked my way down, piece by piece, slowly descending until I finally set my feet on the ridge of the church's slate roof. That descent from the Greek tower was the scariest thing I did in the whole time I worked for Hriko Brothers.

I spent about two months doing this type of job, going home to Toledo every weekend. Then one Monday morning Frank took me and three other guys down to Massillon, Ohio, about 40 miles south of Akron. The Catholic church there was badly in need of repair and the Hriko brothers had the job. We lodged in a hotel and ate in restaurants at company expense, finishing out the week there and reporting back on Monday. When Frank told me I would be in charge of the job until it was finished which would take a few months, I decided to move my family to Massillon.

I found a small apartment only a few blocks from the church, and a week later borrowed a trailer and moved Maggie and Mike to Massillon. This was not a very exciting place, a steel mill town where the residents' chief interest in life seemed to be high school football. But we soon made some friends and were enjoying life on a somewhat slower track than in Toledo.

The work at the church went as planned. We installed a two-inch-diameter steel rod that ran across the 60-foot breadth of the church above the ceiling to tie together the two transept towers that had started to lean, parting company with the nave and threatening to topple into the churchyard.

Then each morning when I got to the job, I would take one turn on each of two four-foot-long turnbuckles that applied pressure on the big steel plates at each end of the rod, bearing against the outside of the two leaning towers. These plates were one-inch-thick, four-foot-wide, six-point stars. The parish priest was quite amused that the Hriko brothers had decorated his church with huge Jewish stars. Gradually we were pulling the towers back into place and the steel rod would keep them there.

We repaired or replaced a number of small broken panes in a huge leaded stained-glass rose window high above the apse, trying to match the original colors as closely as possible. We replaced many slate shingles and stopped the roof from leaking, and we had started to replace a lot of dead mortar in the stonework of the exterior walls.

Then one morning my crew didn't show up and I decided to work alone. That was my first mistake of the day. We had reached a point where we had to move a swing stage suspended over one of the side entry structures. I went up a ladder to the roof over the entry. It was a low roof, only about 20 feet from the ground, but steep. I left my ladder and walked up the steep roof to its peak where I could reach the ropes from the stage falls. That was my second mistake.

I had maneuvered the stage into the position where I wanted it when one of the lines drifted slightly out of reach. Sitting on the slates I leaned back to catch the rope — my third mistake. I started sliding down the slippery slates. My feet hit the top of my ladder and it moved out from the eaves. I caught hold of it and balanced there like a circus acrobat, the ladder straight up in the air. I went down a few steps, the ladder rocking back and forth. So far, so good. I made it down the ladder to about ten feet from the ground and decided to jump.

This was my last mistake, because my feet got entangled in some shrubbery and I pitched head first toward the sidewalk. I partially broke my fall with my hands, but my chin struck the pavement.

The parish priest happened along about the time I hit the ground. He called an ambulance and they took me to the hospital where they patched up my chin. They couldn't do much for my wrists as they weren't broken, but they were very badly sprained and I wasn't able to use them for anything for a while. This effectively put an end to my climbing career, much to Maggie's relief. Not long after that Frank Hriko fell and was crippled for life. I ran into Paul a few years later and he told me about Frank. Paul was still carrying on — the last Hriko in the steeplejack business.

Now that I wasn't able to do anything else, I did what I should have done long ago. I settled down to study for the State of Ohio engineer's license examination. This test was not unlike those I had taken to get my seaman's engine-department certificates of qualification, only longer and much harder, and they gave applicants all day to complete the exam. I had a lot of studying to do. I couldn't hold a book, but I could sit at a table and turn the pages. So while my chin was healing and my wrists becoming again functional, I studied, determined to get a job on the ground level.

Of course Maggie was all for this. While I was laid up, she got a job in Canton handling advertising for a big furniture store. I was able to take care of the baby with the help of the landlady who liked baby-sitting Mike so much I think she would have paid us for the privilege.

I got my engineer's license on October 5, 1947, and went looking for a job. Ford Motor Company was building a new plant, a foundry, in Canton and that's the first place I tried. They had just opened the power plant and I was hired as a shift engineer, one of four, working under the chief. Maggie quit her job at the store to stay home with Mike.

Though Canton was only about ten miles from Massillon, we decided to move there to be closer to the job. We found a small apartment near the Ford plant and moved in. The apartment was small, poorly laid out, but Maggie performed wonders in making it homelike despite the physical limitations.

Work at the Ford plant went well and I was very highly regarded there for a while. Then the UAW started an organization drive in the new plant. Of course I joined and attended all the meetings. Soon I was elected president of the local, and soon after that I was fired, along with the other union officers.

The union filed a brief with the National Labor Relations Board and the case dragged on for months. Ford had the money and lawyers to fight it, and they seemed determined not to have the auto workers union in their new plant. The company eventually lost, but it took more than a year to settle, much too late to be of any help to me. By the time our case with Ford was won, we had already moved from Canton to Cleveland and I'd lost all interest in returning to my job at the Ford foundry.

Once Maggie and I decided we wanted a family, our second son, Timothy, and our two daughters, Ann and Susan, were born in rapid succession over a period of a little more than four years. We have never regretted it, enjoying our children, playing with them, teaching them and observing their development into strikingly different individuals. And they were, each of them, distinct, dissimilar and unique.

Mike was quick, competitive and sometimes intractable. Tim was gentle, equable and thoughtful, reminding me of my brother, Norman. Ann was sweet, agreeable and so sensitive that a mild scolding would devastate her. And Susie was eager, curious, buoyant, and stubborn as a mule when she made up her mind about something. They were all a delight to be with and we had some wonderful times together.

Maggie's folks had made some guarded overtures, seeking to end the long chill caused by our marriage. Though they had never seen their grandsons, we heard from Dana that they would like to. Then, when Ann was born, Maggie's mother came to take care of the boys and stay with Maggie during her convalescence. She came again for Susie's birth and gradually her husband thawed out. I was pleased that Maggie became reconciled with her parents.

Though I had to leave Toledo to find a job and give up full-time political activity, we still maintained an active interest in national and international affairs. As we had predicted, the end of the war did not bring an era of global peace and harmony. Now that there was no longer a need for a joint effort against a common enemy, there developed increasing dissension among the former allies, each trying to maintain or expand its own sphere of influence or control in Europe. Britain and the U.S. contended with Communist guerrillas in Greece and the "Truman Doctrine" was proclaimed to "support free peoples who are resisting attempted subjugation by armed minorities."

A Communist Party coup in Czechoslovakia overthrew the nascent democratic regime of Eduard Benes and Jan Masaryk. The Marshall Plan was aimed at rebuilding the economies of western Europe. Alarmed at the unification of the U.S., French and British sectors of occupied Germany into a single economic unit and issuance of a new currency, the USSR retaliated by blockading land and waterway routes to Berlin. Truman responded by ordering military planes to relieve the blockade. A North Atlantic Treaty Organization (NATO) was created to counter Soviet power in Eastern Europe.

In November, 1948, Harry Truman beat Tom Dewey in an upset victory in the presidential election. Former Vice-President, Henry Wallace, running on the Progressive Party ticket was soundly thrashed, drawing fewer votes than Strom Thurmond running as a Dixiecrat. Though Truman pledged continuing pursuit of his "Fair Deal" policies, emphasis turned more and more toward obsessions with communist infiltrations and threats of subversion.

The Taft-Hartley Act, enacted in 1947, placed many restrictions on the operations of the union movement, including a provision that every union officer had to swear he was not and had never been a member of the Communist Party. Enforcement of this provision eliminated many leaders of CIO unions and the red-baiting hysteria, whipped up by the employers and embraced by many right-wing union leaders, resulted in the expulsion of 11 International unions from the CIO. This meant the virtual destruction of many of them, and their replacement by new organizations approved by the right-wing CIO leadership.

In the maritime industry the government entered directly through the instrumentality of the Coast Guard which issued a new seaman's passport required for anyone employed aboard an

American ship. This was an open move to eliminate all radicals from the industry in the name of national security. In the subsequent screening, all known or suspected members of the C.P. were refused passports, and so were members of all other radical parties. Our small cadre aboard merchant ships was also wiped out.

In 1949 the Chinese communist forces finally routed the Kuomintang and drove Chiang Kai-shek from the mainland. Feeding the cold-war paranoia in the U.S., in the same year the USSR exploded an atomic bomb and the U.S. monopoly of nuclear weapons was at an end. Washington's strategists seemed to be losing ground all over the world and scapegoats had to be found. So it was surely no mere coincidence that at this time the leaders of the U.S. Communist Party were indicted under the same Smith Act they had thought was properly used against the SWP. We denounced the use of the Smith Act against the CP, but its leaders went to trial and were convicted.

In June of 1950 the forces of North Korea moved south of the 38th parallel, Truman sent troops to counter them, invoking the specter of the red Chinese hordes swarming just across the border. Wisconsin Senator Joe McCarthy announced that he had a list of 57 card-carrying communists in the U.S. State Department. Or maybe it was 205; he couldn't seem to make up his mind. Former state department official Alger Hiss was charged with transmitting state secrets to the Soviets. He was convicted and went to prison after a lengthy and highly publicized trial. Julius and Ethel Rosenberg were convicted of transferring the atomic secrets that enabled the USSR to make its nuclear bomb, and they were duly executed.

Roosevelt's New Deal and Truman's Fair Deal were dead. The Cold War Deal took their place. Our party continued to hold meetings, conduct classes and forums for the few who were attracted to our ideas. Though we were not daunted, there was an atmosphere of intimidation abroad in the land, affecting many who might otherwise have listened. The economic crises of world capitalism, and the resulting political upheavals, did not occur as we had predicted and the wave of labor militancy begun in the 30's was now at ebb tide. Most of the workers attracted to the party during those years now dropped out. The Toledo branch ceased to be a vital functioning center and would revert to its status before I went there in 1944 — a handful of like-minded people in sporadic contact. I would not learn until much later (reading Tim Wohlforth's memoir, *The Prophet's Children,* Humanities Press, 1994) that the party's national membership peaked at 1,600 in 1946, my last year in Toledo when I ran for governor of Ohio. By 1954 it would be down to 500 according to SWP figures prepared for the National Committee at the 1979 convention.

During this period of decline, I still attended some meetings, accepted assignments to deliver an occasional lecture on current affairs. I attended the 1952 national convention of the SWP as a delegate from the Cleveland branch. I sometimes regretted not being more active, but at the same time I was aware that we talked mostly to ourselves. The workers were either uninterested in our message or intimidated by the cold-war atmosphere. Also, during this period, another factional dispute raged in the party. A group led by George Clarke, Bert Cochran and Harry Braverman , allying themselves with some European leaders of the Fourth International, believed that the SWP had misjudged the potential of the unorthodox "Stalinist" parties of Yugoslavia and China to accomplish lasting social transformations. All three had been highly regarded intellectual leaders of the party and the issues they raised were certainly valid. But the interminable debate distracted the members from outside activities, bred ill feeling in the ranks and did little to arouse my enthusiasm.

Senator Joe McCarthy continued his reckless and sometimes ridiculous posturing in the public press. His persecutions ruined the lives of a number of blameless people. His attacks on General George Marshall and the U.S. Army intimidated many of his senate colleagues, and for a while even President Eisenhower. The press blazoned his charges in sensational front-page headlines and many joined his anti-communist bandwagon, including such ex-socialist communist haters as James Burnham and Max Eastman.

The House Un-American Activities Committee (HUAC), one of the most despicable instruments ever devised by the U.S. Congress, was running amok in the land, issuing subpoenas to labor leaders, screen-play writers, actors, authors, and anyone whose radical background or activity might get them headlines and feed their publicity machine.

Many of those subpoenaed placed themselves under the protection of the Fifth Amendment, refusing to answer any questions on the grounds of self-incrimination. Others, intimidated by HUAC, fearing they would be blackballed from their industry or profession, gave the testimony demanded by the inquisitors, naming former associates, thereby earning themselves the title of stool-pigeon. Some few defied the committee, incurred contempt citations and paid for their defiance.

Maggie and I had discussed what course to take if we were called by HUAC, which at one point seemed possible because of the prominence our activities had enjoyed in Toledo. In consultation with Ted Selander we decided on a course of defiance. If called we would testify openly about our socialist activities, defending them as legitimate and appropriate, just as our leaders had done when tried under the Smith Act. As for naming colleagues and associates, we would tell the inquisitors that it was none of their damn business and refuse to name anyone.

We saw this as the only honorable way to go, but there were obvious risks. HUAC had power and seemed to enjoy exercising it, intimidating and humiliating witnesses, sending to jail those who refused to cooperate. Under these circumstances, it was easy to become somewhat paranoid and we asked ourselves what would happen to our family if we had to go to prison?

Ted gave me the name of a lawyer who, though he was not a party member, could be relied on to give sound advice and come to our defense if needed. I went to see the attorney who lived and had his offices in a Cleveland suburb with the unlikely name of Chagrin Falls.

I explained the situation to the lawyer, whose name I don't recall, and asked him if he could devise a legal instrument whereby our children would become wards of my brother, Norman, if Maggie and I were jailed for contempt of HUAC. He told me he could do that but didn't recommend it. He said that it seemed highly unlikely they would call us because they were concentrating on those who could be linked to the Soviet Union, the current bugaboo, and most especially on those whose names were well enough known to get them big newspaper headlines. If they were to reach the point of subpoenaing Trotskyists, we would have plenty of warning and then would be time enough to take protective measures for the family. Convinced by his analysis and relieved by his assurances, we took no action. The lawyer made no charge for his advice.

However, we continued to keep a wary eye on HUAC and Joe McCarthy over the next couple of years. Then finally, the Senate voted in December 1954 to censure Joe McCarthy for conduct "contrary to Senate tradition," thus putting an effective end to his long reign of terror. Soon after that, HUAC also seemed to run out of steam, though the cold war itself continued for many years.

27

Looking Back and Summing Up

I don't remember when we first started talking about moving to California, but it may have been soon after Susie was born. I know we had read books about California, including one called, *California, Where Life Is Better*. Our closest friends in Cleveland, Ted and Dot Selander, had lived out there and talked about going back. I had good memories of California from my visit in 1938, and I had never cared much for cold weather. A place where the children could play outside all year and never need snow suits sounded good.

In the spring of 1953, we decided we would work toward the move. With the help of a neighbor who was a welder, I built a trailer to haul our furniture and other goods. We bought a 1949 Ford Country Squire station wagon with wooden bodywork and a powerful V-8 motor to pull the trailer. On December 14th we loaded the trailer with everything we were going to take and held a yard sale to get rid of the rest. That night we put the children to bed at a neighbor's house, then had a farewell party for our friends and neighbors in the empty house. The next morning we headed for California, going directly south to get out of the winter as soon as possible and avoid driving on ice and snow.

When we left Toledo, Mike was five months old. That departure meant the end of our full-time devotion to political activity. When we left Ohio for California, Mike was just two months short of seven years, Maggie and I were 34 and had four children. This trip marked the end of active participation in the socialist movement. Again, this cessation did not result from any major disagreements with the party or disillusionment with the ideals of socialism.

It had its roots first of all in our increasing involvement in family affairs, in the struggle to raise four children. At the same time we also observed the decline of the movement from the peaks enjoyed during our most active days, and the concomitant factional warfare over doctrinal issues that accompanied this decline. This, along with our increasing isolation during the McCarthy era, could only give rise for us to a strong sense of futility.

In retrospect, and almost 50 years later, I feel grateful that we left the party while we could still believe in the general correctness of its program. We were not caught up in the intense factional disputes, over issues both political and personal, that have ravaged the Trotskyist movement in its subsequent years of isolation.

The national leadership of the party, in its desperate need for a mass movement it could identify with, embraced the Cuban revolution. What started as defense of Cuba against U.S. intervention, soon evolved into uncritical support for Castro, excusing all of Castro's tyrannical misdeeds, even when he seized the Trotskyists' print shop, banned their paper and jailed all their leaders. One SWP faction, headed by Arne Swabeck, became Maoists, hailing the revolutionary genius of Mao Tse Tung.

These moves did not occur without opposition, and there have been mass expulsions of old-time leaders, dozens of splinter groups breaking away, then fracturing into even smaller sects. Our faith could not have survived either the programmatic changes or the internecine warfare.

Although we drifted away from the party, we have remained acutely aware of what was going on in the world. We have observed the decline of the labor movement and the increasing marginalization of its radical wing. Thus, over time, watching the continuing failures of our ideals, there has been a gradual erosion of some long-held beliefs.

The workers of the world, whose cause we had championed, for the most part had shown no interest in socialism.

Among my mates in the unions in which I remained active, those with good jobs were primarily interested in power boats and second homes and cared little if their less fortunate brethren had bread on the table or a roof over their heads. And over the years since, wherever the masses of workers have emerged from a state of apathy, they have not espoused international solidarity. Instead they have embraced divisive nationalism, ethno-centric separatism or religious fanaticism. And they have identified socialism with Stalinism — a criminal despotism which masqueraded as a workers' state on its way to an idealistic society of the future, a foul excrescence having nothing in common with Marx's concept of socialism nor with the intentions of the leaders of the Russian Revolution.

The American union movement has never recovered from the expulsion of all the most militant, outspoken workers from their ranks during the Taft-Hartley purge years of 1949-50. Whatever our differences with those under the sway of the Communist Party, and however misled they were by the minions of Stalin, these rank and file union members had been in the forefront of many progressive battles and organization drives. Their elimination silenced the most militant voices and its effect is still felt.

Down all these subsequent years our idealism has been challenged and our expectations blunted as we observed the fall of empires and beheld the terrible genocidal crimes of Hitler and Stalin. We have seen colonial revolutions end in new home-grown despotisms; beheld hopeful "new left" movements arise, only to collapse in farce or tragic bloodshed. We have seen the "old left" disintegrate of schismatic distemper, a plague endemic in movements isolated and impotent. We have looked on aghast as ordinary people, workers and farmers, inflamed with tribal, religious or nationalist frenzy have slaughtered millions of their neighbors, e.g., Uganda, Bosnia, Cambodia, Indonesia; and here at home we have seen a proliferation of doomsday cults, nutty militias and reactionary Christian crusaders. We see 50 percent of our country's eligible voters express their cynicism by boycotting elections while others go to the polls to elect, time and again, the bought-and-paid-for agents of big business who then proceed to legislate in favor of their owners, while increasing numbers of young people, disillusioned and cynical, turn to drugs and crime.

We have watched as our planet is despoiled, its water and earth polluted and its air poisoned, with the so-called "socialist states" being guilty of some of the most flagrant defilement. Even the upper atmosphere has been damaged by mankind's carelessness and greed, and holes in the ozone layer threaten all life on earth. More species become endangered each year and mankind is driving the fish of the seas toward extinction as remorselessly as we eradicated the bison from the plains and the caribou from the tundra.

Living through all this has inevitably raised considerable doubts about convictions of "scientific socialism" once firmly held. What we once considered a logical and historically ordained progression of human society through ever higher stages of development — from primitive communism to slavery, to feudalism, to capitalism, to socialism, giving way to communism, the classless society in which the state would "wither away" — has taken detours not foreseen by Marx, Engels, Lenin or Trotsky.

We believed that socialism was the only rational answer to an irrational system and that a trained cadre of class-conscious workers would be able to lead our society through a successful socialist transformation. We had only to stay on course and be ready to take advantage of the opportunities sure to come. But capitalism, despite periodic cataclysms and chronic malaise, has shown remarkable and unforeseen recuperative powers. New technologies have evolved, including the capacity for nuclear destruction of all life on our planet, never dreamed of by our ideological forebears. It is no longer science fiction that a single madman could bring an end forever to "inevitable" progress.

The international working class as the motive force of progress, an engine of history which would surely lead humankind out of the morass of capitalism into the classless society of the future, has shown little inclination to date to lead anything, least of all a dramatic transformation of society. Where socialists have been voted into office in western Europe they have become, despite some progressive legislation, caretakers for their capitalist system, then voted out again. When radical parties have come to power elsewhere (as in Eastern Europe or Africa), their least worthy leaders have risen unerringly to the top like scum in a cesspool and established themselves as a new ruling hierarchy, intent on pelf and privilege, proving once again the validity of Lord Acton's century-old epigram, "Power tends to corrupt; absolute power corrupts absolutely."

Many of my generation have watched their dreams of an ideal society achieved through political action turn into nightmares of ignominy, and they have reacted variously. There are those who still think Joseph Stalin and/or Mao Tse Tung were humanitarians and great revolutionary socialist leaders. Such people refuse to recognize what the rest of the world finds self-evident. They cannot admit the truth — that these "working class heroes" were world-class criminals — and they cling to their old convictions as a drowning man to the proverbial straw.

At the opposite end, there are those intellectuals who started as leftist critics of Stalinism, then lost the ability to distinguish between their socialist opposition and the "anti-Stalinism" of the likes of Joe McCarthy. They have swung with the pendulum to the other extreme to embrace their former enemies with burning right-wing fervor. Witness Max Eastman, Louis Budenz, Sidney Hook, John Dos Passos, Eugene Lyons, James Burnham, Lewis Corey, Ralph DeToledano, Irving Kristol, Norman Podhoretz and David Horowitz (a latecomer to the list), to name only a few of the better known.

Occupying a special sort of halfway house are people like Al Richmond who spent nearly forty years, most of his adult life, in fervent and generally effective activity in the American Communist Party and the YCL. I cite him only as a typical example, one of many who finally broke with the Communist Party, gave lengthy accounts of their careers, and apparently learned little or nothing from experience or blocked out the obvious conclusions.

Richmond related his life experiences in a long and very readable book, *A Long View From the Left* (Houghton Mifflin, 1972). Young Richmond, whose mother had been active in the Russian revolutionary movement, went directly from high school into full time, unpaid field work for the YCL. On-the-job training turned him into an accomplished journalist and he worked on the staff of the *Daily Worker* before becoming editor of the *People's World,* west coast organ of the Communist Party.

During the CP's ultra-left "Third Period", Richmond denounced Roosevelt as a fascist and organized for the Marine Workers Industrial Union, the CP's "revolutionary" dual union on the waterfront. When Stalin switched signals, Richmond along with all the other party faithful, changed to uncritical support of Roosevelt, exhorting the organized workers not to rock the boat of "collective security." Though somewhat shaken by the Stalin-Hitler pact, he swallowed his qualms, scuttled the "people's front," and joined the "Yanks are not coming" crusade. In retrospect, 30 years later, he concludes that "diplomatic necessity" justified the pact. He recalls that the pact led to the Nazi invasion of Poland but conveniently forgets that the Soviet armies invaded also, occupying half of Poland and sending a million and a half Poles into slavery in Siberian gulags.

And so it went. Richmond recalls in his memoir how disturbed he was by Khruschev's 1956 revelations of Stalin's criminal career as leader of the Soviet Union. He remembers being shaken by the use of Soviet troops to thwart the democratic aspirations of the Hungarian workers. He saw many of his old comrades quit the CP in disgust, but still he accepted the flimsy excuses and stuck to his guns. It was 12 years later that he went to Prague and found that Aleksander Dubcek and the Czechoslovak party leadership were supported by the overwhelming majority of the workers with whom he talked. He witnessed the brutal crushing of that leadership by Stalinist stooges supported by Russian tanks.

Returning to his post in San Francisco, Richmond told the truth about what he had seen in Czechoslovakia, was bitterly attacked by his own party leadership, and resigned his position as editor of *People's World*. Summing up his life experience he finds nothing wrong with any of the often contradictory policies he pursued over the years at Stalin's behest.

Al Richmond devoted his life to this movement with no prospects for material gain. I believe he was sincere, however mistaken, and that all his sacrifices were made in the honest conviction that they furthered the cause of the revolutionary transformation of our society. I have often had occasion to ponder the mystery of how a basically honest, decent person can blindly follow an indecent course for a lifetime and at the end find nothing wrong with it.

Besides those like Al Richmond in the wide spectrum between the die-hard Stalinist loyalist and the born-again neo-conservative there are a myriad of tints and shades of political opinion held by those of us who have retained any political interest at all. I have a few old friends (though fewer all the time due to the attrition of age) who are steadfast in their faith in the invincibility of Marxist doctrine. They can present lengthy, strong and convincing arguments which demonstrate their complete understanding of everything that has gone wrong in every country where political disaster has befallen. Based on a Marxist analysis, they know what programs are needed to rectify all these situations and how to snatch victory from the jaws of defeat.

However, the workers whom they address continue to ignore their appeals and they talk primarily to themselves, often sharply disagreeing with one another on arcane matters of interpretation or application of Marxist doctrine. I have no quarrel with their intentions; I applaud their commitment to fight injustice wherever they find it; I honor their idealism and respect their courage. I regret that I cannot accept their faith.

For every person, there is a considerable psychological loss involved in the death of certainty, whether these certainties be religious or political, rational or irrational. I think this is the reason many find it so difficult to turn their backs on the true beliefs that have lighted their paths, ordered their lives and filled their days with meaning, their futures with significance. It may the need for absolute certainty that explains why so many of those whose "god had failed" hastened to fervently embrace another true belief, often the polar opposite of the one abandoned. Thus ex-Socialists became neo-conservatives, apologizing for the reactionary right and defending Joe McCarthy (Burnham, Eastman, Schlam) or editing far-right magazines (Podhoretz, Kristol). I knew Jim Burnham and Irv Kristol as Trotskyists in the '30s.

I find tragedy as well as pathos in the spectacle of once-sincere champions of the poor and oppressed becoming tools of their former enemies. I can only be saddened when I learn that Albert Goldman, a party leader and brilliant, renowned radical lawyer became so demoralized he had to take a job driving a taxicab and became an informer for the FBI. Or that Felix Morrow, able party theoretician and a revolutionary socialist for most of his life, became a CIA collaborator, occultist, and publisher of soft-core pornography.

And what did the death of certainty mean to me? I had no doubt derived a large measure of psychological satisfaction from the certainty that I had a firm grasp on the general trends of history and knew how to intervene in its processes. I held the key to an accurate analysis of societal and political questions and knew just what was needed to bring socialist order out of capitalist chaos. As my grandfather might have put it, I "had history by the tail and a down-hill start." However, I do not need and never have wanted certainty so much that I would cling to a credo whose tenets I seriously questioned. Nor do I need to seek another to replace that which was lost.

Also, like all people who join movements large or small, I certainly enjoyed the emotional support that comes from belonging. For more than fifteen years I was a member of a close-knit group of congenial, like-minded people, an elite corps of cognoscenti whose vision of the future would surely be validated by historical developments. However, despite the benefits that naturally accrue to "belonging," the camaraderie and emotional support, I would rather be alone than dependent for comradeship on a sodality in which I no longer felt comfortable.

So, like many others, including the late scholar, Irving Howe, my old friend and former associate in the Young Peoples Socialist League, I have retired from the political wars but without renouncing my principles or apologizing for my past participation. My political activism was inspired by an idealistic urge to bring about a better, more humane society, and I have no regrets. I believe I owe a considerable debt to the movement in which I spent so many of my early years. It was there I learned to reason and think seriously about the social problems that still beset us. If my "science" was flawed and my optimism mistaken, I do not find that a cause for self-reproach or shame. I would rather have been wrong than to have seen injustice all around me and done nothing.

We live in a nation where million-dollar-per-year corporate executives lay off thousands of workers, then vote themselves huge bonuses as reward, while tens of thousands of homeless people scavenge in garbage cans, huddle in doorways and sleep under bridges. I have never lost my conviction that this is an unjust society. I find its extreme inequities intolerable, its predatory logic and its ethic of greed repellent. Reacting against the injustices that surround us, I still try to do my bit where I see some prospect of making a difference.

We can take encouragement from the existence of thousands of nonconforming groups and alternative publications supported by millions of dissenters of every variety working for social justice and environmental salvation. Though they differ from one another about many things, they still offer a small counterweight to the preponderant military/industrial behemoth and its Republican/ Democrat flunkies. They win few victories but they do persist and keep the cause of freedom and justice alive.

Though the union movement has suffered serious decline over the past half-century and segments have fallen under the control of self-serving bureaucrats or racketeers, millions of workers are still loyal to their organizations and continue the fight for economic justice. Despite some recent successes in organizing service and public-sector employees, the labor movement today conducts primarily a rear-guard action. However, I believe it still has potential as an instrument of progress.

I believe that ultimately human beings will always seek freedom from tyranny. So, despite all current indications to the contrary, I still hope that humankind will find a better way of ordering its affairs, without warfare or destruction of our planet, without poverty and exploitation, and without racial, religious or gender discrimination. I want this for all our children, our grandchildren and generations yet to come.

Mark Walker is author of a suspense novel, *Cassis, Resort to Vengeance* and a childhood memoir, *Maine Roots: Growing up Poor in the Kennebec Valley*, which was on the Maine best-seller list for two years. One of his plays, *Charade*, was produced in summer stock and off-Broadway. He has also been a regular contributor to national magazines including *Popular Science* and *Readers Digest*. He has been an organizer for the International Association of Machinists, edited union journals and trade magazines and written electrical technical books and pamphlets as a consultant to a national trade association. He now lives in California and, with his wife, Maggie, is working on a biography of Arthur Henry, a literary figure of the early years of the last century.